THE UNIVERSITY COLLEGE OF
RIPON AND YORK ST. JOHN

Please return this book by the date stamped below
– if recalled, the loan is reduced to 10 days

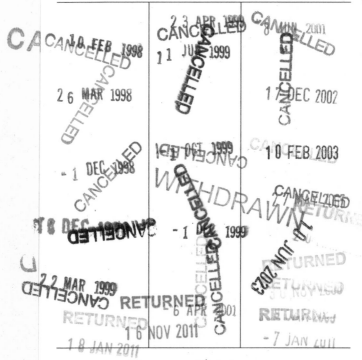

Fines are payable for late return

*The Dramatic Use
of Bawdy
in Shakespeare*

The Dramatic Use of Bawdy in Shakespeare

E. A. M. Colman

Longman

LONGMAN GROUP LIMITED
London

Associated companies, branches and representatives
throughout the world

© Longman Group Limited 1974

First published 1974

ISBN 0582 50456 2
Library of Congress Catalog Card Number: 73–86132

Set in 11 on 12pt Bembo
and printed in Great Britain
by Western Printing Services Ltd, Bristol

Contents

Abbreviations used in the Bibliography and footnotes

EC   *Essays in Criticism*

ELH   *English Literary History* (Johns Hopkins Press)

MLR   *Modern Language Review*

N&Q   *Notes and Queries*

SEL   *Studies in English Literature 1500–1900*

SQ   *Shakespeare Quarterly*

SS   *Shakespeare Survey*

As to the poetical Character itself ... it is not itself—it has no self—it is every thing and nothing—It has no character—it enjoys light and shade; it lives in gusto, be it foul or fair, high or low, rich or poor, mean or elevated —It has as much delight in conceiving an Iago as an Imogen. What shocks the virtuous philosopher, delights the camelion Poet. It does no harm from its relish of the dark side of things any more than from its taste for the bright one; because they both end in speculation.

John Keats to Richard Woodhouse,
27 October 1818

Preface

Shakespeare's use of salacious, licentious, scurrilous or lewd dialogue and reference is an aspect of his artistry that literary critics have left in comparative neglect. The two best known investigations, Eric Partridge's *Shakespeare's Bawdy* (1947, 1955, 1969) and Helge Kökeritz's more scholarly *Shakespeare's Pronunciation* (1953), approached the whole matter from angles other than that of critical assessment: with Partridge the main emphasis was psychological and conjecturally biographical, while with Kökeritz, as the title of his book made clear, it was phonological. As modern psychology has gone on reducing the inhibitions surrounding sexual discourse in our particular culture, editors of Elizabethan plays have become increasingly ready to provide footnotes explicating salacious passages. Yet it is my impression that editorial éclaircissements have been slow to influence contemporary *critical* writing on Shakespeare, where there lingers a feeling that anything scurrilous must also be trivial. A glance through the Shakespearean criticism of the past fifteen to twenty years would suggest that the middle-class upbringing of many a sensitive critic has impelled him to hurry past the obscene in Shakespeare—to hurry past it at least in what he publishes, if not in what he thinks.

The attempt to establish a new microclimate of thought in this highly specialised area at once faces certain dangers. There is the risk, first of all, of falling into obsessive or onesided criticism, of assuming that sex, for example, must be *the* informing principle of some particular play or group of plays. This would be an equal as well as opposite reaction to nineteenth-century reticence, and it would constitute the critic's equivalent of what a leader-writer in *The Times Literary Supplement* (8 July 1965) diagnosed as a special affliction of novelists in the 1960s—'the acceptance of sex as the master metaphor for problems of existence: the notion that with it the writer may drill through to the undiscovered deposits of the collective unconscious'. He went on to warn authors against what he called the 'positivist' fallacy: 'That is, that if you describe people copulating rather than kissing, you have inevitably said something of greater profundity about man's estate.' The caveat can usefully be taken to heart by any post-Freudian busying himself with the evaluation of significance in Shakespeare's plays and poems.

Put baldly, the thesis of the following chapters is that Shakespeare, as his career developed, quickly became a discriminating user of bawdy, and eventually made it one of the most potent weapons in his dramatic armoury. Yet it is still not the case that *all* Shakespearean indecencies are artistically significant, even among the late plays. I believe it can be demonstrated, for example, that *Antony and Cleopatra* is one of his greatest dramas, while it can also be shown to be one of his most 'sexy', but to claim a simple causal relationship between the sexuality and the poetic and dramatic force would be to assert a clumsy half-truth.

In practice, this enquiry has involved two closely related but separable sets of questions. Those in the first set, posed in chapter 1, are designed to clarify precisely what we mean when we talk of indecency in the context of Renaissance drama. After the first chapter, the query 'Is such-and-such a word or phrase, in such-and-such a setting, indecent or not?' continues to recur, but I have tried not to let points of semantic detail clog up the wider evaluative discussion. It is for this reason, rather than to create a kind of ready reckoner for the merely prurient, that a glossary has been added at the back of the book. It keeps semantic annotations apart from the main critical essay, while at the same time it saves them from being totally eliminated.

The second set of questions, in chapters 2–10, tries to gauge the contributions of bawdy elements to successive plays and poems. The grouping of the plays under their various chapter headings is in a broad way chronological, but the groupings are also designed to suggest the different discernible trends in Shakespeare's use of sexual indecency. It also seemed more satisfactory to discuss the poems and sonnets in a chapter of their own than to mingle them with the plays. Quite apart from the impossibility of dating the sonnets accurately, their bawdy is 'dramatic' in a slightly different sense of that word from that which applies to the bawdy of the plays. As an intellectual and emotional shock tactic, defiance of sexual inhibition works much more directly between lyric poet and reader than it does between dramatist and audience in a theatrical setting.

Like everyone else who writes on Shakespeare, I have many debts to acknowledge, and only the most specific of them appear among this book's footnotes. In comparing Shakespeare's ribaldry with that of his sources, for example, I have made continual use of Geoffrey Bullough's *Narrative and Dramatic Sources of Shakespeare* (7 vols, Routledge, and

Columbia University Press, 1957–72), and always with gratitude for his great expertise. Quotations from the text of Shakespeare are from the various volumes of the New Penguin Shakespeare (general editor T. J. B. Spencer), supplemented where necessary by Peter Alexander's edition of the *Complete Works* (4 vols, Collins, 1958). The decision to use a modern spelling text was a deliberate one. There are, of course, minor complications in discussing puns and other quibbles from a modernised text: editorial emendations and disputable spellings—*clef/cliff, Holy-Horse/ hobby-horse, housewife/hussif, nothing/no-thing, piled/pilled,* and so on— make it necessary to quote from the early quartos and folio from time to time. But this inconvenience is far outweighed by the advantage of being able to refer readers to an easily read, scholarly and widely available edition such as the New Penguin.

I should also like to record my gratitude to a number of people who have helped me in other ways. Most of the book was written at the Shakespeare Institute, University of Birmingham, during two periods of study leave in 1968–69 and 1970–71. The first of those visits was assisted by a grant from the British Council, the second by a Myer Foundation Grant-in-aid from the Australian Academy of the Humanities. Various parts of the manuscript were read and helpfully criticised by Professor Spencer, Director of the Shakespeare Institute; Professor H. J. Oliver and Dr R. W. Powell of the University of New South Wales; Miss Doreen Gillam and Miss Dorothy Jones, Wollongong University College; Dr A. W. James of the Department of Greek, University of Sydney; Mr F. W. Bateson, Emeritus Fellow of Corpus Christi College, Oxford; and Professor Arthur Brown of University College, London. Also in my debt for skilled and patient help are Mrs Alice Bray, Librarian of the Shakespeare Institute, and (as indefatigable proofreader) my daughter Juliet.

Sydney,
January 1973   E. A. M. Colman

1

What is Indecency?

Now it is quite undeniable, that there are many passages in Shakespeare, which a father could not read aloud to his children—a brother to his sister—or a gentleman to a lady:—and every one almost must have felt or witnessed the extreme awkwardness, and even distress, that arises from suddenly stumbling upon such expressions, when it is almost too late to avoid them, and when the readiest wit cannot suggest any paraphrase, which shall not betray, by its harshness, the embarrassment from which it has arisen. Those who recollect such scenes, must all rejoice, we should think, that Mr Bowdler has provided a security against their recurrence; and, as what cannot be pronounced in decent company cannot well afford much pleasure in the closet, we think it is better, every way, that what cannot be spoken, and ought not to have been written, should now cease to be printed.[1]

Thus Francis Jeffrey, advocate, Lord Rector of the University of Glasgow, and formidable editor of *The Edinburgh Review*. True to character, the future law lord was pronouncing sentence on Shakespeare's indecency with a good deal less circumspection than Dr Bowdler himself. Bowdler, in a preface to his edition, drew a careful distinction between the editor of a literary text and any presumptuous artist who might take it upon him to retouch a painting or sculpture. With literature, Bowdler pointed out, 'the original will continue unimpaired', to be reprinted *in toto* if the expurgated version is consigned to oblivion, whereas in the plastic arts, 'if the endeavour to improve the picture or the statue should be unsuccessful, the beauty of the original would be destroyed, and the injury be irreparable'.[2]

For all its modest good intent, however, *The Family Shakespeare* let its editor in for generations of ridicule, much of it from people who had not read his well-meaning preface. Such are the penalties of having one's name give rise to a household word. But what poor Bowdler's whole exercise makes clear—and Jeffrey's forceful support of it clearer still—is that the bawdy passages in Shakespeare should not be shrugged aside as merely frivolous. They can produce a strong emotional effect in certain readers simply by the fact of being bawdy. This remains true even in the comparatively uninhibited 1970s. The cultural world of Lord Jeffrey and the Bowdlers lies at an immense distance, and from the heights of what a John Updike character has called 'the post-pill paradise' we may smile down on their stern pronouncements with detached tolerance. Yet such evidence as we have from sociologists and psychologists suggests that the verbal expression of ideas connected with sex and non-sexual coprology does still elicit a marked emotional response from most English-speaking readers. References to sexual activity, urination and defecation may have lost much of their power to startle, but they remain the literary counterparts of what the law continues to call 'indecent exposure'. People think them healthy, comic, improper, distasteful, offensive or sinister as a result of their tending to defy widely respected (if ill-defined) standards of chastity or propriety. These standards depend on a robust but fluctuating system of taboos—a system that varies between different social groups at any one time and varies still more markedly between one 'generation' and another. Perhaps the most obvious fluctuations in ideas of what is proper, at least as far as the English-speaking nations are concerned, can be seen in conversations about pregnancy, childbirth, contraception, and even just the female legs and feet. All those unmentionables of the nineteenth-century English middle classes are now largely free of taboo: the draped piano limbs of Queen Victoria's Windsor have become only a joke.

Given, then, that standards of propriety, and hence of its opposite, do genuinely shift, it becomes necessary to establish three things before tackling Shakespeare's bawdy. First, exactly what do we now mean when we describe any piece of writing as 'indecent'? Secondly, how far did Elizabethan and Jacobean notions of indecency differ from those most readily acknowledged—permissively or otherwise—among English-speaking people today? And thirdly, how far do Shakespeare's plays themselves draw attention to the special nature of their own indecent passages?

An initial distinction must be made between sexuality in general and indecency in particular. Quite obviously, not all sexual writing is indecent. A medical textbook or a manual on birth control will be much concerned with the sexual organs and their functioning, but cannot be described as bawdy. It lacks both salacity and salacity's usual motive—a desire to shock, even if only fleetingly or mildly. In literature too, a great deal of writing about sex and sexual mores is rendered, by its seriousness, utterly remote from bawdy. Consider, for instance, *Madame Bovary*. This was, in its day, accused of being indecent and subversive, yet not even the Imperial Attorney claimed that Flaubert's literary depravity had extended to his treating sex flippantly or grotesquely. Bawdy, as distinct from straightforward sensuality, always partakes of the comic, whether through absurdity, grossness or a startling ingenuity. It need not actually be funny, any more than a pun needs to be funny in order to be recognised as a pun, but it often consists in that form of the absurd in which something physical is unexpectedly introduced when something spiritual is at issue. Again, in its least humorous forms, bawdy can be identified by its quality of caricature. It exaggerates, sometimes to the point of being downright bizarre, but sometimes only quite mildly. As with other forms of the grotesque in literature, the reader or listener has to be alert to fine differences in context and fine gradations of tone. To my mind, Macbeth is being neither gross nor (consequently) bawdy when he envisages withered murder who

> with his stealthy pace,
> With Tarquin's ravishing strides, towards his design
> Moves like a ghost

II.i.54

—but I imagine that not everybody would accept my opinion. I think most people would agree, on the other hand, that Iago is being bawdy when he implicitly invites Othello to picture Desdemona 'naked with her friend in bed'. Such a phrase is rolled on the tongue, as one critic has put it,[3] while its speaker savours both the picture evoked and the torture it inflicts. Similarly, Othello himself is being bawdy, though with deadly seriousness, when he speaks to Emilia and Desdemona as if they were in a brothel. The sexual accusations become indecent by being perversely distorted.

So we have an axiom: to be bawdy, a piece of talk or writing has to have behind it the intention to startle or shock. It also has to be at once more and less than sensual. Inasmuch as it labours the physical, it is sensual; but its other aspect is the exercise of wit, and this requires that the speaker remain partly at a distance from what he contemplates. Bawdy is often indirect, metaphorical or allusive. Only at its least subtle does it use blunt, unequivocal terms of sexual description, the familiar four-letter words. Shakespeare invariably suppresses these in favour of euphemistic or pseudo-euphemistic substitutes: a man's *yard* (*penis*, as an English word, came later) will less often be joked about under its own name than under the thin disguise of *prick* or *pike* or *weapon*. *Cunt* and *fuck* do not reach print in Shakespeare's text at all, except through puns (*count, focative*). Again you find substituted words carrying the ideas—*case, foin* and the like. Shakespeare's indecency might well be described metaphorically as a linguistic region, a zone situated between the real and the imagined, between the clinical and the pornographic. The area is shady and ill-defined. Its borders are always uncertain, and they can waver mercurially from moment to moment as a conversation or poem proceeds. The region provides breeding grounds for fantasy, as we have already seen with Othello. If Don John, Iago or Iachimo hints vaguely at a sexual offence ('Even she—Leonato's Hero, your Hero, every man's Hero'), the imagination of the hearer is stirred but still left free to envisage attitudes worthy of the most practised and inventive of concubines.

At an opposite extreme from the bawdy jibe and innuendo you find Shakespeare's non-scurrilous sexual references. Most of his allusions to the consummation of marriage are of this neutral kind, as also are his references to childbirth, suckling and, quite often, illegitimacy. In the history plays particularly, a character's bastardy will often be discussed simply in the matter-of-fact terms of his limited rights, obligations and social standing. The same is true of adultery when it is discussed with legalistic formality at certain points in the trial scene of *The Winter's Tale*. Some of this sexually slanted, but non-bawdy, material receives attention in the chapters that follow, but only when it has proved to have a bearing on genuinely indecent passages. More often, serious unexaggerated sexuality can be passed over without special mention. Yet the distinction between the two modes of sexuality will have to be made continually, so it will be worth while at this stage to consider in general terms how far Elizabethan notions of the indecent differed from some of those of the present day. In this, as in any other matter, Shakespeare is not always bound by convention, but we do at least have to be aware of the prevailing conventions of his time if we are to interpret his words sanely.

Non-sexual obscenity has changed comparatively little in England across four centuries. We have no difficulty in recognising, and gauging the force of, Shakespeare's references to chamber-pots, close-stools or flatulence. More remote from a twentieth-century viewpoint, but clear enough from the attitudes of characters within the plays, is the medieval and Renaissance cherishing of bad breath as a source of ribald humour. The joke has lost its popularity—progressively, I would suppose, with the advance of modern dentistry—though like nose-picking and scratching, halitosis remains a topic widely avoided in everyday conversation.

Since these asexual types of impropriety are only marginal to investigation of the sexual, this book could have disregarded them without serious loss. But it happens that when Shakespeare resorts to non-sexual indecency he nearly always does so in a context that is already bawdy in a sexual way. Yeats's Crazy Jane is less than precise, anatomically, when she assures the Bishop that 'Love has pitched his mansion in / The place of excrement', but she would seem truthful enough to most of Shakespeare's characters, as their cheerfully indisciminate use of such a word as *tail* makes clear (see glossary). While it would be perfectly logical, then, to rule copro-philous indecency out of this whole discussion, on the grounds of its being asexual, it is easy and usually helpful to consider it alongside the sexual scurrility which tends to accompany it in the plays.

Turning to sexual indecency itself, we find a much wider range of Elizabethan subject matter. To begin with, almost any Renaissance comedy, Shakespearean or not, draws on much the same sources of sexual humour as any mid-twentieth-century television farce. There are likely to be jokes about the male and female reproductive organs; about articles of clothing that have sexual implications (codpieces, points, hose, plackets, smocks, and bodices low-cut or tight-laced); about lust, and especially the lust of bachelors, husbands or widows; about frigidity, and especially the frigidity of wives; about adultery and prostitution; and of course about sexual promiscuity generally. Where the Elizabethan selection does differ noticeably from the parallel list one might compile from popular entertainment of the present day it is chiefly in a preference for jokes about cuckoldry, castration or itinerant friars as opposed to, say, birth control, homosexuality or seductive typists. The causes of some of these differences are too obvious to need comment. The Elizabethans did not have typists or reliable methods of birth control—though some of them had ambitions to contraception:

> EPICOENE   . . . And have you those excellent receipts, madam, to keep
> yourselves from bearing of children?
> LADY HAUGHTY   O, yes, Morose. How should we maintain our youth
> and beauty else? Many births of a woman make her old, as many
> crops make the earth barren.[4]

For our part, we do not have itinerant friars. We do, on the other hand, still have adultery, and this makes it interesting that cuckoldry has lost much of the mirth-provoking force which it clearly possessed four centuries ago. Its decline may perhaps be attributable to the loosening of patriarchal ties in a society that has, in general, grown less concerned than it used to be with questions of inheritance. As the first act of *King John*, with its dispute between the Faulconbridge half-brothers, reminds us, a man's true paternity used to be a matter of pressing importance, both socially and economically. Any act of adultery on the part of a married woman was a potential destroyer of lineage and hence of that ordered security which nowadays depends much more on the independently earned incomes of successive generations. In a milieu where much is at stake when paternity is doubted or challenged, society's fear of the adulterer may well find expression indirectly, both through a high valuation of the notion of 'honour' in relation to sexual behaviour and through a popular view of the deceived husband as a butt, a figure for the time of scorn to point his slow unmoving finger at. The cuckold's horns survive today only vestigially, represented by a two-finger gesture of increasingly vague opprobrium; yet there is abundant documentary evidence to show that our Elizabethan ancestors not only found the horns idea funny but also felt sensitive to its implication of cuckoldry whenever it was used against them. A passage in the anonymous compilation *Tarlton's Jests*[5] describes how the famous comic fell out with 'one in the Gallerie':

> It chanced that in the midst of a Play, after long expectation for *Tarlton*, (being much desired of the people) at length he came forth: where at his entrance, one in the gallerie pointed his finger at him, saying to a friend that had never seene him, that is he: *Tarlton* to make sport at the least occasion given him, and seeing the man point with one finger, he in love againe held up two fingers: the captious fellow jealous of his wife (for he was maried) and because a Player did it, tooke the matter more hainously, and askt him why hee made Hornes at him: No quoth *Tarlton*, they be fingers:
>
>> For there is no man which in love to mee
>> Lends me one finger, but he shall have three.
>
> No, no, says the fellow, you gave me the hornes: true saies *Tarlton*, for my fingers are tipt with nailes which are like hornes, and I must make a shew of that which you are sure of: this matter grew so, that the more he medled, the more it was for his disgrace: wherefore the standers by counselled him to depart, both he and his hornes, lest his cause grew desperate: so the poore fellow plucking his Hat over his eyes, went his wayes.

Humour dealing with homosexuality shows up another shift in social attitudes, though here the evidence from Elizabethan drama is harder to weigh. In the first place, emotional friendships between men were an accepted part of Renaissance life, and the gradations between simple admiration and homosexual lust seem to have been even wider in range and subtler in kind than they are now. When young men shared a bed, it was likely to be regarded as a matter of mere convenience rather than as the indulgence of a sexual inversion. The same was true, and remained so for much longer, of pairs of young women. To an Elizabethan audience, the friendships between Valentine and Proteus, Antonio and

Bassanio, Menenius and Coriolanus ('I tell thee, fellow, / Thy general is
my lover', V.ii.13), would have seemed no more homosexual than those
of Rosalind and her cousin Celia, Beatrice and her cousin Hero—
'although, until last night, / I have this twelvemonth been her bedfellow'
(*Much Ado* IV.i.146). The Sonnets carry us into a different sphere, since
the relationships between the poet's persona and one or more young men
do suggest active sexual involvement. At least one of the sonnets (number
20, to be discussed in detail in chapter 9) shows Shakespeare rebutting
the suggestion of physical homosexuality, but, viewed in the light of the
sequence as a whole, that attempt to etherealise the love affair looks
specious.

When the plays glance at sodomy it is with reticence and distaste. The
one fully explicit reference comes from Thersites in *Troilus and Cressida*
when he curses Patroclus as Achilles' male varlet:

PATROCLUS   Male varlet, you rogue! What's that?
THERSITES   Why, his masculine whore. Now, the rotten diseases of the
south, the guts-griping ruptures, . . . incurable bone-ache, and the
rivelled fee-simple of the tetter, take and take again such preposterous
discoveries!

V.i.15

The word *preposterous* here is being used quite literally—'backside fore-
most'—and this bluntness, like so much else in *Troilus*, is in marked
contrast with Shakespeare's usual treatment of the topic. Generally, his
allusions to buggery are few in number and ambiguous in tenor. A
typical instance is in *Henry V* (III.ii.129) where Gower exclaims 'Gentlemen both, you will mistake each other' and Jamy comments, 'Ah, that's
a foul fault!'" Jamy's remark is ambivalent. It could be condemning only
the art of deliberate misunderstanding, as cultivated by Fluellen and
Macmorris, but the considerable force of the word *foul* in early modern
English, and the frequent occurrence of a sexual flavour in *fault*, together
suggest a *double entendre*. If my suspicion is right and this is a joke based
on the idea of the two disputants homosexually mis-taking one another,
its very ambiguity looks defensive, a kind of evasion.

So far as one can judge, then, Shakespeare seems to have shared in the
conventional disapproval of sodomy which found further theatrical
expression through Jonson, Middleton, Tourneur and others.[6] But the
evidence for this is mostly of a negative type: the subject was one that he
seems to have preferred to avoid—as is scarcely surprising if one considers
official attitudes to homosexuality in the reign of Elizabeth I. From 1563
until 1861 buggery 'committed with mankind or beast' was a felony that
could, and quite often did, incur the death sentence. Among the many

ugly sidelights on the death of Christopher Marlowe in 1593 was the informer Richard Baines's report that Marlowe had affirmed 'That all they that love not Tobacco & Boies were fooles'. If Marlowe had escaped Ingram Friser's dagger, this piece of careless talk would not in itself have hanged him—Baines and Thomas Kyd, between them, had notes of far more heinous items of table-talk—but an accusation of homosexuality would at the very least have added weight to charges of atheism. From 1603 to 1625 the official outlook on homosexual activity was presumably less searching than in Elizabeth's reign, if only because James I himself was said to be homosexually inclined, as also was his eventual Lord Chancellor, Francis Bacon. The practice of sodomy in such high places, however, would not have been likely to make the dramatists more outspoken about it. And the law remained unchanged: in 1628, the third part of Sir Edward Coke's *Institutes of the Laws of England* surveyed the history of punishments for buggery, confirming that 'the judgement of felony doth now belong to this offence, *viz.* to be hanged by the neck till he be dead'. Coke mentions only one Jacobean prosecution for a homosexual offence: in 1608 a man called Stafford had been indicted 'for committing buggery with a boy, for which he was attainted and hanged'.[7]

If Elizabethan and Jacobean dramatists were more nervous of sexual inversion on the stage than are their later-twentieth-century descendants, they were a good deal *less* squeamish over venereal disease. Their comments on 'the pox' are numerous and, on the whole, cheerful, with an unpleasant and dated air, not unlike that of the same period's jocularity over madmen. It was not that the deadly nature of syphilis went unrecognised. The new and virulent strain of this infection that seems to have been brought to Europe by Columbus's men on their return from the New World in 1493 had been recognised as a killer by a number of sixteenth-century physicians. But the writers of medical treatises were not yet able to distinguish between syphilis and the other sexually transmitted diseases—infections that were much less dangerous, but which simultaneously affected many of the syphilitic patients.[8] From gonorrhoea, in the absence of syphilis, a man or woman might recover, and it was perhaps because of this that the physicians' warnings about brothelry went largely unheard, very much as in our own time cigarette smokers have widely disregarded the findings of research into lung cancer. Shakespeare's plays embody the popular attitudes: up to about 1599 (the probable year of *Henry V*) they treat the pox as a source of fun; thereafter, they have a good deal to say about death from it, speaking sometimes sombrely, sometimes with a brittle kind of hilarity.

Interesting though they are, these various changes in the prevailing

modes of sexual humour over the centuries are only a part of what has
to be taken into account for the assessment of Shakespearean indecency.
An equally important kind of change is the purely semantic. In sexual
matters, more than in most others, individual words have tended to
change their meaning or force, often under the pressure of changing
fashions in slang. *Aunt*, for example, can no longer mean *prostitute*, unless
in some special stage situation which explicitly sets up the euphemism.
Aching bones, coughing, a cracked voice and whitening or thinning
hair do not nowadays suggest venereal illness, as they do for Timon of
Athens and for Pandarus in *Troilus and Cressida*. The *cart* is no longer a
standard punishment for prostitutes. *Appetite*, in modern usage, has lost
the sense *sexual appetite* or *lust*, just as *light* no longer invites semantic
punning on a secondary meaning *forward, wanton*. Contrariwise, *bastard*
has lost much of its scabrous weight by declining into common usage as a
vague expletive. Such broadening and weakening, the normal fate of
abusive terms, can be seen affecting *whoreson* in the course of Shakespeare's
own lifetime. Thereafter the word fails to hold its place in the spoken
language even as a soldierly expletive. *Cuckold* and *bawd* have also vanished
from everyday speech, while *bawdy* and *bawdry* survive only in comparatively sophisticated (usually literary) contexts, and *pox* only in medical
compounds such as *chicken-pox*.

As regards our recognising sexual indecency when we come to it,
however, neither old-fashioned subject matter nor obsolete vocabulary
represents the major difficulty. The archaic and the puzzling at least
alert us, as we read, to the need for research. The trickiest problem lies
rather in responding accurately to the sexual *innuendo* of a bygone age.
Two quotations, one from our own day and one from Shakespeare's,
will perhaps illustrate this.

> What about these crooners, eh? What about these crooners? I don't know
> what we're coming to. I don't, honest. Look at the stuff they sing.
> Look at the songs they sing! "The Dark Town Strutters' Ball", "The
> Woodchoppers' Ball", "The Basin' Street Ball"—it's a lot of rubbish,
> isn't it?

John Osborne, equipping his Entertainer with that music-hall joke, can
count on us to see it, and to appreciate its hackneyed quality, because it is
rooted in the subsoil of a popular culture which is still familiar. But
with this, compare Ben Jonson inviting a friend to supper.

> Yet shall you have, to rectifie your palate,
> An olive, capers, or some better sallade
> Ushring the mutton; with a short-leg'd hen,
> If we can get her, full of egs, and then,

> Limons, and wine for sauce: to these, a coney
> Is not to be despair'd of, for our money;
> And, though fowle, now, be scarce, yet there are clarkes,
> The skie not falling, thinke we may have larkes.

For the twentieth-century reader there is nothing in these lines that points immediately to a secondary meaning behind the surface promise of gustatory joy, yet several possible ambiguities of a *risqué* kind are treading on one another's heels. *Capers* can suggest kidlike (even goatish?) leapings as well as a herbal relish: in *As You Like It* Touchstone patronises Audrey with 'I am here with thee and thy goats, as the most capricious poet, honest Ovid, was among the Goths' (III.iii.5). *Sallade* is the same word as *sallet*—something improperly tasty, as we know from Hamlet's warning the players not to have 'sallets in the lines to make the matter savoury' (II.ii.435). *Mutton* crops up frequently in the Elizabethan period as a cant term for *prostitute*, or at any rate to denote a sexually available woman. A short-legged hen is more innocent, but *playhouse poultry* are prostitutes in *Bartholomew Fair* (II.v.96), and eggs are aphrodisiacs to Falstaff (*Merry Wives* III.v.25–6). *Coney*, although commonest in its straightforward sense *rabbit* and its slang extension to *gull* or *naive victim*, sometimes becomes a term of endearment for a woman, decently or indecently (*OED*, *cony*, sb. 5 and 5b). *Larks* are amongst the 'Good poultry' served to Cocledemoy and the procuress Mary Faugh, in strict privacy, in Marston's *Dutch Courtesan* (ed. M. L. Wine, I.i.13–18). Now, none of this *proves* that Jonson's epigram has an underlying pattern of mock bawdy enticement; but the coincidence of half-a-dozen salacious nether-meanings available within almost as many lines does open up some such possibility. Reference to Jonson's source, the forty-eighth Epigram of Martial's tenth book, neither strengthens nor weakens the possibility. The Martial poem is not in any way erotic, but Jonson is, as usual, adapting, not merely translating, so he is not in any way bound by the limits of his Latin original. Again, it may be objected that he himself was not habitually bawdy in his writing, and that he more than once inveighed against 'the immodest and obscene writing of many in their plays'. But he was not so solemn as to practise consistently what he preached, as anyone reading 'On the Famous Voyage' quickly discovers. Where that account of a journey up the noxious Fleet Ditch differs radically from 'Inviting a Friend to Supper' is in the blunt obviousness of most of its ribaldry. Yet if a strain of indecency does run through the invitation, its cryptic, muted quality is exactly what one might expect from that kind of poem. Jonson would have taken care not to expose it plainly, since that would have taken away from the poem's wit. Hilda

Hulme has explained the principle well in a discussion of *double entendres* in Shakespeare:

> The more skilfully the improper sense is suggested, the less likely it is
> that we can prove that such a sense is present. The art of the speaker and
> of the dramatist will be shown, so to say, by concealment, in the exactness
> with which the innocent and less innocent meanings can counterchange,
> the preciseness with which one sense fits the space taken by the other.[9]

So it is with the Ben Jonson epigram. One is left suspicious, but unsure, because the available evidence is indecisive. We live close enough in time to *The Entertainer* to feel certain of Osborne's calculated suppression of the expected word *balls* in favour of *rubbish*, but we are too far removed from the everyday verbal humour of Jonson's world to know for certain whether he is doing something similar.

With Shakespeare, then, page by page and line by line, the possible bawdy ambiguities must be weighed carefully if their value is to be judged at all accurately. On the one hand there is the risk of reading past them; on the other, there is the risk of being so determined to grasp at every innuendo that we proceed to read in to the text lewd meanings which its wording and phrasing will not reasonably support.

An amusing instance of the first of these errors affected the editorial handling of a line in *Romeo and Juliet* for over two hundred years. One of Mercutio's milder indecencies is his reference to 'Young Abraham Cupid' (II.i.13), which occurs when he is 'conjuring' the hidden Romeo to reappear and join his friends instead of skulking in the Capulets' garden. Puzzled by the apparently incongruous attachment of Abraham to the son of Venus, Lewis Theobald, in 1733, aired a suspicion that Shakespeare had really written 'Young *auborn* Cupid,—i.e. *brown-hair'd*'.[10] Other eighteenth-century editors changed *Abraham* to *Adam*, having accepted the 'explanation' put forward by John Upton:

> Shakespeare wrote, *Young* Adam *Cupid*, &c. The printer or transcriber,
> gave us this *Abram*, mistaking the *d* for *br*: and thus made a passage direct
> nonsense, which was understood in Shakespeare's time by all his audience:
> for this *Adam* was a most notable *archer*; and for his skill became a
> proverb.[11]

Ingenious, very. And the habit of printing *Adam* instead of *Abraham* survived right to the middle of our own century—despite the fact that as long ago as 1838 Charles Knight had solved the artificial crux: 'The "Abraham" Cupid is the cheat—the "Abraham man"—of our old statutes.'[12] Mercutio is likening the near-naked Cupid to the rogues who wandered the country stealing and begging, many of them with faked sores showing through their scanty rags. Dekker's book *Lantern and*

Candelight describes with gusto how these villains went without breeches quite deliberately, and how their 'going *Abr'am* (that is to say, "naked") is not for want of clothes but to stir up men to pity and in that pity to cozen their devotion'.[13] This combination of the ideas of nakedness and cozenage exactly fits the tone of Mercutio's bawdily derisive speech. Theobald and Upton were unintentionally bowdlerising Shakespeare.

To illustrate the converse, the editorial *creation* of an indecent innuendo, the eighteenth century may be quoted again. Sir Thomas Hanmer, perplexed over Lear's use of the expression *good-years* ('The good-years shall devour them, flesh and fell', V.iii.24), was apparently unwilling to connect it with the vague imprecation 'What the good-year!' which occurs in *Much Ado*, *2 Henry IV*, *The Merry Wives* and other plays. Instead, he 'emended' Lear's use of it to *goujeres*. This intriguing but imaginary word he glossed as 'The *French* disease', and alleged its derivation to be from the French *Gouje*, 'a common Camp-Trull'.[14] One cannot help admiring the ingenuity of all this. It seems slightly un-chivalrous of *Chambers's Dictionary* to dismiss it drily as 'an editor's would-be improvement upon *goodyear . . .*, from a spurious Fr. *goujère*'.

At the same time, it would be unjust to create the impression that distortion of Shakespeare's indecency, one way or the other, has been any more common among Shakespeare's editors than among his other commentators. If anything, the reverse has been true, at least in recent decades. The very nature of the modern textual scholar's expertise makes him less likely to corrupt Shakespeare's meaning than are critics who lack such training, and the twentieth-century equivalents of Theobald's or Hanmer's well-meant solecisms are to be found, for the most part, out-side the confines of formal textual study. Eric Partridge's book *Shake-speare's Bawdy* is their best-known repository—not so much through being positively misleading as through failing to provide explicit defence for interpretations which, as H. W. Fowler might have said, will require to be defended every time they are put forward. It might have been possible for Partridge to justify the inclusion of *come* in his glossary, but the entry under the word certainly does not succeed in justifying it. The gloss 'To experience a sexual emission' is supported by two Shakespearean quotations:

MARGARET   Well, I will call Beatrice to you, who I think hath legs.
BENEDICK   And therefore will come.

Much Ado V.ii.23

OLIVIA   Wilt thou go to bed, Malvolio?
MALVOLIO   To bed! 'Ay', sweetheart, and I'll come to thee!'

Twelfth Night III.iv.28

Neither of these, I suggest, is anything like convincing as evidence for the modern orgasmic usage of *come* which Partridge is attributing to Shakespeare. It is a usage that does occur in Dekker—'a wench that will come with a wet finger', *1 Honest Whore* I.ii.4—but that does not make it Shakespearean.

Much the same thing happens with *eye*, for which Partridge in 1947 claimed a Shakespearean sense of *pudendum muliebre*. Shakespeare uses the word *eye*, in singular or plural form, 1311 times. Given the associative habit of the poet's mind, it is not impossible that once or twice amongst all those occurrences the opening or closing movement of this moist, hair-fringed organ—conventionally, with Elizabethan writers, the point of entry for love—could suggest the appearance or function of the vulva. As G. I. Williams has pointed out, *eye* is used in this way by Middleton and Rowley:

> I'll never leave the love of an open-hearted widow for a narrow-eyed
>   maid again.
>
> Middleton, No Wit Like a Woman's I.ii.295

> ... for a woman, they say, has an eye more than a man.
>
> Middleton and Rowley, The Changeling III.iii.74

But the very clarity of these two examples is instructive, for if the limited similarity between eye and vulva is to be part of the sense-pattern in any play, its wording, or at least that of its context, must surely indicate that the comparison is being made. Partridge, in the single Shakespeare quotation he invoked, could point to no such indication.

> A whitely wanton with a velvet brow,
> With two pitch balls stuck in her face for eyes;
> Ay, and, by heaven, one that will do the deed,
> Though Argus were her eunuch and her guard.
>
> Love's Labour's Lost III.i.186

The last two lines are indisputably bawdy, but it would take more than that, with or without an *eyes/ay* pun and a mention of balls, to supply for *eyes* the pudendal significance that Partridge asserted. The weakness of his case becomes still more apparent when his cross-reference to O ('For the semantics') is followed up. From O in the glossary we are further referred to *circle*, where 'the semantics' consist of a note stating, '*Magic circle* and—physiologically inaccurate—sexual circle'. When yet another cross-reference leads us back, via *ring*, to the entries at *circle* and O, we might be excused for suspecting an elaborate leg-pull.

Even outside the Partridge glossary there have been a number of inadequately supported attributions of indecencies to Shakespeare in

recent years. For a long time after the appearance of Dover Wilson's New
Cambridge edition of *Hamlet* (1934; second edition 1936), the repeated
use of the word *nunnery* in III.i was widely accepted as meaning *brothel* as
well as, if not indeed instead of, *convent*. That a jocularly inverted use of
the word would have been available to Shakespeare is not in doubt:
OED (*nunnery*, 1b) quotes its use by Nashe, by Fletcher and on an
eighteenth-century title-page. But to know that such a usage was possible
in the early seventeenth century is not in itself enough to demonstrate that
Shakespeare avails himself of it for Hamlet. As A. L. French has shown,[15]
this usage simply does not lend itself to the antithesis that Hamlet is
making when he harangues Ophelia—an antithesis, not simply between
marriage and the avoidance of marriage, but between sexual activity and
its avoidance. 'He cannot be saying "avoid sex by going to a brothel"!'

The *nunnery* instance effectively demonstrates the importance of the
general tone of a passage in determining what is indecent and what is not.
William Empson and the New Critics have made us readier than preceding generations to appreciate Shakespeare's habit of combining apparent
incompatibles, whether in verse or in stage effect. We have come to
accept, too, that the author who devised the mock suicide of Gloucester
and Imogen's despair over the corpse of Cloten seems capable of almost
any mingling of emotions, however bizarre. But there is nothing to
suggest that he would set up such tensions casually, let alone unconsciously, as some of the more avid bawdy-hunters would seem to imply.
Take, for example, Cleopatra's lament on the death of Antony.

> O, see, my women,
> The crown o' th' earth doth melt. My lord!
> O, withered is the garland of the war,
> The soldier's pole is fallen! Young boys and girls
> Are level now with men. The odds is gone,
> And there is nothing left remarkable
> Beneath the visiting moon.   [*Swoons*
>   IV.xv.62

Commenting on these lines, Virgil K. Whitaker writes of 'an all too
appropriate though indecent double meaning of the kind that Shakespeare
uses elsewhere to deflate the emotion of a potentially tragic situation'.[16]
The alleged double meaning is, I take it, in the phrase 'The soldier's pole
is fallen', which in a comic context could no doubt make reference to a
detumescent penis. To accept that as an available meaning here, however,
is to read with the distorting eye of early adolescence. At a literal level, one
could oppose the sexual reading by remarking Cleopatra's steady emphasis on soldierly triumph as contrasted with ordinariness. Young boys

and girls find a place in the flow of images not because they are sexually
immature but because they are powerless, uncelebrated; grown men have
become like them, unremarkable. But Whitaker's interpretation can
surely be disposed of more simply. In the theatre, where Cleopatra has to
faint ('She's dead too, our sovereign'), a joke would either prove un-
actable or, if actable, atmospherically ruinous. To suppose that Shakespeare has blundered so absurdly at this of all moments in the play is to
carry critical openmindedness to the point of vacuity.

Not all allegations of indecency can be so firmly proved or disproved.
Bawdy, as I have said, is an indefinite region, and between the demonstrably decent and the demonstrably indecent lies much that is neither.
It is hard to be sure, for example, whether Cleopatra is being flippant or
serious, improper or heedlessly urgent, when Shakespeare has her exclaim

> Ram thou thy fruitful tidings in mine ears,
> That long time have been barren.
>
> II.v.23

Then again, what does one decide about two of the most famous lines of
song in *Twelfth Night*?

> Journeys end in lovers meeting,
> Every wise man's son doth know.
>
> II.iii.41

If the word *son* were to be given the heavy stress that the tetrameter
allows, it could conceivably be argued that progression from *lovers
meeting* to *son* implies copulation—and hence a *risqué* insinuation of the
kind which pointedly omits explicit reference to sexual activity, as in the
John Osborne passage I quoted earlier. Yet it seems doubtful, to say the
least, whether many readers or audiences would detect so muted a hint;
and to ignore it would not necessarily be imperceptive, especially in view
of the near-proverbial commonness in Elizabethan literature of phrases
like 'every wise man's son' and 'every mother's son'. This is also why
such sayings as 'woo her, wed her, and bed her' (*The Taming of the Shrew*
I.i.141) are rarely if ever indecent.

A more complex illustration of the same interpretative difficulty may
be drawn from the title *Much Ado About Nothing*. This lends itself to at
least two possible interpretations, and perhaps also a third. First there is
the obvious sense of the phrase, appropriate as the name of a light comedy
in which characters fuss over what seems to have occurred but in fact
amounts to nothing. Secondly there could be the *nothing/noting* pun which
occurs only innocently within the play itself (II.iii.52–5) but which is
to be found in a context of prostitution in Marston:

FRANCESCHINA   . . . You ha' brought mine love, mine honor, mine
body, all to noting!

MARY FAUGH   To nothing! I'll be sworn I have brought them to all the
things I could. I ha' made as much o' your maidenhead—and you had
been mine own daughter, I could not ha' sold your maidenhead
oft'ner than I ha' done.

                                        The Dutch Courtesan, ed. cit., II.ii.7

This would give us not only much ado about nothing but also much ado
about noting—*noting* in the sense *observing* or 'branding with disgrace'
(*OED, note,* v., *1,* 7b, 7c).

But there still remains the third possibility, that *Nothing* carries the
bawdy implication *vulva,* as the letter O probably does when Juliet's
Nurse demands of Romeo, 'Why should you fall into so deep an O?'
(III.iii.91). Another possible parallel is in *Hamlet*:

HAMLET   Do you think I meant country matters?
OPHELIA I think nothing, my lord.
HAMLET   That's a fair thought to lie between maids' legs.
OPHELIA What is, my lord?
HAMLET   Nothing.

                                        III.ii.112

After the pun in *country,* we need not doubt that Hamlet is making a
further bawdy joke with 'Nothing.' But what joke, precisely? Does this
nothing, with or without a circular gesture of the fingers, represent the
female pudend, as Dover Wilson and Thomas Pyles both proposed?[17]
Or does Shakespeare only mean—as F. W. Bateson has suggested to me—
that no-thing, no penis, ought to be lying between maids' legs? Either
meaning is possible, and neither seems provable.

The difficulty of finding solid corroboration for *Nothing* as a pudendal
joke in *Much Ado* increases rather than decreases when we face the
bewildering variety of *nothing*-quibbles displayed by Shakespeare and his
contemporaries. Many are based on the idea of somebody's lacking sexual
organs (male or female) altogether. In *The Lover's Melancholy* III.i.74,
Ford has the foolish courtier Cuculus exclaim, 'I will court any thing;
be in love with nothing, nor no-thing'. Essentially the same idea, this
time in a quibble conflating the want of a vagina with the want of a
dowry, occurs in the anonymous *King Leir* (printed 1605):

RAGAN
She [Cordella] were right fit to make a Parsons wife:
For they, men say, do love faire women well,
And many times doe marry them with nothing.
GONORILL
With nothing! marry God forbid: why, are there any such?

RAGAN
  I meane, no money.
GONORILL
  I cry you mercy, I mistooke you much . . . .

  B4

Many other *nothing*-jokes only approach the physiological, steering clear
of it at the last moment. When Pistol asks, 'Come we to full points here,
and are etceteras nothings?' (*2 Henry IV* II.iv.174) his meaning is un-
mistakably sexual, but it is also obscure. The same applies to Leontes's
ranting to Camillo in *The Winter's Tale*:

                    Is whispering nothing?
  Is leaning cheek to cheek? Is meeting noses?
  Kissing with inside lip? Stopping the career
  Of laughter with a sigh?—a note infallible
  Of breaking honesty. Horsing foot on foot?
  Skulking in corners? Wishing clocks more swift?
  Hours minutes? Noon midnight? And all eyes
  Blind with the pin and web but theirs, theirs only,
  That would unseen be wicked—is this nothing?
  Why, then the world and all that's in't is nothing;
  The covering sky is nothing; Bohemia nothing;
  My wife is nothing; nor nothing have these nothings,
  If this be nothing.

  I.ii.284

A speech like this would seem to be the last word in what Thomas Pyles
called 'pudendal suggestiveness': *nothing, note, foot, honesty* in a hymenal
form that will break—all these are words which, in one place or another,
Shakespeare uses sexually. But in the pell-mell flow of Leontes's diseased
imagination, 'suggestiveness' is the most we can claim. Of the nine
nothings in those twelve lines, we cannot point to a single one and say with
confidence, 'Just there he means vulva.'

  The whole matter is further complicated by the fact that *nothing* is
synonymous with *nought*, which Elizabethan spelling did not consistently
differentiate from *naught*. Such a quibble as Flute's 'A paramour is—God
bless us—a thing of naught', or Richard III's 'Naught to do with Mistress
Shore?' is not necessarily anatomical. It may simply be invoking the
general idea of sexual sin (as in *naughty*). The same is true of *nothing* itself
when Iago dwells on it. 'Nay, but be wise: yet we see nothing done, /
She may be honest yet. . . . So they do nothing, 'tis a venial slip' (*Othello*
III.iii.429, IV.i.9).

  We arrive, then, at a semantic impasse. If Shakespeare had called his
comedy *Much Ado About Nought* we could at least have claimed one ribald
nether-meaning, *nought/naught/naughty*, with some confidence. As it is,

Much Ado About Nothing might conceivably involve a sexual *double entendre*, since the plot is concerned with Hero's virginity and, in a way, with Beatrice's. Hero, although doing nothing wrong, finds herself accused of 'doing nothing' in a conceited sense of that phrase. But since not even Borachio or Don John anticipates Iago's quibble, we have to face the fact that the play itself does not establish this kind of connection between its title and its content. A reader comparing that title with the quite un-conceited names of companion pieces—*The Merchant of Venice, Twelfth Night, All's Well That Ends Well*—has no choice but to return the same verdict as for the Ben Jonson poem: non-proven.

Enough has been said to indicate the hazards surrounding the analysis of indecent material in Shakespeare's plays and poems. As I hope several of the foregoing quotations have made clear, not only single words and phrases but even whole speeches, whole episodes, will sometimes steer close to being bawdy, yet will just shave past its true sexual-absurd tone. An 'averagely indecent' Shakespeare play (*As You Like It*, perhaps, or *1 Henry IV*) is likely to have roughly as many near-bawdy lines as it has actually bawdy lines. Fortunately, Shakespeare himself gives extensive help towards our telling the difference. As has often been remarked in other connections, he was never an author to waste his effects by allowing them to pass unnoticed. Whatever the dramatic functions of his sexual references—whether made lightly (*The Two Gentlemen of Verona, Love's Labour's Lost*), in aggressive jest (*Hamlet, Troilus, Cymbeline*) or in grim earnest (*Othello, Lear, Timon*)—they are very often shaped and pointed by their context. Key words or phrases are sometimes repeated to give the theatre-audience time to grasp double meanings.

> HOSTESS   Here's a goodly tumult! . . . Alas, alas! put up your naked
> weapons, put up your naked weapons. . . . Are you not hurt i'th' groin?
> Methought 'a made a shrewd thrust at your belly.
>
> 2 *Henry IV* II.iv.194–201

Besides the guidance given by the general tone and drift of meaning, we also get, in the plays, the explicit responses of a variety of characters, 'registering' indecency in their different ways. Sometimes the speaker of a bawdy line will hesitate over it or apologise for it in advance:

> BURGUNDY   Pardon the frankness of my mirth, if I answer you for
> that. If you would conjure in her, you must make a circle; if conjure
> up love in her in his true likeness, he must appear naked and blind.
>
> *Henry V* V.ii.287

POMPEY   Sir, she came in great with child, and longing—saving your
   honour's reverence—for stewed prunes.

Measure for Measure II.i.86

On other occasions the apology comes after the lapse into impropriety,
and it will often be addressed directly to the audience.

> NURSE
>   Sleep for a week. For the next night, I warrant,
>   The County Paris hath set up his rest
>   That you shall rest but little. God forgive me!
> Marry, and amen!

Romeo and Juliet IV.v.5

In some of these comic passages, Shakespeare's characters will pointedly
bowdlerise their own expressions. Touchstone avoids saying *jakes* by
calling Jaques 'Master What-ye-call't'; Lafew refers delicately to Lavache's
'lower part', and Launce to 'another thing' that his milkmaid may
perhaps be liberal with; Pompey speaks of the pox as 'the thing you wot
of'; and in the brothel at Mytilene, Boult suppresses *thorn* or *prick* when he
is praising the fresh rose, Marina, to Lysimachus.

On the occasions when a suggestive remark is not signalled by the
character speaking it, there should still be small danger of our missing the
point if the dramatist has another character at hand to clarify the line for
the audience through his or her reception of it, whether amused, guffaw-
ing, coy, reproving, shocked, brusque or indignant. Reproof comes most
commonly—as one might expect—from the women.

MARIA   Come, come, you talk greasily; your lips grow foul.

Love's Labour's Lost IV.i.130

KATHERINE   Le foot, et le count? O Seigneur Dieu! Ils sont mots de son
   mauvais, corruptible, gros, et impudique, et non pour les dames
   d'honneur d'user. Je ne voudrais prononcer ces mots devant les
   seigneurs de France pour tout le monde. Foh! Le foot et le count!

Henry V III.iv.48

Needless to say, Shakespeare's females vary widely in their attitudes to
verbal impropriety, but the variations are based on a recognisable
Elizabethan norm. Once again it is Marston who expresses it most
plainly:

> Fie, Crispinella! you speak too broad. . . . Faith, sister, I'll be gone if
> you speak so broad. . . . Good quick sister, stay your pace. We are
> private, but the world would censure you; for truly severe modesty is
> women's virtue.

The Dutch Courtesan, ed. cit., III.i.24, 28, 45

Shakespeare is invoking this social inhibition when he has Lavinia, in
Titus Andronicus, seek a euphemism for some such word as *ravishment*
('one thing more, / That womanhood denies my tongue to tell'), and
when he has Desdemona hesitate over saying *whore*: 'Am I that name,
Iago? . . . I cannot say "whore": / It does abhor me now I speak the
word'. In *Much Ado*, the stock convention is simultaneously acknowledged
and disrupted. It rules Hero, but not her lively cousin Beatrice or the
blunter Margaret.

> HERO   God give me joy to wear it [her wedding gown], for my heart
> is exceedingly heavy.
> MARGARET   'Twill be heavier soon, by the weight of a man.
> HERO   Fie upon thee! Art not ashamed?
> MARGARET   Of what, lady? Of speaking honourably? Is not marriage
> honourable in a beggar? Is not your lord honourable without
> marriage? I think you would have me say, 'saving your reverence, a
> husband'; an bad thinking do not wrest true speaking, I'll offend
> nobody. Is there any harm in 'the heavier for a husband'? None, I
> think, an it be the right husband and the right wife; otherwise 'tis light,
> and not heavy; ask my Lady Beatrice else, here she comes.
>
> III.iv.22

A similar difference in freedom of expression between ladies of comparable social position can be seen in *Henry VIII* (II.iii) when the Old
Lady teases Anne Bullen about chastity and ambition. More likemindedness and a still less 'refined' attitude can be noticed in Cleopatra's attendants:

> CHARMIAN   Well, if you were but an inch of fortune better than I,
> where would you choose it?
> IRAS   Not in my husband's nose.
> CHARMIAN   Our worser thoughts heavens mend!
>
> *Antony and Cleopatra* I.ii.55

The well-bred female's sense of propriety is thus a highly variable, but
also very useful, indicator of Shakespearean indecency.

Scoldings for outspokenness are not always well deserved. Sometimes
it is the reprover, not the reproved, who has invented the indecency that
Shakespeare is pointing up. In *The Taming of the Shrew*, for example,
Petruchio's lackey Grumio (madcap servant to a madcap master) abuses
the already victimised tailor by making him the butt of a series of quite
imaginary scurrilities:

> PETRUCHIO [*to the tailor's man*]   Well sir, in brief, the gown is not for me.
> GRUMIO   You are i'th'right, sir, 'tis for my mistress.
> PETRUCHIO   Go, take it up unto thy master's use.
> GRUMIO   Villain, not for thy life! Take up my mistress' gown for thy
> master's use!

PETRUCHIO   Why sir, what's your conceit in that?
GRUMIO
    O sir, the conceit is deeper than you think for.
    Take up my mistress' gown to his master's use!
    O fie, fie, fie!

                             IV.iii.151

The whole process of imputing indecency is at its most intricate with those characters whose scurrilising tendencies go deepest. Mistress Quickly could vie with any police prosecutor in the art of uncovering what she—but scarcely anyone else—would take to be cunningly worded sexual innuendo. Much the same is true, in a more serious way, of Othello and Leontes in their jealous phases. Luckily, this habit of mind is easy to gauge.

Finally, we have to consider those instances of possible bawdy in which the speaker makes no hesitation or apology, and no other character is suitably placed to register licentiousness. When this happens, the reader will be thrown back on his assessments of mood, connotation, implication, dramatic circumstance and the nature of the person speaking. The occurrence of several potentially indecent words in rapid succession can also strengthen one's suspicions, as we saw with Ben Jonson. Even then, at any one time, our reading of 'doubtful' bawdy will embrace a whole range of semantic possibilities, with the result that our precise interpretation can differ between one reading (or performance) and the next. These ambiguous indecencies, fortunately, are seldom crucial to the interpretation of an entire speech or scene.

One result of this whole enquiry into indecency has been my own growing conviction that the golden rule is to be slow in *assuming* ribald significance anywhere in Shakespeare—above all when reading or directing the plays in the sex-conscious and irony-loving atmosphere of the later twentieth century. There has been unintended warning for us all in productions of *Othello* rendered nonsensical by tarty, ogling Desdemonas; in some orgiastic *Midsummer Night's Dreams*; and in the odd extensions of homosexual emphasis in at least one *Troilus and Cressida*. The lesson needs to be written plain: only where the text of Shakespeare fully supports a bawdy interpretation can we make deductions of any worth regarding his dramatic or thematic use of indecency.

NOTES

1. *The Edinburgh Review*, xxxvi (1821–22), 52–3: part of an unsigned notice of Thomas Bowdler, ed., *The Family Shakespeare* (10 vols, London, 1818). In an article in *Notes and Queries* (n.s. xiii (1966), 141–2) Noel Perrin pointed out that, strictly speaking, the 1818 *Family Shakespeare* was not the first but the second

edition. The true first edition, containing only twenty of the plays, had appeared in 1807 and had been the anonymous work of Bowdler's sister, Henrietta Maria Bowdler.

2. *The Family Shakespeare* (London, 7th edn, 1839), p. vii.

3. G. I. Williams, 'Serious uses of sexual imagery in the Elizabethan drama', Ph.D. thesis, University of Wales, 1964, p. 313.

4. Ben Jonson, *Epicoene*, ed. Edward Partridge (1971), IV.iii.50.

5. *Tarlton's Jests* (edn of 1613), [B2ᵛ]. In this extract, as in all other old-spelling quotations in this book, I have adopted modern typographical conventions, expanding Elizabethan contractions and altering *v*, *u*, *i* and long *s* to *u*, *v*, *j* and short *s* wherever modern usage would have them so. (I am grateful to Professor P. H. Davison for drawing my attention to the Tarlton incident.)

6. See, for example, Jonson, *Sejanus*, ed. J. A. Barish (1965), I.i.212–16, or *Epicoene*, *ed. cit.*, I.i.23–4; Middleton, ed. A. H. Bullen (London, 1885–86), *More Dissemblers besides Women* V.i.190ff., or *A Game at Chess* IV.ii.108–10; Tourneur, *The Revenger's Tragedy*, ed. R. A. Foakes (1966), I.iii.35, or *The Atheist's Tragedy*, ed. Irving Ribner (1964), IV.iii. 205–10; Dekker, ed. Fredson Bowers (1953–61), *Satiromastix* I.ii.21–166; Webster, *The White Devil*, ed. J. R. Brown (1960), V.i.122–4.

7. The quotations from Sir Edward Coke are taken from H. Montgomery Hyde, *The Other Love* (1970), pp. 37–41.

8. See, for example, William Clowes, *Treatise, touching the cure of the disease called Morbus Gallicus* (London, 1579; 1585).

9. Hilda M. Hulme, *Explorations in Shakespeare's Language* (1962), p. 118.

10. Lewis Theobald, ed., *The Works of Shakespeare* (7 vols, London, 1733–34), vii, 151–2.

11. John Upton, *Critical Observations on Shakespeare* (London, 1746), pp. 234–5 (quoted, with slight alterations, in H. H. Furness's Variorum *Romeo and Juliet* (Philadelphia, 1874), p. 87).

12. Quoted in Variorum *Romeo and Juliet*, p. 88.

13. Thomas Dekker, *The Wonderful Year, The Gull's Horn-Book, Penny-Wise Pound-Foolish, English Villainies Discovered by Lantern and Candlelight, and Selected Writings*, ed. E. D. Pendry (1967), p. 289.

14. Sir Thomas Hanmer, ed., *The Works of Shakespear* (6 vols, Oxford, 1743–44), vi, Aaaa.

15. A. L. French, 'Hamlet's Nunnery', *English Studies* (Amsterdam), xlviii (1967), 141–5.

16. Virgil K. Whitaker, *The Mirror up to Nature* (1965), p. 295.

17. Cf. J. Dover Wilson, ed., New Cambridge *Hamlet* (2nd edn, 1936), p. 199, and Thomas Pyles, 'Ophelia's "Nothing"', *Modern Language Notes*, lxiv (1949), 322–3.

2

Bawdy as simple Farce

Prithee say on. He's for a jig, or a tale of bawdry, or he sleeps.
Hamlet II.ii.493

In view of the impossibility of assigning firm dates to most of Shakespear's early plays, a case could be made out for making *Titus Andronicus* or one of the early histories the starting-point for examination of his bawdy. It happens, though, that some of the early comedies present both a simpler picture and a fuller one so far as ribaldry is concerned. It is there more than anywhere else that cheerful indecency finds a home as an end in itself, to make those laugh whose lungs are tickle o' the sere. As Hilda Hulme has remarked, it sometimes seems that one or two lines of dialogue gain a place in Shakespeare's text only for the sake of the small firework display that they contain.[1]

While the metaphor of the firework display is, I think, particularly apt for much of what goes on in the early comedies, a distinction needs to be made between those displays that are primarily verbal and those that might be called 'notional' or 'situational'. Roughly it is the distinction between the quip and the prank, except that no practical joking is involved. *Love's Labour's Lost*, for example, is especially rich in verbal display, word-play for its own sake—so much so, that I shall be considering it in the next chapter rather than here. In *The Comedy of Errors*, on the other hand, as also in *The Two Gentlemen of Verona* and a little later in *A Midsummer Night's Dream*, we more often encounter mild indecencies of the situational kind. Most of them are inherent in plot material concerned with the interchange of lovers or acceptance of substitute husbands, whether through magical agency or because of mistaken identity. And it is immediately striking that whereas *A Midsummer Night's Dream* mines this vein of humour fairly thoroughly, *The Comedy of Errors* (notoriously hard to date, but certainly the earlier of the two plays) shows the dramatist going to some trouble to limit, rather than expand, the salacious element of his sources.

Shakespeare's main source for *The Comedy of Errors* was the *Menaechmi* of Plautus. In softening many of the original play's indecencies he may to some extent have been following a lead from William Warner, whose English version of the *Menaechmi* is known to have circulated in manuscript before being printed in 1595: 'A pleasant and fine Conceited Comædie, taken out of the most excellent wittie Poet *Plautus: Chosen purposely from out the rest, as least harmefull, and yet most delightfull.*'[2] But there is some evidence that Shakespeare had read the original Latin, and none to indicate that he followed Warner rather than *vice versa.*[3] In the present state of our knowledge we can make no reliable deductions about Warner's influence, if any, on the ribald touches in *The Comedy of Errors*. What we can observe, in comparing Shakespeare directly with Plautus, is the near-elimination of the prostitute, Erotium. She speaks sixty-four lines in the Latin play and only twenty-six—most of them about jewellery —as the nameless Courtesan in *The Comedy of Errors*. Similarly, her maid has no part whatever in the Shakespeare play, whereas in Plautus she is not above a little prostitution on her own account:

> amabo, mi Menaechme, inauris da mihi
> faciendas pondo duom nummum, stalagmia,
> ut te lubenter uideam, quom ad nos ueneris.[4]

The same tendency to eliminate potential salacity can be seen in Shakespeare's handling of his second Plautine source, the *Amphitryon*. *Amphitryon* seems to have suggested the idea of having identical servants in addition to identical masters, and it clearly supplied the plot-material for Shakespeare's III.i, the locking-out of Antipholus of Ephesus. In Plautus the door is barred by Mercury in the likeness of the slave Sosia, and the messenger-god becomes an outright pander. He assumes Sosia's form in order to procure Alcmena, Amphitryon's wife, for Jupiter. Jupiter, in turn, takes the shape of Amphitryon, and duly spends the night with Alcmena. Only on the following day (that is, the day in which the action of the play is set) does the real Amphitryon return from the war, to find himself locked out of his own house while Jupiter spends a further hour with the lady. Shakespeare, in taking over the locking-out incident for *The Comedy of Errors*, eliminates the overnight stay. In doing so, he gains the advantage of heightening suspense. 'What error drives our eyes and ears amiss?' asks the innocent interloper, Antipholus of Syracuse, bewildered by Adriana's wifely possessiveness.

> Until I know this sure uncertainty,
> I'll entertain the offered fallacy.

II.ii.184

He waits to see what will happen next: and we wait too, throughout the door-barring scene. As Michel Grivelet has remarked, we are on the brink of the irreparable, and our comic pleasure owes much to the extreme precision and the extreme precariousness of the equilibrium.[5] The interesting question of the Syracusan's relationship with Adriana is resolved in III.ii, where Luciana's reproaches to the visitor for his coolness towards her sister make it clear that sexual integrity has been preserved. But this in turn makes possible a new ambiguity. Far from following through his advantage with Adriana, Antipholus of Syracuse has fallen in love with Luciana herself—to her great consternation, since she believes him to be her brother-in-law. Shakespeare thus adds a complete new loop to the play's chain of 'errors', while still safeguarding his characters from the opprobrium that convention would attach to sexually immoral acts. Indeed, the promotion of the gentle Luciana to something approaching main character status makes the play engage more fully with the theme of marital duty and sympathy, and thus takes it further than ever from the simple farce of the *Amphitryon's* dénouement, in which Alcmena bears twins, one to each husband. Shakespeare's ending, with Emilia coming from her priory to be reunited with her long-scattered family, is much more fully resolved in emotional terms.

So much, then, for the potential ribaldry eliminated, or at least excluded, from *The Comedy of Errors*. How much does Shakespeare add? Not very much. Most of what he does add is given to the two Dromios, who in this, as in much else, are true to their Plautine role as comic servants. Dromio of Ephesus quibbles about horns and cockolds (II.i.57-9) and about the dubious virginity of Nell the kitchen-maid ('the kitchen-vestal', IV.iv.72). Dromio of Syracuse has two lengthier bouts of word-play— one on syphilitic alopecia and unsound testicles (II.ii.82-106), and one on the geography of Nell:

DROMIO OF SYRACUSE ... she is spherical, like a globe; I could find out countries in her.
ANTIPHOLUS OF SYRACUSE In what part of her body stands Ireland?
DROMIO OF SYRACUSE Marry, sir, in her buttocks. I found it out by the bogs.
ANTIPHOLUS OF SYRACUSE Where Scotland?
DROMIO OF SYRACUSE I found it by the barrenness, hard in the palm of the hand.
ANTIPHOLUS OF SYRACUSE Where France?

DROMIO OF SYRACUSE   In her forehead, armed and reverted, making
war against her heir.

III.ii.113

Syphilis is involved here too, since France, mythical home of 'the French
disease', is punningly said to be in Nell's forehead, attacking her hair. (In
fact it was not necessarily syphilis itself but more probably the Elizabethan
treatment of it, by fumigation and sweating, that led to the rapid loss of
hair.) It might well seem that Dromio is somewhat preoccupied with
venereal infection, since he glances at it again with the equivocal warning
'Light wenches will burn' (IV.iii.51); but jokes based on cooking, roasting
or accidental burning, and likening this to the burning sensations symptomatic of gonorrhoea and urethritis, are an Elizabethan commonplace, as
may be seen from the entries in the glossary under *burn*, *heat* and *roast
meat for worms*. Dromio's venereal jokes are in fact no more than the stock
material of an Elizabethan comic, as also is the coprological couplet
flung at him by his brother: 'A man may break a word with you, sir;
and words are but wind; / Ay, and break it in your face, so he break it
not behind' (III.i.75–6). In an encounter in which two servants are
exchanging abuse, this finds as natural a place as might otherwise be
filled with some insult based on bad breath or pimples, and it is of no
significance to the play as a whole. The same is true of the Dromios'
sexual scurrilities. When extended, as in II.ii and III.ii, they help to
fulfil one of the standard functions of sub-plot in covering a supposed
lapse of time in the main action of the play. Otherwise they are simple
farce, art for laughter's sake.

Outside the servants' quarters in *The Comedy of Errors*, references to
sexual matters tend to be direct, non-humorous, and therefore non-bawdy.
One exceptional moment is when Antipholus of Ephesus attacks his wife
with 'You minion, you, are these your customers?' (IV.iv.57). He is
taking up bawdy here as a rhetorical weapon of the most emotionally
formidable kind—a kind that Shakespeare is to use more extensively much
later, in *Hamlet*, *Othello* and other distinctively 'Jacobean' plays. In this
early comedy, however, it plays only a fleeting role. Like the servants'
more unbuttoned scurrilities, it does little to disturb the prevailing non-
bawdy tone. Indeed, *The Comedy of Errors* prompts a negative hypothesis
that most of the other early comedies will strengthen. The hypothesis is
that as the writers of stage comedy in the 1590s went, Shakespeare was
not even averagely bawdy; not, at any rate, as a matter of general habit.
Although willing enough to use bawdy in an incidental and occasional
way—in witticisms and byplay, in the puns, metaphors and allusions
making up the small firecracker displays that Hilda Hulme referred to—

his earlier comedies do not rely on bawdy plots or situations or characters or themes. Some of these will come later, especially in the problem plays, but even then Shakespeare will offer us no bedroom farce or comic cuckoldry apart from the frustrated efforts of Falstaff in *The Merry Wives of Windsor*. Compare this dramatist with Marston or Middleton, Molière or Wycherley, and it becomes clear that his chaste handling of *The Comedy of Errors* is broadly typical of him. It is a comedy in which salacity is remarkable in just the same way as the barking dog of Conan Doyle's 'Silver Blaze':

> 'Is there any point to which you would wish to draw my attention?'
> 'To the curious incident of the dog in the night-time.'
> 'The dog did nothing in the night-time.'
> 'That was the curious incident,' remarked Sherlock Holmes.

Just as, in *The Comedy of Errors*, bawdy is almost exclusively a property of the servant class, so also in *A Midsummer Night's Dream* it attaches mainly to Bottom, Quince and their 'crew of patches, rude mechanicals'. There are in the play, at a cautious estimate, about nine demonstrable instances of bawdy,[6] and all but two of these come from the artisans. Like their stubbornly English, un-Athenian manner, their comparatively frequent scurrilities help to set the working-men apart from the play's aristocratic and magical groups of characters. But here the similarity with the bawdy of the Dromios abruptly ends. The Dromios' sexual and coprological jokes were conscious, contrived, even (in a crude sense) witty. The *Dream's* mechanicals, on the other hand, are very rarely allowed to show any awareness of their own comic lines. Peter Quince, carpenter and play-producer, is permitted one deliberate quibble over French-crown-colour—once again the secondary reference is to baldness as a supposed symptom of syphilis—and Bottom is being lumpishly facetious with Peaseblossom when he asks to be commended 'to Mistress Squash, your mother, and to Master Peascod, your father': behind the primary meaning of *squash*, an unripe peascod, there lurks a suggestion of the human female squashed by the male in coitus, and the hint is strengthened by the nearness of *peascod* itself, since *cod* can have the secondary sense *testicle*. Apart from these two instances, however, the amateur actors reveal no special aptitude for *risqué* linguistic hair-splitting.

Their unconscious humour is a different matter. 'We will meet, and there we may rehearse most obscenely and courageously,' declares Bottom as the palace-wood rendezvous is settled. In the event, his malapropism turns out to be less prophetic of the 'Pyramus and Thisbe' rehearsal than of the actual performance:

BOTTOM *as Pyramus*
O, kiss me through the hole of this vile wall!
FLUTE *as Thisbe*
I kiss the wall's hole, not your lips at all.

V.i.197

Shakespeare's choice of the word *hole* seems quite deliberate here. In the one obvious source for 'Pyramus and Thisbe', Arthur Golding's translation of Ovid's *Metamorphoses*, an edition of which came out in 1593, the wall, being inanimate, has simply a 'crany'. Similarly, Thomas Mouffet's poem *The Silkworms and their Flies*, which has been claimed as a further possible source,[7] has nothing as physically suggestive as 'the wall's hole'. Nevertheless, I balk at a suggestion, put forward in a letter to *The Times Literary Supplement* (29 January 1971), that Bottom and Flute should converse through Snout's legs rather than through the 'chink' of two fingers. The Pyramus-and-Thisbe interlude is farce, but it need not decline into circus clowning. Flute's line about kissing the 'wall's hole' surely works best as a *verbal* infelicity, unintended by its speaker and comparable with Bottom's later line 'Since lion vile hath here deflowered my dear'. Like *deflowered* for *devoured*, the *wall's hole* becomes part of the mechanism by which Shakespeare widens the gap between the artisan actors and the classically 'tragic' tale they are presenting. 'Tongue-tied simplicity' is precisely what Philostrate is eager to censure, Theseus to forgive.

Bottom's honest unsubtlety also complicates his other entanglement with royalty, the affair with Titania. This has nothing to do with his name, or at least nothing bawdy to do with it. The modern sense of *bottom* as buttocks is never so much as glanced at in the *Dream*, and it does not appear in the quite generous lists of synonyms for *the rump* given in the Italian and French dictionaries of John Florio and Randle Cotgrave (1598–1611).[8] The *OED's* earliest record of *bottom's* being written in this modern sense is dated 1794–96. Shakespeare's Bottom is a weaver, and Elizabethan weaving gives him his name: a bottom was the object on which thread was wound. If that suggests a certain wooden stolidity, this is indeed the quality that dominates his scenes in the forest. In III.i, unaware of his newly acquired ass's head, and deserted by his fellows, he advertises his equanimity by singing.

> The finch, the sparrow, and the lark,
>   The plainsong cuckoo grey,
> Whose note full many a man doth mark
>   And dares not answer 'Nay'

III.i.123

—dares not, because any man may, for all he knows, be a cuckold; but Bottom, riding rough-shod over this implication, 'explains':

> for indeed, who would set his wit to so foolish a bird? Who would give a bird the lie, though he cry 'cuckoo' never so?

> III.i.127

The cuckoo verse, with its bawdy implication unnoticed by the singer, has emphasised the asinine streak in Bottom at the very moment when Titania is awakening to become infatuated with him. 'Thou art as wise as thou art beautiful,' she sighs, with unconsciously ironic truth. The twentieth-century audience might well be put in mind of Emma's reflection about Harriet Smith, 'Humph—Harriet's ready wit!... A man must be very much in love indeed, to describe her so.' Bottom is a man of parts, but he can hardly be praised for finesse—as we may notice again two scenes later when, as Ernest Schanzer has put it,[9] he is proceeding to hold a levee in his new role of Prince Consort: 'I have a reasonable good ear in music. Let's have the tongs and the bones.'

The whole Titania–Bottom episode throws light on the handling of sex in Shakespeare's play as compared with its apparent sources. *The Comedy of Errors* showed him reducing the salacious element of his raw material. *A Midsummer Night's Dream* suggests, if anything, a cautious tendency in the opposite direction, especially in so far as the play seems to derive from Reginald Scot's book *The Discovery of Witchcraft* (1584). Scot, fervently attacking 'the popish beliefs' of earlier writers on witches, fairies and magic, insists on the non-material nature of spirits.

> Where there is no meate eaten, there can be no seed which thereof is ingendred: although it be granted, that Robin [Goodfellow] could both eate and drinke, as being a cousening idle frier, or some such rog[u]e, that wanted nothing either belonging to lecherie or knaverie, &c. Item, where the genitall members want, there can be no lust of the flesh: neither dooth nature give anie desire of generation, where there is no propagation or succession required. And as spirits cannot be greeved with hunger, so can they not be inflamed with lustes. ... But the power of generation consisteth not onlie in members, but chieflie of vitall spirits, and of the hart: which spirits are never in such a bodie as *Incubus* hath, being but a bodie assumed, as they themselves saie. And yet the most part of writers herein affirme, that it is a palpable and visible bodie; though all be phansies and fables that are written hereupon.[10]

We have no means of determining for certain whether this particular passage encouraged Shakespeare in the notion of depicting his fairy king and queen in the throes of a marital quarrel. We may be sure, though, that the sexual propensities of Oberon and Titania represent a 'phansie' that would have disgusted the Calvinistic Scot more than ever. These spirits seem to be in no want of genital members when, in clear contrast with the sexually experienced but ever-reticent Theseus and Hippolyta, they wrangle in public over a loved boy and fling off reciprocal accusations of adultery. Oberon goes further: sending for the juice of love-in-idleness to apply to Titania's eyes, he maliciously hopes to see her dote on 'lion, bear, or wolf, or bull, / On meddling monkey or on busy ape' (II.i.180). The animalism envisaged here is itself a form of bawdy. To an Elizabethan audience the inclusion of 'meddling monkey' in the list would set the seal on that, since the monkey, like the goat and the sparrow, typified lechery, and the verb *to meddle* often implied sexual activity.

Yet in recognising this, one surely need not feel driven into viewing the play, or even Titania's part in it, through the baleful spectacles of Jan Kott:

> The *Dream* is the most erotic of Shakespeare's plays. In no other tragedy or comedy of his, except *Troilus and Cressida*, is the eroticism expressed so brutally. . . .
> It is this passing through animality that seems to us the midsummer night's dream, or at least this aspect of the *Dream* is the most modern and revealing. This is the main theme joining together all the three separate plots running parallel in the play. Titania and Bottom will pass through animal eroticism in a quite literal, even visual sense. But even the quartet of lovers enter the dark sphere of animal love-making . . .
> I imagine Titania's court as consisting of old men and women, toothless and shaking, their mouths wet with saliva, who sniggeringly procure a monster for their mistress. . . . Since antiquity and up to the Renaissance the ass was credited with the strongest sexual potency and among all the quadrupeds is supposed to have the longest and hardest phallus.[11]

If we were to accept such guidance as this, we could obviously travel a long way from, say, Dover Wilson's picture of 'Titania's delicate courtship' or Frank Kermode's of a quasi-regal Bottom who has known the love of the triple goddess in a vision.[12] But with Kott's image of Bottom wholly metamorphosed into priapic quadruped, and of Moth, Cobweb, Peaseblossom and Mustardseed creeping from their acorn cups as decrepit panders, Shakespeare too is being left behind.

Sexuality and bawdy do, of course, have a role to fill in *A Midsummer Night's Dream*, and it is at once more extensive and more disconcerting than a polite Mendelssohnian interpretation of the play will recognise. But surely here, as so often elsewhere, Shakespeare is having the best of two thematic worlds? Oberon's bear, bull and meddling monkey remind us that midsummer madness is amoral and that there is a distasteful side to Titania's doting *mésalliance* with the ass-headed Bottom. Yet Titania and Oberon become reconciled well before the end of the play, and the fogs of night disperse, 'No more yielding but a dream'. With Duke Theseus using his benign authority to bring reason and love into company once again, it does not even matter that the Pyramus-and-Thisbe venture has been less than a total artistic success. Shakespeare's comedy ends with a blessing, and Bottom cannot have scaped sixpence a day.

Turning to *The Two Gentlemen of Verona*, one finds that in the distribution of bawdy lines amongst its characters it follows much the same social pattern as *The Comedy of Errors* and *A Midsummer Night's Dream*. There are some thirteen clear instances of indecency, and roughly the same number of probable but uncertain instances. As always, an exact count is impossible, but even an approximate survey shows up a clear contour line. Of the twenty-six or twenty-seven lines that can reasonably be considered either bawdy or quasi-bawdy, twenty are shared between the two clowns, Speed and Launce. Of the remainder, Lucetta (Julia's waiting-woman) speaks one, the Duke of Milan reads one in Valentine's intercepted letter to Silvia, and the rest are all Julia's.

A good deal of scepticism is needed in the interpretation of these 'statistics'—partly because they are not in fact statistics in any proper sense of the term, and partly also because the pattern of characterisation, when we read or see the play, is not what the simple counting of definable indecencies would suggest. It might seem, for example, that Julia is of a bawdy turn of mind; but if one re-reads her full part in the play, her occasional bawdy lines turn out to be both innocuous and unobtrusive:

> ... maids, in modesty, say no to that
> Which they would have the profferer construe ay.
>
> I.ii.55

> [*with the pieces of Proteus's torn-up letter*]
> Lo, here in one line is his name twice writ:
> *Poor, fororn Proteus, passionate Proteus,*
> *To the sweet Julia* . . . .
> Thus will I fold them one upon another.
> Now kiss, embrace, contend, do what you will.
>
> I.ii.123, 128

There is nothing of the proto-Cressida about Julia. There is, on the other hand, something of the sexual realist, a proto-Rosalind or -Helena. Her sane awareness of love's physicality saves her from the cloudy idealism that envelops her changeable Proteus and his friend Valentine.

Contrast between the ordinarily physical and the romantically ideal does not stop there. Launce's dog Crab is making the same essential point when he 'thrusts me himself into the company of three or four gentleman-like dogs under the Duke's table' and proceeds to make water against a

gentlewoman's farthingale. No gentlemanlike dog, no ideal dog, would
do such a thing at any time, least of all when he had just been sent as a
present from a courtly wooer to the Duke's daughter. And just as Crab
will not conduct himself like a toy dog, so also Launce and Speed will not
readily sympathise with their masters' air of being toy lovers and toy
gentlemen. On noticing how high a proportion of the play's bawdy
lines Shakespeare gives to the two servants, one comes to see the combined
function of the pair as one that counterpoints and even criticises the
affected behaviour of their employers when 'metamorphosed with a
mistress'. Harold Brooks[13] has pointed out that love in the courtly
manner, if we entertain an inadequate, everyday view of it, is very
liable to arouse mere mockery and impatience. Aware of this, Shakespeare embodies those hostile feelings within the play itself, so as to
control and place them. Speed's cheeky jibes at Proteus and Julia in I.i—
'a laced mutton . . . you were best stick her'—are laughed aside by
Proteus, whose eagerness to hear a reply to his love-letter more than
counteracts Speed's clownish cynicism. Proteus threatens punishment
for the messenger's impertinence (' 'twere best pound you'), but he is
really more intent on courting Julia than he is on beating another man's
servant. So far, so good. But Speed's callowness seems to have proved
insufficiently robust for Shakespeare's purpose, and it is Launce who
gradually takes over the role of lower-class anti-romantic cynic:

> SPEED   I tell thee my master is become a hot lover.
> LAUNCE   Why, I tell thee, I care not though he burn himself in love.
>
> II.v.44

Besides being older than Speed, Launce is sharper-tongued—there may
be point in his name—and by the third act Speed has become little more
than his 'feed-man'. The second half of III.i consists of a lengthy clowning
session for Launce, who detains Speed in conversation for as long as he
needs a foil. Thus belated, poor Speed hurries off to Valentine, from whom
he will suffer 'correction' for arriving so late: he has already kept his
master waiting in the first scene of the play. The main point of III.i,
however, is not Speed's lateness but Launce's catalogue of his inamorata's
qualities:

> 'tis a milkmaid; yet, 'tis not a maid, for she hath had gossips; yet 'tis a
> maid, for she is her master's maid and serves for wages.
>
> III.i.267

Gossips, in such a context as this, are not so much godparents as just
women friends invited to attend a confinement. Add this to the plain
denial of the girl's virginity, and her *serving* of her master could be

ambiguous, copular as well as domestic. Similarly, not all of her neatly listed virtues are ladylike, though Launce takes a philosophic view:

SPEED   *Item: She is too liberal.*
LAUNCE   Of her tongue she cannot, for that's writ down she is slow of; of her purse, she shall not, for that I'll keep shut. Now, of another thing she may, and that cannot I help. Well, proceed.

III.i.338

Once again we are at the other end of the scale from romantic and aristocratic ardours, and once again the contrast supports Harold Brooks's contention about the function of built-in satire. Launce's woman, who never appears on the stage, has only the kind of shadowy presence in the play that Luce/Nell, the kitchen vestal, had in *The Comedy of Errors*; but she comes a degree closer to Audrey, whose role in *As You Like It* will stand in dramatic contrast to Rosalind's, Celia's and Phebe's.

The case should not be pushed too far. Shakespeare is feeling his way towards the use of bawdy as a significant element in characterisation, yet *The Two Gentlemen of Verona* still does not show this at all consistently. As with thematic contrast—the servants' bawdy juxtaposed with the masters' idealism—Shakespeare has not yet developed the technique to a point at which it becomes artistically important. So far, it is only something which, by the benefit of hindsight, can be recognised as a foretaste of skills that are to come. Such recognitions have led Norman Sanders to describe *The Two Gentlemen* in terms of an Elizabethan 'anatomie', a show-through version of Shakespeare's comic art. Because it is managed with a beginner's lack of expertise, Sanders suggests, it gives us a chance to see, more clearly than anywhere else in the canon, what were to become characteristic techniques.[14] So far as bawdy elements are concerned *The Comedy of Errors* and even *A Midsummer Night's Dream* could share in that description. The *Dream* is, inarguably, the most accomplished of the three, but seen from this particular viewpoint it too is significant for what it foreshadows rather than for any careful complexity in the manner in which its bawdy is put to work. To detect a new stage in the emergence of such complexity, we need to turn to the sex-war comedies that are the subject of the next chapter.

NOTES

1. Hulme, *Explorations in Shakespeare's Language*, p. 126.
2. From title-page reproduced as frontispiece in W. H. D. Rouse, ed., *The Menaechmi* (1912).
3. The probability that Shakespeare had read Plautus in Latin is accepted by Geoffrey Bullough, ed., *Narrative and Dramatic Sources of Shakespeare*, i, 3–5; and by R. A.

Foakes in his New Arden edition of *The Comedy of Errors* (1962), pp. xxiv-xxviii.

4. *Menaechmi*, ed. Rouse, III.iii.17. 'My dear Menaechmus, it would be nice if you would give *me* some earrings, with the pendants made two didrachms in weight, just so that I'll be really pleased to see you whenever you come around to our place.'

5. Michel Grivelet, 'Shakespeare, Molière, and the Comedy of Ambiguity', *SS* 22 (1969), 18.

6. I.ii.90, II.i.54 and 181, III.i.124–6 and 181–2, IV.ii.13–14, and V.i.198, 234 and 284.

7. Kenneth Muir, 'Pyramus and Thisbe: a study in Shakespeare's method', *SQ*, v (1954), 141–53, quoting Mouffet on p. 149. For the relevant extract from the Ovid–Golding *Metamorphoses*, see Bullough, *op. cit.*, i, 405–9.

8. John Florio, *A World of Words* (London, 1598, 1611); Randle Cotgrave, *A Dictionary of the French and English Tongues* (London, 1611).

9. Ernest Schanzer, '*A Midsummer-Night's Dream*', in Kenneth Muir, ed., *Shakespeare, The Comedies* (1965), p. 30.

10. Bullough, *op. cit.*, i, 395.

11. Jan Kott, *Shakespeare Our Contemporary* (2nd edn, 1967), pp. 175–83.

12. John Dover Wilson, *Shakespeare's Happy Comedies* (1962), p. 216. Frank Kermode, 'The mature comedies', in Brown and Harris, eds, *Early Shakespeare* (1961), p. 219.

13. Harold F. Brooks, 'Two clowns in a comedy (to say nothing of the dog): Speed, Launce (and Crab) in *The Two Gentlemen of Verona*', *Essays and Studies*, n.s. xvi (1963), 94–5.

14. Norman Sanders, ed., *The Two Gentlemen of Verona* (1968), p. 15.

3

Verbal Gymnastics

The tongues of mocking wenches are as keen
As is the razor's edge invisible,
Cutting a smaller hair than may be seen,
Above the sense of sense; so sensible
Seemeth their conference; their conceits have wings,
Fleeter than arrows, bullets, wind, thought, swifter things.
Love's Labour's Lost V.ii.256

Love's Labour's Lost and *The Taming of the Shrew* mark themselves off from Shakespeare's other early comedies in being much more extensively given over to the art of the wit combat. Conflict between the sexes dominates the action in almost all of these plays, but *Love's Labour's Lost* goes further than any of the others in making the conflict pre-eminently verbal and quite often bawdy. Anatomical jesting is so evenly and liberally spread in the play that it seems at first glance as if no character is without a share of it. On looking more closely one finds that, leaving aside those with merely walk-on parts (Dull, Sir Nathaniel, the Forester), only one speaker—the Princess of France—avoids ribaldry quite consistently. King Ferdinand, true to his nature as a fairly likable prig, comes close to matching this high sense of decorum, but is beguiled into one faintly *risqué* rejoinder to the masked Rosaline:

> KING
> Will you not dance? How come you thus estranged?
> ROSALINE
> You took the moon at full; but now she's changed.
> KING
> Yet still she is the Moon, and I the Man.

V.ii.213

Otherwise, everyone in the play, from aristocrat to clown, quibbles unrestrainedly and at times obscenely. Now and again, when they feel that licentious chatter has gone far enough, the courtiers call one another to order. Maria's scolding of Boyet ('you talk greasily') comes at the end of a lengthy set-to in IV.i, when Boyet has, as Maria puts it, wrangled with Rosaline, watched by an admiring if sometimes baffled Costard. The basic metaphor for most of their innuendos is deer-shooting, which admits of the puns *shooter/suitor* and *deer/dear*, together with various quibbles over *horns, hitting, upshoot, prick, mark* and *bow*. Since the last two almost certainly refer to the vulva—parallels are suggested in the glossary—Boyet's line 'An if my hand be out, then belike your hand is in' is accusing Maria of masturbation. Little wonder that she now, at last, protests.

Later, it is Longaville's turn to recall his friends to practical matters when Berowne's monologue 'Have at you, then, affection's men-at-arms' has launched them into a rush of phallic word-play:

> KING
> Saint Cupid, then! and, soldiers, to the field!
> BEROWNE
> Advance your standards, and upon them, lords;
> Pell-mell, down with them! But be first advised,
> In conflict, that you get the sun of them.
> LONGAVILLE
> Now to plain-dealing; lay these glozes by.
> Shall we resolve to woo these girls of France?
>
> IV.iii.362

Elsewhere, the copular tittle-tattle flows on unchecked. In the play, as in life, quibbling becomes one of the occupational diseases of academe. (It is a point that we can scarcely miss when in the pedantic presence of Holofernes.) Some of the jokes are predictable: six times Shakespeare puns on *light* in the sense *easy* or *unchaste*; three times he invokes the familiar horns of cuckoldry. Yet what is most striking is not the familiarity of the sexual word-play but its sustained intricacy: with Berowne in III.i describing Dan Cupid, for example,

> Dread prince of plackets, king of codpieces,
> Sole imperator, and great general
> Of trotting paritors
>
> III.i.174

—the paritor being an apparitor, an officer who summoned offenders to appear in the bishop's court.

Critics of this comedy, friendly and hostile alike, have been almost unanimous in reading it as an extended revel in words, something more concerned with language than with life. Recent commentators have gone on to stress the formal precision with which it enacts, not the experience of being in love, but what C. L. Barber has called a particular sort of folly—

> the folly of amorous masquerade, whether in clothes, gestures, or words. It is the folly of acting love and talking love, without being in love. For the festivity releases, not the delights of love, but the delights of expression which the prospect of love engenders—though those involved are not clear about the distinction until it is forced on them; the clarification achieved by release is this recognition that love is not wooing games or love talk. And yet these sports are not written off or ruled out; on the contrary the play offers their delights for our enjoyment, while humorously putting them in their place.[1]

This is well said, and it does much to take the chill off what could otherwise be mistaken for a somewhat thin-blooded comedy of the *Much Ado* or *As You Like It* kind. Yet we are still left with the minor aesthetic problem of unrelated bawdy: bawdy that has nothing more solid to reflect than Costard's, Armado's and Holofernes' interests in Jaquenetta—all earthy enough, but scarcely commanding emotional engagement on the part of the theatre audience. That this is a real difficulty, and not merely one that we manufacture in the process of singling out bawdy for special scrutiny, is confirmed by such a response to the play as Johnson's.

> In this play, which all the editors have concurred to censure and some have rejected as unworthy of our poet, it must be confessed that there are many passages mean, childish, and vulgar; and some which ought not to have been exhibited, as we are told they were, to a maiden queen.[2]

Even though the twentieth-century reader or playgoer is likely to feel less confident of the canons of bad taste, Dr Johnson's strictures cannot simply be shrugged aside. The man was no prude. What he was registering, essentially, was the view that in this particular comedy, far too often for comfort, 'words get in the way'. When some of them turn out to be bawdy words, a kind of spiritual desiccation sometimes results. For those who share Johnson's disenchantment over this, consolation lies in the thought that perhaps Shakespeare needed to go through some such experimental phase in comedy—as he had already gone through the uglier phase marked by *Titus Andronicus* in tragedy—before being ready to turn bawdy to better integrated theatrical ends.

With that possibility in mind, let us move on from love lost to love tamed. In that world of surmise where the literary student necessarily spends a part of his time, *The Taming of the Shrew* has long contended with other plays, known and unknown, for identification as the *Love's Labour's Won* mentioned by Francis Meres in his *Palladis Tamia: Wit's Treasury* (1598):

> As *Plautus* and *Seneca* are accounted the best for Comedy and Tragedy among the Latines: so *Shakespeare* among the English is the most excellent in both kinds for the stage; for Comedy witnes his *Gentlemen of Verona*, his *Errors*, his *Love labors lost*, his *Love labours wonne*, his *Midsummers night dreame*, & his *Merchant of Venice*.[3]

In its immediate outcome, Petruchio's achievement in wooing and taming Katherina becomes the converse of Berowne's frustrating experience with Rosaline: no twelvemonth's jesting in a hospital this time. It may even seem bizarre to want to compare the two comedies, considering the chattiness of *Love's Labour's Lost* as against the large element of slapstick in *The Shrew*. Nothing that happens in Navarre parallels Hortensio's entry with a smashed lute round his neck, or the livelier moments of the wedding-night scene at Petruchio's house. But Petruchio's combination of wit and realism in the pursuit of his aim is not unlike Berowne's, and a survey of the play's bawdy also reveals a general pattern surprisingly similar to that of *Love's Labour's Lost*. There are two set-pieces of indecent wit. One is found in the wooing scene:

> PETRUCHIO
> Women are made to bear, and so are you.
> KATHERINA
> No such jade as you, if me you mean. . . .
> PETRUCHIO
> Come, come, you wasp, i'faith, you are too angry.
> KATHERINA
> If I be waspish, best beware my sting.
> PETRUCHIO
> My remedy is then to pluck it out.
> KATHERINA
> Ay, if the fool could find it where it lies.
> PETRUCHIO
> Who knows not where a wasp does wear his sting?
> In his tail.
> KATHERINA   In his tongue.
> PETRUCHIO   Whose tongue?
> KATHERINA
> Yours, if you talk of tales, and so farewell.
> *She turns to go*

PETRUCHIO
> What, with my tongue in your tail? Nay, come again.
> *He takes her in his arms*
> Good Kate, I am a gentleman. . .

KATHERINA
> What is your crest—a coxcomb?

PETRUCHIO
> A combless cock, so Kate will be my hen.

KATHERINA
> No cock of mine, you crow too like a craven.

> > > > > > > > > > > > > > > > > > > II.i.200, 209, 223

As G. R. Hibbard points out in his New Penguin edition of the play, the word *jade*, by implying easy tiring, impugns Petruchio's virility as well as glancing at his rustic manners; while the suggestion that he is impotent may well be caught up again in Katherina's use of *craven*. The *tail-tongue-tale* sequence is more complicated. *Tail*, in Shakespearean slang, denotes the female sexual organ just about as often as the male, so there need be no doubt that Petruchio, in his crudely flirtatious way, is trying to interest Katherina in the proposition of cunnilingus. She, for her part, is concentrating more on squashing his attempts to talk bawdy, particularly when she pretends to take *tail* as meaning *tale*—assuming we can accept the First Folio's spelling ('Yours if you talke of tales') at face value.

The one other sustained barrage of indecencies comes in the wedding-feast that ends the play.

WIDOW
> He that is giddy thinks the world turns round.

PETRUCHIO
> Roundly replied.

KATHERINA> > > > > Mistress, how mean you that?

WIDOW
> Thus I conceive by him.

PETRUCHIO
> Conceives by me! How likes Hortensio that?

HORTENSIO
> My widow says thus she conceives her tale.

PETRUCHIO
> Very well mended. Kiss him for that, good widow. . . .

BAPTISTA
> How likes Gremio these quick-witted folks?

GREMIO
> Believe me, sir, they butt together well.

BIANCA
  Head and butt! An hasty-witted body
    Would say your head and butt were head and horn.
VINCENTIO
  Ay, mistress bride, hath that awakened you?
BIANCA
  Ay, but not frighted me, therefore I'll sleep again.
PETRUCHIO
  Nay, that you shall not. Since you have begun,
  Have at you for a bitter jest or two.

                                                V.ii.20, 38

Bianca's 'head and horn' joke is obscure—appropriately, I suppose, since she is fuddled and sleepy. 'Head and butt' may mean 'head and bottom', as Hibbard suggests. If, on the other hand, Bianca is playing on the idea of a goat's butting, and making a cuckoldry joke of this, it is less likely that she is aiming at Gremio (who is still unmarried) than at Petruchio. The implication that he will be cuckolded by Katherina would account satisfactorily for his counterattack on Bianca in the last two lines of the quotation.

Apart from the wooing scene and the wedding-feast, *The Shrew's* scurrilities are only intermittent and inessential. Petruchio has the lion's share of them—out of sixteen demonstrably bawdy lines in the play, he speaks or is reported to speak ten; the remaining indecent jokes or insinuations are scattered quite loosely among the rest of the *dramatis personae*.

Within this broad pattern, a couple of particular points are worth noting. First, Shakespeare has once again left aside almost entirely the bawdy content of a source play. George Gascoigne's *Supposes* (1566)[4] not only has in Polynesta a pregnant and unmarried heroine but also presents a more than usually quarrelsome and ribald servant class. Only the faintest traces of all this can be discerned in *The Taming of the Shrew*. Bianca is perhaps more amenable to Lucentio's advances than would be entirely proper, though she is never incautious; and the fondness for Ovid that Lucentio shares with Tranio (I.i.33, IV.ii.8) may derive from the tastes of the corresponding figures in *Supposes*, Dulypo and Erostrato:

> DULYPO Nay you can tell, you are better scholer than I.
> EROSTRATO In deede you have lost your time: for the books that you tosse
> now a dayes, treate of smal science.[5]

One phrase of Grumio's, 'an old trot with ne'er a tooth in her head, though she have as many diseases as two and fifty horses' (I.ii.78–9), may also have been suggested by a bawdy line in Gascoigne, 'Go that the gunne pouder consume thee olde trotte' (*Supposes*, III.v). Yet, considering how many more lines of such abuse the older play had to offer, it becomes obvious that Shakespeare preferred to do without them.

The other point that strikes one in contemplating the bawdy touches in *The Shrew* is that they have a definable role to play in the relative 'placing' of characters. As in so much else, it is Petruchio who makes the running, but both Katherina and Bianca have some share in the sexual humour too. During Petruchio's rough courtship, as we have seen, Katherine is ready to give as good as she gets. Even before that, when she has been only a few moments on the stage, she has lashed back in sexual terms at a sour jibe from Gremio:

> BAPTISTA
> ... Because I know you well and love you well,
>   Leave shall you have to court her at your pleasure.
> GREMIO
>   To cart her rather. She's too rough for me.
>   There, there, Hortensio, will you any wife?
> KATHERINA (*to Baptista*)
>   I pray you, sir, is it your will
>   To make a stale of me amongst these mates?

I.i.53

This kind of thing, however, comes from the heroine in her shrewish phase only. By the end of her taming, scurrility has vanished from her conversation, even when others try to provoke her to it. Thus the Katherina who is ashamed to kiss in the open street, but who does it for love's sake, takes no part in the wedding-breakfast banter of V.ii. Not so Bianca. It becomes increasingly apparent that in the course of the action the two sisters have begun to change places, morally speaking. Katherina defends Petruchio against snide attack from Hortensio's wife (V.ii.20–35), but otherwise remains entirely docile, and at the same time keeps well clear of the suggestive remarks that flit about the banquet-table. Bianca, on the other hand, now emerges as a potential minx, and the widow as more than a potential one. Their combined contrast with Katherina serves as dramatic preparation for her climactic speech of reprimand to them and submission to her husband.

We may detect in this final scene of *The Shrew* the beginnings of something that is to become a regular habit with Shakespeare—the controlled use of bawdy as one indicator of dissident or anarchic traits in a personality. Here, by establishing this key difference between Katherine and the other two brides, he is finally merging his two plots—Katherina's and Bianca's—to form a single whole. He is also creating a helpful stage-atmosphere in which to state outright the play's central thematic point, such as it is: that for harmonious and orderly living, wifely submission is prerequisite.

Among Shakespeare's more mature comedies, the one that may be seen as the direct successor to *Love's Labour's Lost* and *The Taming of the Shrew* is *Much Ado About Nothing*. *Love's Labour's Lost* stands unchallengeably as the most word-conscious of all the plays, but *Much Ado* is scarcely less witty, besides being, in my view, much funnier. In Messina as in Navarre there assembles 'a college of witcrackers'. Now that the military campaign is over, these leisured ladies and gentlemen can devote their full energies to the engineering of marriages, masques, dances and wilful misprisions of meaning. They have not, of course, reckoned with the continuing malevolence of Don John, just as the Princess of France, in the earlier play, had not expected the death of her sick father. As a result, we have the troubled and troubling episode in which Claudio rejects Hero, an episode which serves as a valuable dramatic foil to the love story of Beatrice and Benedick, and also provides occasion for these characters themselves to gain 'depth' by becoming tensely earnest in IV.i and V.i: 'Kill Claudio.' Nevertheless, viewed as a whole, the play is still comedy rather than tragi-comedy. Critics have surely been right in finding its vitality mainly in the bright hardness of its wit and the dancing spray of its dialogue.[6] Beatrice and Benedick often look like a polished, high-life version of Katherina and Petruchio—

> BEATRICE I wonder that you will still be talking, Signor Benedick; nobody marks you.
> BENEDICK What, my dear Lady Disdain! Are you yet living?
>
> I.i.108

There is the important difference, however, that for this later play a happy outcome requires that the man be tamed as well as the woman. When peace is eventually declared it is not at the cost of surrender by either contestant.

Bawdy has a larger part to play in all this than in *The Shrew*. Benedick's distrust of the married state—or perhaps his fear of his own attraction towards it—repeatedly finds expression through the stock metaphor of the cuckold's horns. 'Is't come to this?' he cries, on hearing of Claudio's wish to marry Hero. 'Is't come to this? In faith, hath not the world one man but he will wear his cap with suspicion? Shall I never see a bachelor of threescore again?' (I.i.184). Reminded by Don Pedro that even he,

Benedick, may change his views about marriage, he grows still louder in protestation:

> DON PEDRO   Well, as time shall try:
> 'In time the savage bull doth bear the yoke.'
> BENEDICK   The savage bull may; but if ever the sensible Benedick bear
> it, pluck off the bull's horns and set them in my forehead, and let me
> be vilely painted; and in such great letters as they write 'Here is good
> horse to hire', let them signify under my sign 'Here you may see
> Benedick the married man.'

I.i.240

This establishes two of the play's recurrent motifs: Benedick the untamed bull and Benedick the (labelled) married man. The second of these jokes, having solid support from the plot, has survived the passage of time with that longevity which is characteristic of comedy of situation. Quoted against Benedick at the end of the play, it can still earn laughter in the theatre or the study today. With the 'horns' convention, on the other hand, we run into a critical hazard of *Much Ado* that few commentators have faced up to. The joke is dead. Audiences that still laugh at it usually do so in a dutiful fashion: they have been studying footnotes or programme notes and are eager (as W. G. McCollom has neatly put it[7])to enjoy what their piety has brought them to witness. In the theatre, one way out of the difficulty is for directors simply to cut some or all of the stock joke's repetitions. But with Shakespeare it often happens that the elimination of something apparently trivial turns out to be damaging to some other thing that is important. Shorn of its recurring cuckoldry joke, *Much Ado About Nothing* loses some of its irony. It is, after all, Claudio rather than Benedick who comes to believe himself cuckolded and who then behaves with bullish aggressiveness. The thoughtless reiteration of the 'savage bull' witticism by Claudio and Don Pedro helps to focus attention on the fact that whereas they look with cheerful cynicism on adultery as a general notion, they view it with horror and indignation when it seems to have come nearer home. How far this ambivalence must have been deliberately contrived by Shakespeare is not easy to estimate. While his probable sources for the rejection of Hero would have given him a serious Claudio ready-made, most of what he invents for Claudio to do in the Beatrice–Benedick plot naturally leans towards the jocular. However it came about, there is a disparity between the serious and the skittish sides of Claudio, and it is never resolved. Perhaps the best that can be said is that Claudio, being immature and uncertain, is at least consistently inconsistent. And his brusque treatment by Benedick on the final appearance of the wild bull image suggests that Shakespeare did at least recognise how thin this particular jibe had worn by now:

DON PEDRO
    Good morrow, Benedick. Why, what's the matter,
    That you have such a February face,
    So full of frost, of storm and cloudiness?
CLAUDIO
    I think he thinks upon the savage bull.
    Tush, fear not, man, we'll tip thy horns with gold,
    And all Europa shall rejoice at thee,
    As once Europa did at lusty Jove,
    When he would play the noble beast in love.
BENEDICK
    Bull Jove, sir, had an amiable low;
    And some such strange bull leaped your father's cow,
    And got a calf in that same noble feat
    Much like to you, for you have just his bleat.

                                                          V.iv.40

Turning to the question of how the play distributes its bawdy lines, it is not surprising to find roughly half of them concentrated in the speeches of only two characters, Beatrice and Benedick. Very much as in *Love's Labour's Lost*, the wit contests of the upper class are marked by an aristocratic freedom of language, and Shakespeare lets his hero and heroine make the most of it. One's general sense of this freedom is heightened by a marked absence of bawdy at the artisan level in *Much Ado*. Neither Dogberry nor Verges speaks a single indecent line, consciously or unconsciously. Among their associates of the Watch, only the Second Watchman gets jolted—by the excitement of apprehending villains—into what might be considered a ribald exclamation: 'We have here recovered the most dangerous piece of lechery that ever was known in the commonwealth.' The malapropism *lechery* for *treachery*, scarcely bawdy in itself, probably becomes so when followed by '*common*wealth', but even then the speech could hardly be said to shatter the framework of august verbal propriety in which Shakespeare sets Dogberry.

On the intermediate grades of the social scale, only Margaret and Borachio show any clear inclination towards bawdy, and in both cases it makes significant contribution to the plot. Margaret's easy ways make her a suitably unenquiring accomplice for Borachio in his midnight deception of Claudio and the Prince, very much as Emilia's facile morality proves helpful to Iago's handkerchief plot. Borachio's bawdy, by contrast, is characterised by a shrillness of phrase that fits him well for the role of chief propagandist against Hero. As a villain he shows himself to be at once more inventive and less comic than his master Don John. Don John, type figure of all envious bastards,[8] is at least as funny as he is sinister: 'Let us to the great supper; their cheer is the greater that I am subdued.

Would the cook were o' my mind!' It is Borachio—drunken, motiveless, busy—who raises the emotional temperature, priming Don John with such phrases as 'a contaminated stale, such a one as Hero . . . the semblance of a maid'. Here in II.ii bawdy is merging into serious sensuality of the kind that reappears in Claudio's speeches of scathing reproach in IV.i— and again, later in Shakespeare's work, whenever a Hamlet, a Thersites, or a Timon makes it the outlet for an uncontrollable sense of disgust.

Meantime, to sum up, it can be said that in those of Shakespeare's comedies most marked for their verbal humour, sexual impropriety takes its place amongst a wide variety of witty contrivance, and tends on the whole to be used 'antiseptically'. Badinage, polite or impolite, generally leaves its participants emotionally uninvolved. Occasionally, though, these plays use bawdy as a way of making it clear to the audience that larger issues are at stake than those which the dialogue is explicitly acknowledging. Such a moment is Bianca's touch of pertness about head, butt and horns at the wedding-feast, or Beatrice's admission (II.i.21) that a cow too curst may find herself left single. In *Much Ado About Nothing*, to a far greater extent than in the earlier comedies, bawdy has begun to contribute to characterisation and hence to plot development. To chart Shakespeare's progress in these areas more fully, it is necessary to turn away from the genre of comedy and consider the use of the indecent in *Titus Andronicus* and the early history plays.

NOTES

1. C. L. Barber, *Shakespeare's Festive Comedy* (1959), p. 93. For a similar view of the play, but one that places the emphasis squarely upon its preoccupation with language, see James L. Calderwood, '*Love's Labour's Lost:* a wantoning with words', *SEL*, v (1965), 317–32.
2. *Dr Johnson on Shakespeare*, ed. W. K. Wimsatt, Penguin Books (1969), p. 108.
3. Francis Meres, quoted in Bentley, *Shakespeare: a biographical handbook* (1961), p. 201. Quite apart from Meres, a reference to what is called *loves labor won* occurs in manuscript, as part of a list of plays by Shakespeare, on a bookseller's leaf bound up in a copy of Thomas Gataker, *Certain Sermons* (London, 1637). See T. W. Baldwin, *Shakespeare's 'Love's Labor's Won'* (1957).
4. George Gascoigne, *Supposes*, ed. Bullough in *Narrative and Dramatic Sources*, i, 111–58. Professor Bullough also reprints *The Taming of A Shrew* (Q 1594), which he accepts as 'a badly printed version of the old play which Shakespeare used as his main source for *The Shrew*'. I have preferred to exclude *A Shrew* from the present discussion, however. Whatever the true nature of its relationship with *The Shrew*, it is recognisably a patched-up quarto, as its inner confusions and its echoes of Marlowe make clear. This being so, its comic passages are likely to

possess the least integrity of all. Jokes, bawdy or otherwise, being the basic stock-in-trade of the professional clown, are only too easily transferred from one play to another.

5. Bullough, i, 122.

6. These phrases are from A. P. Rossiter, *Angel with Horns* (1961), p. 80, and M. C. Bradbrook, *Shakespeare and Elizabethan Poetry* (1951), p. 181.

7. W. G. McCollom, 'The role of wit in *Much Ado About Nothing*', SQ, xix (1968), 166.

8. R. A. Foakes, in his New Penguin edition of *Much Ado About Nothing* (1968), p. 128, quotes aptly from Bacon's essay 'Of Envy': 'Bastards are envious: for he that cannot possibly mend his own case, will do what he can to impair others.'

4

Bawdy in Character

Is it possible he should know what he is, and be that he is?
All's Well That Ends Well IV.i.43

At first glance, the historical plays of Shakespeare's early years in the theatre seem more inconsistent in their use of bawdy than the earliest comedies. Here again eroticism is illustrative and auxiliary rather than fundamental to any play's structure, and the dramatist often appears to be deploying indecent humour simply for its immediate appeal to a theatre audience, regardless of whether it fully matches the general behaviour of the character speaking. As time goes on, however, the seemingly arbitrary flashes of bawdy can be seen to be following patterns that fit increasingly well into the full portrayal of the characters concerned. This trend in the chronicle plays is strikingly confirmed in the earliest of the tragedies, *Titus Andronicus*, where even Lavinia's two or three bawdy lines prove to be less out of character than one might at first suppose.

While this chapter, like chapters 2 and 3, confines itself mainly to a group of early plays—*Titus* and the first tetralogy—it should not be thought that Shakespeare later jettisons the use of bawdy as an element of characterisation. On the contrary, it remains one of his regular devices in serious drama as well as comic; but to trace it in detail through every play would try the reader's patience. This chapter therefore aims at indicating the *kind* of relationship that comes into being between bawdy and character-portrayal in Shakespeare's histories and tragedies. Once the process has been illustrated, the reader of the later plays will need no prompting to notice its recurrence, even when bawdy is simultaneously fulfilling some of the more complex functions to be outlined in subsequent chapters.

*　　*　　*

Ribaldry in *The First Part of King Henry VI* centres almost entirely on two important characters—Humphrey, Duke of Gloucester, and Joan la Pucelle.

In the opening scenes of the play Gloucester is shown at his most aggressive in his running quarrel with another of the young king's uncles, the Bishop of Winchester. The historical Winchester, later Cardinal Beaufort, was Henry VI's *great*-uncle, and so uncle to Duke Humphrey, but Shakespeare[1] at this stage shows little or no interest in this difference of a generation. His emphasis is on their rivalry, and on its antiprelatical implications. Yet the anticlericalism of these first scenes is oddly blurred, since Winchester's demeanour, although polemical, is made relatively dignified, while Gloucester's becomes downright scurrilous. Having first alleged that churchmen had prayed for Henry V's death, Gloucester soon converts this into a direct accusation of murderous conspiracy, and adds a charge of a more lubricious kind:

> Stand back, thou manifest conspirator,
> Thou that contrived'st to murder our dead lord,
> Thou that giv'st whores indulgences to sin.
>
> I.iii.33

Calling on his followers to attack Winchester's men, he repeats the taunt about brothel-keeping with a shout of 'Winchester goose!' To modern ears this sounds strange, but it has a certain quaint logic. The cant association of the goose with prostitution is very ancient, and the specific phrase '*Winchester* goose'—meaning a syphilitic chancre, a sufferer from syphilis, or just a prostitute—seems to owe its origin to the licensing, in the reign of Henry II, of eighteen bawdy-houses in Southwark (John Stow, *A Survey of London*, edn of 1603; ed. C. L. Kingsford (1908), ii, 54–5). Since the see of Winchester held most of the land in the whole district, it may be that successive bishops also owned the very buildings used as brothels. This would make Gloucester's calling this bishop a syphilitic (with a suggestion also, perhaps, of pimp) less far-fetched than it now looks.

The jokes about Winchester and whores may also have had topical force for the original audiences at *1 Henry VI*. First, in general, allusions to clerical tolerance of brothels were not uncommon among the Elizabethans as a form of anti-Catholic propaganda. Ben Jonson satirises this type of Puritan sermonising in 'An Execration upon Vulcan':

> The Brethren, they streight nois'd it out for Newes,
> 'Twas verily some Relique of the Stewes:
> And this a Sparkle of that fire let loose

> That was lock'd up in the Winchestrian Goose
> Bred on the Banck, in time of Poperie,
> When Venus there maintain'd the Misterie.[2]

Secondly, if A. S. Cairncross is right in suggesting 1590 as the likely date of composition for *1 Henry VI*,[3] there may be in Gloucester's rather schoolboyish series of taunts an echo of the Martin Marprelate controversy. 'Martin's' opening salvo, fired at the Bishops of London *and Winchester* in October 1588, had been aimed 'To the right puissant and terrible priests, my clergy masters of the Confocation-house, whether fickers general, worshipful paltripolitan, or any other of the holy league of subscription'.[4] In the absence of any more definite links, one has to be tentative in conjecturing a possible connection between this and the anticlerical bawdy in *1 Henry VI*; but the possibility is there.

Topical or not, Duke Humphrey's scabrousness in his attacks on Winchester does have one dramatic function within the play itself. It matters to the whole plot that the royally begged reconciliation in III.i should be plainly hollow, merely the first of Henry's many and harmful illusions. For this to be obvious to an audience, it is necessary that Gloucester's insults to Winchester must be of such a kind that they will be, from the prelate's point of view, quite unforgivable. They are. In this way, their indecency is integral to the play, and not to be dismissed as merely topical matter thrust in to please the antiprelatical patriots of 1590.

What, though, of Joan la Pucelle? Can the same kind of thing be said of the salacious material surrounding her in the play?

To feel that there is something unsatisfactory about this portrayal of the legendary Jeanne d'Arc is not, I think, to succumb to the unconsciously Protestant heroine-worship that Shaw complained about in the preface to *Saint Joan*. One does not ask that any Elizabethan should be historically accurate in a chronicle play, or that he should be fair to the French; but the Talbot–Pucelle conflict is crudely presented, for all its Marlovian *éclat*.

> Frenchmen, I'll be a Salisbury to you.
> Pucelle or puzzel, dolphin or dogfish,
> Your hearts I'll stamp out with my horse's heels
> And make a quagmire of your mingled brains.

> I.iv.106

The reader who would like to admire this play finds himself searching for any flashes of irony that might mercifully separate Shakespeare from the jingoism. What irony there is, however, works just the other way. Joan may be pucelle or puzzel, virgin or whore: the two different versions

of the same word epitomise the squarely conflicting French and English
views of her, and it is the French estimate that comes to be increasingly
undercut by bawdy. While the Dauphin Charles claims her as a holy
patron ('No longer on Saint Denis will we cry, / But Joan la Pucelle
shall be France's saint'), it is nevertheless a lecherous interest that fires his
speeches of public acclaim.

> Divinest creature, Astræa's daughter,
> How shall I honour thee for this success?
> Thy promises are like Adonis' gardens,
> That one day bloomed and fruitful were the next.
>
> .   .   .   .
>
> A statelier pyramis to her I'll rear
> Than Rhodope's of Memphis ever was.
>
> I.vi.4, 21

Since Rhodope of Memphis has connotations of courtly prostitution, and
Adonis of fertility ritual, there runs beneath the formal hyperbole an
undercurrent of sexual indulgence that washes away some of the saintli-
ness. Again in II.i, when the English have taken Orleans and the factious
commanders of the French have fallen to mutual recrimination, Charles
gets into difficulties in explaining how he spent the night:

> And, for myself, most part of all this night,
> Within her quarter and mine own precinct
> I was employed in passing to and fro
> About relieving of the sentinels.
>
> II.i.67

Among the quarrelsome lieutenants this leaves room for a snigger, the
more readily because the Bastard of Orleans has already given signs of
sharing the English cynicism about la Pucelle: 'Tut! holy Joan was his
defensive guard.' She partially extricates herself from the backbiting by
making practical proposals for regrouping the scattered French army,
but only a moment later she has to share the farcical disarray of the
others under what look like authorial stage directions: 'Alarum. Enter an
English Soldier, crying "A Talbot! A Talbot!" They fly, leaving their
clothes behind.' It is no surprise, consequently, when Shakespeare afterwards gives la Pucelle no words in which to deny Talbot's charge of
being 'Encompassed with . . . lustful paramours' (III.ii.53).

This is not to say that the dramatist by this time sees nothing further
to be said for Joan. Sexually corrupted she may be, but she still puts new
courage into the French leaders after the fall of Rouen, and in her role of

clearsighted realist she sees the ambivalence of martial glory. It is she who castigates Sir William Lucy for his pompous listing of Talbot's honours in IV.vii. 'Him that thou magnifiest with all these titles, / Stinking and fly-blown lies here at our feet.' In using Joan la Pucelle to register this tellingly ugly contrast, the Elizabethan play allows her to come close to the perceptiveness of her Shavian *alter ego*.

In depicting the final events of Joan's life, however, *1 Henry VI* reverts to satirical bawdy. Condemned to burn for witchcraft, she rejects her peasant father, claims to be a virgin, abandons the claim (to plead instead that she is pregnant), and finally goes out to her death with a most unsaintly parting curse. This choice of material for dramatisation shows Shakespeare picking out from the chronicles the mixture of elements that will most damage la Pucelle's moral standing. In making her manifestly guilty of sorcery—V.iii sees her in action as a witch, complete with thunder and fiends of 'accustomed diligence'—the dramatist is precisely following Raphael Holinshed, whose *Chronicles of England, Scotland, and Ireland* (2nd edn, 1587) make no effort to question the metaphysical nature of 'hir campestrall conversation with wicked spirits'.[5] Edward Hall, in *The Union of the Two Noble and Illustre Families of Lancaster and York* (1548), had been a good deal more sceptical about these familiars. It was only as his account of Joan grew vituperative towards its end that he described her as 'an enchanteresse, an orgayne of the devill, sent from Sathan, to blind the people and bryng them in unbelife'.[6] As regards the historical Joan's chastity, on the other hand, the chroniclers agree on her innocence —however grudging its admission by Hall:

> a rampe of suche boldnesse, that she would course horses and ride theim to water, and do thynges, that other yong maidens, bothe abhorred & wer ashamed to do: yet as some say, whether it wer because of her foule face, that no man would desire it, either she had made a vowe to live chaste, she kept her maydenhed, and preserved her virginitie.[7]

Holinshed confirms this in his account of Joan's interrogations, where the prisoner, 'found though a virgin' when examined, claims to be a strumpet, and pregnant, only 'to eetch out life as long as she might . . . though the shift were shamefull'.[8] Shakespeare, faced with this substantial agreement between the two historians, in effect rejects both. His Pucelle is very far from keeping her maidenhead, and when he includes in the play her admission of harlotry, it is to take it at face value, omitting Holinshed's mention of her having proved to be a virgin. The last-minute confessions of pregnancy and promiscuity are also made to interweave with ribald jokes from the English lords:

YORK
  Now heaven forfend! The holy maid with child!
WARWICK
  The greatest miracle that e'er ye wrought:
  Is all your strict preciseness come to this?
YORK
  She and the Dauphin have been juggling.
  I did imagine what would be her refuge.
WARWICK
  Well, go to; we'll have no bastards live;
  Especially since Charles must father it.
PUCELLE
  You are deceived; my child is none of his:
  It was Alençon that enjoyed my love.

                                                          V.iv.65

She is given no final word of refutation for York's further taunt, 'Strumpet, thy words condemn thy brat and thee'. Apparently guilty in full, she is dragged out cursing.

So the Shakespearean version of Jeanne d'Arc goes to her death, morally tainted and self-tainting. If we find this handling of the character unsatisfactory, it is not necessarily because we are failing to allow for the differences between Elizabethan and nineteenth- or twentieth-century modes of characterisation. Rather it is because we sense a near miss in an attempt to achieve true dramatic and moral complexity. There are, as it were, two separate Pucelles—neither of them a saint, but one certainly a loyal and full-hearted patriot, whether eloquently converting Burgundy to the French cause (III.iii) or bewailing the eclipse of her homeland:

> Now the time is come
> That France must vail her lofty-plumed crest
> And let her head fall into England's lap.

                                                          V.iii.24

Such language lends an imaginative conviction to her claims of royal blood and celestial inspiration, but the play fails to reconcile this imaginatively with the 'other' Pucelle, the malevolent witch and courtesan.

The dramatist's ambiguous attitude to Joan seems at least partly inherited from Holinshed, and his task would have been simpler if he had kept to the sparer, more hostile narrative of Hall. Yet this choice of the more complex account, even at the cost of some confusion, is typically Shakespearean. Later in his career Shakespeare becomes able to combine sexual promiscuity and profoundly sympathetic characteristics within a single convincing figure—a Mistress Quickly, a Cressida, a Cleopatra. It may be that with Joan la Pucelle, in whom he clearly did not want sympathetic characteristics, he was writing against the grain of his own deeper judgement.

It is immediately striking, when one turns from Part 1 to Part 2 of *Henry VI*, that the dialogue of the second play is much the less scurrilous. The English nobles scheme against one another no less energetically than before, but they indulge less in verbal abuse. Even the Duke of Gloucester and Cardinal Beaufort have mellowed. They are now identified firmly as nephew and uncle, as distinct from their much vaguer presentation simply as 'cousins' in *1 Henry VI*, and in keeping with this change Shakespeare restrains the vituperative element in their 'ancient bickerings'. Similarly, la Pucelle's role of ambitious witch now passes to Eleanor Cobham, Duke Humphrey's wife, and she, for all her guilty traffickings with conjurors, is not one to demean herself with smutty talk. When sexually suggestive insinuations do appear, it is with the quasi-adulterous Suffolk and Queen Margaret—in their encounter with the petitioners, for instance:

> FIRST PETITIONER   Mine is, an't please your Grace, against John Goodman,
>   my Lord Cardinal's man, for keeping my house and lands, and wife
>   and all, from me.
> SUFFOLK   Thy wife too! That's some wrong indeed.
>
> I.iii.16

But even at their least sympathetic, as in the dismissal of Gloucester in II.iii, Suffolk and Margaret tend to strike a chord of complicit sensuality rather than outright bawdy.

Elsewhere in *2 Henry VI*, scabrous or salacious talk is used mainly to indicate the low social rank and general irresponsibility of the speakers from whom we hear it. This is a natural extension of the kind of bawdy that characterises servants and artisans in the early comedies. Its inclusion in crowd scenes as part of the mob's idle chatter becomes Shakespeare's normal practice, as indeed it does for any dramatist who writes into stage dialogue the style of talk that he can hear around him in a working-class crowd to this day. In both *Julius Caesar* and *Coriolanus* it will express the moods of the citizens at their most malleable:

> Truly, sir, all that I live by is with the awl: I meddle with no tradesman's
> matters, nor women's matters; but withal I am, indeed, sir, a surgeon
> to old shoes: when they are in great danger, I recover them. As proper
> men as ever trod upon neat's leather have gone upon my handiwork.
>
> *Julius Caesar* I.i.21

Just how specious is the innocence of this discourse on cobbling will become clear if the reader consults the glossary under *meddle, women's matters,* and *surgeon.* Similarly with *Coriolanus*:

> THIRD CITIZEN   Nay, your wit . . . if it were at liberty 'twould sure southward.
> SECOND CITIZEN   Why that way?
> THIRD CITIZEN   To lose itself in a fog, where being three parts melted away with rotten dews, the fourth would return for conscience' sake to help to get thee a wife.
>
> II.iii.26

Essentially the same type of placing can be observed in the armourer of *2 Henry VI* (II.iii). Imbued with Dutch courage, he runs true to proletarian type with 'I'll pledge you all; and a fig for Peter!'—almost his last words, poor Horner, before his man Peter kills him in combat.[9]

Scurrility again becomes a social indicator, but with darker implications, on the eruption into the play of Jack Cade and his followers. Shakespeare clearly had familiarity with what may seem to us an exclusively modern custom, the use of obscenity to give expression to socio-political protest. The Jack Cade scenes would suggest that, even allowing for inhibiting effects from the Elizabethan system of political censorship, it was a mode of protest with which the dramatist had little sympathy. At first he makes Cade less licentious than one might perhaps expect. A reference to the gelding of the commonwealth (IV.ii.160) and a mildly indecent nickname for the Dauphin, 'Mounsieur Basimecu' (= Baisez-ma-queue, = Kiss-my-arse)[10] are thrown off lightheartedly enough not to cost Cade any of the audience's affection. But this energetic leader of men is also an ambitious rebel, and bawdy has its part to play in revealing his hubris. At the height of his shortlived power in IV.vii, he has no sooner announced 'My mouth shall be the Parliament of England' than he is claiming the *droit de seigneur*: 'there shall not a maid be married, but she shall pay to me her maidenhead ere they have it.' If that can be dismissed as just randy high spirits, the same cannot be said of the ugly business with the heads of Say and Cromer at the end of the scene.

> *Re-enter One with the heads*
> CADE   But is not this braver? Let them kiss one another, for they loved well when they were alive. . . . Soldiers, defer the spoil of the city until night; for with these borne before us instead of maces will we ride through the streets, and at every corner have them kiss. Away!
>
> IV.vii.122

Shakespeare allows his Cade plenty of courage and considerable *élan*. He presents him as a formidable personality, especially in contrast with his unstable followers: 'Was ever feather so lightly blown to and fro as this multitude?' Yet, anarchist first and last, Cade finds only a dunghill for his grave, and Iden comes under no authorial criticism as he mutilates the dead body. Shakespeare is making sure that Jack Cade's earlier gusto will not take away from the moral opprobrium of rebellion. The character of Cade leaves us, nevertheless, with an odd mixture of impressions. Once again one looks forward to Shakespeare's presenting similar figures with a surer touch later in his career.

In *The Third Part of King Henry VI* we have a play that bristles with open baronial conflict, and, as we might expect, it employs most of its bawdy in direct exchanges of personal invective. According to the Duke of York in I.iv, his tormentor Queen Margaret is triumphing 'like an Amazonian trull'; and the younger Richard—of whom we are to see much more, first as the new Duke of Gloucester, then as King Richard III—repeats the charge of whoredom by casting the standard kind of aspersions on the legitimacy of Margaret's son: 'Whoever got thee, there thy mother stands; / For well I wot thou hast thy mother's tongue' (II.ii.133). Richard's brother Edward pursues the insinuation a few lines later.

> A wisp of straw were worth a thousand crowns
> To make this shameless callet know herself.
> Helen of Greece was fairer far than thou,
> Although thy husband may be Menelaus;
> And ne'er was Agamemnon's brother wronged
> By that false woman as this king by thee.

II.ii.144

Superficially, these charges resemble the bawdy abuse heaped on Winchester by Duke Humphrey in *1 Henry VI*, but there is the important difference that whereas that depended on crude anti-Catholic prejudice for its justification, the audience being shown no actual behaviour on Winchester's part that validly laid him open to this particular line of attack, Queen Margaret's adultery with Suffolk in the present instance has been hinted at in both the earlier plays of the trilogy. The accusations from York and his sons fulfil the function of keeping Margaret's infidelity to Henry fresh in our minds. Although defending Henry's throne, she is self-interested and potentially traitorous. The bawdy indictments are thus working alongside the animal imagery describing her: 'She-wolf of France . . . adder's tooth . . . tiger's heart . . . tigers of Hyrcania.' It should be acknowledged that Shakespeare gives Margaret herself similar images in which to depict young Richard—

> thou art neither like thy sire nor dam;
> But like a foul misshapen stigmatic,
> Marked by the destinies to be avoided,
> As venom toads or lizards' dreadful stings.
>
> II.ii.135

This is not without justification, but it does not lessen either our sense of Queen Margaret's own ferocity or our unease in contemplating the state of her England. Soon, after York's death, the country will be torn between such people. H. C. Goddard[11] has aptly compared *Henry VI* in this respect with *King Lear*, where animality, lechery and chaos will again connect imaginatively.

A second notable function of bawdy in *3 Henry VI* is in helping to delineate Edward, the eldest of York's three surviving sons. In this play and in *Richard III*, as in the chronicles on which they are based, Edward IV's susceptibility to pretty women proves to be a dangerous gap in his political defences. Warwick's allusive line, 'Did I let pass th' abuse done to my niece?' (III.iii.188) hints at behaviour described more amply by Edward Hall:

> And farther it erreth not from the treuth that kynge Edward did attempt a thyng once in the erles house which was much agaynste the erles honestie (whether he woulde have deflowred his doughter or his nece, the certayntie was not for both their honors openly knowen) for surely such a thyng was attempted by king Edward, which loved well both to loke and to fele fayre dammosels.[12]

The historical Edward's marriage to the beautiful young Elizabeth Wydville (widow of Sir John Grey), and his promotion of the interests of her brothers, sisters and sons, led directly to the estrangement from Warwick, to Edward's six-month exile in 1470–71, and to the battles of Barnet and Tewkesbury after his return to regain the throne. In converting this narrative material into dramatic form, Shakespeare's method, as usual, was to concentrate as far as possible on the clash of antagonistic personalities, and this was one of the instances in which Hall's account offered a clear lead in that direction. According to modern historians, Edward IV's motive for advancing his wife's family to heights of power and influence was at least partly one of self-protection: he was building up a group of magnates who would counterbalance Warwick and the Nevilles.[13] Hall's chronicle, however, throws the whole emphasis onto the king's sexual desire for Elizabeth Grey. Shakespeare, exploiting this in the play, provides Richard and George—now the Dukes of Gloucester and Clarence—with a drily bawdy commentary on the wooing:

GLOUCESTER (*aside to Clarence*)
                   Yea, is it so?
I see the lady hath a thing to grant,
Before the King will grant her humble suit.
CLARENCE (*aside to Gloucester*)
He knows the game; how true he keeps the wind!

   •   •   •   •

GLOUCESTER (*aside*)
Ay, widow? Then I'll warrant you all your lands,
An if what pleases him shall pleasure you.
Fight closer or, good faith, you'll catch a blow.
CLARENCE (*aside to Gloucester*)
I fear her not, unless she chance to fall.
GLOUCESTER (*aside to Clarence*)
God forbid that, for he'll take vantages.
KING EDWARD
How many children hast thou, widow, tell me.
CLARENCE (*aside to Gloucester*)
I think he means to beg a child of her.
GLOUCESTER (*aside to Clarence*)
Nay, then whip me; he'll rather give her two.
LADY GREY
Three, my most gracious lord.
GLOUCESTER (*aside*)
You shall have four if you'll be ruled by him.

                                                   III.ii.11, 21

A prototype for this *sotto voce* commentary is to be found in the Dauphin's seduction of la Pucelle, *1 Henry VI*, I.ii.119–25—'Doubtless he shrives this woman to her smock . . .'. But the ironies of Gloucester and Clarence at Edward IV's expense have been anticipated in a more direct way in *3 Henry VI* itself, where Richard at II.i.41 has a *suns/sons/daughters* joke. Richard's invitation to Edward to breed daughters rather than sons, and an apologetic 'by your leave' with which he quickly follows it, hint at friction between the brothers. The hints are the stronger for serving as cue for the messenger who brings the news of York's death.

Now nobody would maintain, I imagine, that the badinage with which Shakespeare has decorated Hall's basic dialogue between the Yorkist brothers represents comic writing of a particularly high order. What is worth noting is its broad function in the play. It has a place here not simply as comic relief but because the whole dramatic process of *3 Henry VI* now depends partly on the disruptive jealousies within each of the two power-seeking groups and partly on the stage contrast between pious 'shame-faced' Henry and 'sportful Edward', 'lascivious Edward'. The two kings are equal and opposite, as Shakespeare emphasises in juxtaposing

Richard's release of Edward from captivity at Middleham Castle (IV.v) with Warwick's release of Henry from the Tower (IV.vi). It is in this chaotic, cox-and-box realm of rival monarchs that the play's human disasters lie: sons kill their fathers, fathers their sons, and the guile and ruthlessness of the Yorkist brothers prevail. Theirs are the values that will hold sway until, in the final act of the whole tetralogy, Richmond returns from exile to fulfil Henry VI's prophecy that this young man would wear a crown, wield a sceptre, and 'bless a regal throne'. Whatever private doubts Shakespeare may have had about the Tudor myth, the *Henry VI* plays, bawdy and all, endorse Hall's account of the baronial wars.

In view of its comic-macabre atmosphere, especially in the first three acts, *Richard III* is a surprisingly 'unbawdy' play. The reason probably is that the hero's own favourite veins of humour are on the whole asexual. Now that Shakespeare is presenting Richard of Gloucester at full play length, ribaldry forms no important part of the personality he chooses to depict. It is of the nature of scurrilous humour soon to grow monotonous, and monotony would be quite alien to this villain-hero's quicksilver mind.

First and last, Richard is a politician, and when he makes jokes of *any* kind, indecent or otherwise, they are almost always made purposefully, either to influence the hearers or to unnerve them. In conversation with Clarence, for example, he will sneer at Queen Elizabeth and Mistress Shore just as readily for their *nouveau riche* status ('Since that our brother dubbed them gentlewomen') as for their sexual roles—the one as 'o'er-worn widow', the other as king's mistress. The effect on Clarence, the political effect, is what matters, and this, more than the jibe itself, comprises Richard's source of satisfaction. Again, when he constructs an extended witticism on Jane Shore's liaison with Edward, his aim is not simply the comic denigration of the adulterers but also the sudden discomfiting of Brakenbury:

> RICHARD
> ... We say that Shore's wife hath a pretty foot,
> A cherry lip, a bonny eye, a passing pleasing tongue;
> And that the Queen's kindred are made gentlefolks.
> How say you, sir? Can you deny all this?
> BRAKENBURY
> With this, my lord, myself have naught to do.
> RICHARD
> Naught to do with Mistress Shore? I tell thee, fellow,
> He that doth naught with her, excepting one,
> Were best to do it secretly, alone.

BRAKENBURY
>What one, my lord?

RICHARD
>Her husband, knave. Wouldst thou betray me?

>I.i.93

Since this kind of compromising wit is wholly typical of Richard, he is always on the alert to make use of the shadowy Mistress Shore's successive intrigues—partly, no doubt, because Shakespeare could count on his audience to be familiar with them. It suits Richard well that after Edward's death (II.ii) she becomes the mistress of Lord Hastings. Richard's bawdily exaggerated reference to her as 'that harlot, strumpet Shore' (III.iv.71) is what finally springs the trap against Hastings when he has unwarily pressed the matter of Edward V's coronation. The charge against his mistress provokes from Hastings just enough expostulation to give Richard pretext—however slight—for the simulated fit of rage in which he sends this opponent to the block. After the execution it remains fascinating, as E. A. J. Honigmann has remarked, to notice how Jane Shore's infamy becomes a moral touchstone. Every time Richard refers to it we feel that he is manipulating normal ethical attitudes in order to mask the really serious crimes, his own murders of Clarence and Hastings.[14]

The same preposterous yet finely calculated quality characterises the touches of bawdy involved in the propaganda campaign for the crowning of Richard. Buckingham is to hint that Edward IV was both illegitimate by birth and sexually insatiable by temperament:

>urge his hateful luxury
>And bestial appetite in change of lust,
>Which stretched unto their servants, daughters, wives,
>Even where his raging eye or savage heart,
>Without control, listed to make a prey.

>III.v.79

This instruction from Richard shows the lurid sensuality of a Barabas or an Aaron put to a comic use that makes perfect dramatic sense. As Freud was quick to stress, it comes fittingly from a character who feels himself debarred by physical deformity from normal sexual relationships. Paradoxically, too, the directions for the posthumous bastardising of Edward show Richard at his most sympathetic, since they display so well the luxuriant inventiveness of comic genius:

>Yet touch this sparingly, as 'twere far off,
>Because. my lord, you know my mother lives.

>III.v26.

Other references to sex in *Richard III* are numerous, and again are used as instruments of policy—in the wooing of Anne, in the wooing by proxy of Elizabeth, in rousing the royal army to battle—but none of them are strictly bawdy. Indeed, taking the play as a whole, one's final impression is of a calculated economy in the use of sexual innuendo. If *1 Henry VI* had a tendency to use its bawdy clumsily, this last play of the tetralogy stands almost at the other extreme. What little salacity it has is fully integrated with its characterisation and plot structure.

The problems of chronology that surround the composition of *Titus Andronicus* are scarcely less knotty than those affecting *1 Henry VI*, but it is not necessary to trace them in detail here. A practical working assumption is that *Titus*, *1*, *2 and 3 Henry VI* and *Richard III* were all written no earlier than 1589 and no later than 1594. This dating, for all its roughness, invites some comparison between the handling of indecency in the historical group of plays and that in the Roman melodrama.

In a text as much concerned with sexual crime as *Titus Andronicus*, it is no simple matter to determine precisely where, or why, the sexuality turns to bawdy. Even the typical obliqueness of bawdy for once proves an uncertain guide, because the fanciful, flowery nature of much of this play's language can easily be confused with it.[15] Yet rape, for example, is not bawdy. Allusions to rape sometimes are; but in this play only the obvious criminals—Aaron, Tamora, Demetrius, Chiron—strike that note in discussing their treatment of Lavinia, whereas the various motif-references to the Tereus–Philomela–Progne story avoid it.

In Demetrius and Chiron, bawdy provides straightforward expression of a decadent lechery:

> What, man! more water glideth by the mill
> Than wots the miller of; and easy it is
> Of a cut loaf to steal a shive, we know.
> Though Bassianus be the Emperor's brother,
> Better than he have worn Vulcan's badge.

II.i.85

The whole play owes much of its peculiar horror to the tension between such levity and the brutality behind it. At the other end of Shakespeare's career the same method will be applied in the rather similar figure of Cloten, whose unfulfilled plans for the murder of Posthumus and subsequent rape of Imogen closely resemble the actual events of this much earlier play. Here, just as in *Cymbeline*, necrophilous perversion underlies the ravishment-plot, and in this instance its bawdy figurations are shared by the Queen:

DEMETRIUS
   ... This minion stood upon her chastity,
   Upon her nuptial vow, her loyalty,
   And with that painted hope braves your mightiness;
   And shall she carry this unto her grave?
CHIRON
   An if she do, I would I were an eunuch.
   Drag hence her husband to some secret hole,
   And make his dead trunk pillow to our lust.
TAMORA
   But when ye have the honey we desire,
   Let not this wasp outlive us both to sting.

II.iii.124

Tamora's own lust for Aaron merges into her pleasure in the prospect of Lavinia's rape—'Now will I hence to seek my lovely Moor, / And let my spleenful sons this trull deflower'—and the way she equates the two intrigues can leave no room for doubt that what the liaison with Aaron represents on the mythic or symbolic level is an aspect of the Goths' bestiality.

Aaron himself is a more complex figure. True to the English medieval and Renaissance expectations of a Moor, he is both cunning and voluptuous,[16] but Shakespeare adds further qualities. Far from being merely the instrument for Tamora's crimes, Aaron is a partner, and dominant partner at that. His mastery over Chiron and Demetrius comes out even in bawdy: when he joins them in lewd banter, it is to flick it contemptuously aside in the same breath—

AARON
   Why, then, it seems some certain snatch or so
   Would serve your turns.
CHIRON   Ay, so the turn were served.
DEMETRIUS
   Aaron, thou hast hit it.
AARON   Would you had hit it too!
   Then should not we be tired with this ado.

II.i.95

This brusqueness (which is not unlike Richard III's) marks another special attitude to bawdy that will be characteristic of some later Shakespearean figures. Coriolanus shows exactly this mood when he jokes, briefly, with the servants of Aufidius, only to dismiss them the more decisively:

THIRD SERVINGMAN   ... Then thou dwell'st with daws too?
CORIOLANUS   No, I serve not thy master.

THIRD SERVINGMAN   How, sir? Do you meddle with my master?
CORIOLANUS   Ay, 'tis an honester service than to meddle with thy
mistress. Thou prat'st and prat'st. Serve with thy trencher. Hence!
He beats him away from the stage

IV.v.46

Coriolanus's true stature is, of course, apparent to the audience long
before this encounter; Aaron's does not fully emerge until Act IV, when
he preserves the life of his baby son. Here, too, indecency comes into
play to create dramatic contrast. The Nurse brings the newly born,
black-skinned infant from Tamora with instructions for Aaron to
'christen it with thy dagger's point'.

AARON
    Zounds, ye whore! Is black so base a hue?
    Sweet blowse, you are a beauteous blossom sure.
DEMETRIUS   Villain, what hast thou done?
AARON   That which thou canst not undo.
CHIRON   Thou hast undone our mother.
AARON   Villain, I have done thy mother.

IV.ii.71

This ebullient ribaldry makes possible a melodramatic 'switch' to ferocity
—and to a certain primitive splendour—a few lines later, as Aaron defends
the child against their swords:

Stay, murderous villains, will you kill your brother!
Now, by the burning tapers of the sky
That shone so brightly when this boy was got,
He dies upon my scimitar's sharp point
That touches this my first-born son and heir.

IV.ii.88

The sudden change here, with Aaron hurtling from the scabrous to the
defiant, is not only striking as a stage effect but also characteristic of the
man. And the human normality of his protectiveness towards the baby
adds a new, unpredictable streak to what might otherwise have remained
a theatrical stock figure of atheist-barbarian. Much the same emotional
sequence works in reverse, but with like effect, near the end of the play:
Aaron, now Lucius's prisoner, has to be assured that his son will be
cared for, and only then gives vent to a climactic burst of grisly humour.

AARON
    First know thou, I begot him on the Empress.
LUCIUS
    O most insatiate and luxurious woman!

AARON

Tut, Lucius, this was but a deed of charity
To that which thou shalt hear of me anon.
'Twas her two sons that murdered Bassianus;
They cut thy sister's tongue, and ravished her,
And cut her hands, and trimmed her as thou saw'st.

LUCIUS

O detestable villain! Call'st thou that trimming?

AARON

Why, she was washed, and cut, and trimmed, and 'twas
Trim sport for them which had the doing of it.

V.i.87

In a perceptive essay in his book *Shakespeare's Early Tragedies* (1968), Nicholas Brooke has argued that the central theme of *Titus Andronicus* is the confounding of issues of right and wrong, and that its main preoccupation is the truth that Man is at once noble and bestial. Brooke does not claim any share in the nobility for Aaron—'he develops as a beast straight from the earth to which he will finally be condemned'—but he does point to a positive value in the instinctual assurance of behaviour that goes with the fellow's evil. Conversely, says Professor Brooke, suffering corrupts Titus and Lavinia into subhuman revengers. ' "Gentle" Lavinia is the agent of Titus' metamorphosis, and she is his bestial accomplice in Revenge' (p. 39). This is a reading of the play that permits only a distanced sympathy for Lavinia as the victim of outrage, but it provides convincing explanation for aspects of her behaviour that would otherwise be puzzling. One of these is her willingness to become involved in the cheap exchanges of II.iii, where she joins Bassianus in the clumsily ironic upbraiding of Tamora for her adultery with Aaron:

> Under your patience, gentle Emperess,
> 'Tis thought you have a goodly gift in horning,
> And to be doubted that your Moor and you
> Are singled forth to try experiments.
> Jove shield your husband from his hounds today!
> 'Tis pity they should take him for a stag.
>
> II.iii.66

This would seem to be inconsistent with Lavinia's demureness elsewhere. It is she, after all, who snubs Saturninus with chaste firmness when he ventures a lightly improper remark about new-married ladies being late-risers (II.ii.14–17); and even when threatened with imminent rape, she will be too modest to pronounce that word: 'one thing more, / That womanhood denies my tongue to tell' (II.iii.173). Yet the alternation of purity and vulgarity in Lavinia makes good dramatic sense if one bears in

mind Nicholas Brooke's advice that it would be sentimental to look for
a nice little heroine in this play. In the symbolically disruptive atmosphere
of Act II's 'barren detested vale', we gain glimpses of those darker
qualities in Lavinia that will alone explain her part in the ritualistic
murders of V.ii.

Titus himself also has a minute share in the play's bawdy. He is too
much the type figure of ancient Roman ideals to be made light-spoken,
even in his revengeful decline, but IV.iii, the arrow-shooting scene,
brings this:

> O, well said, Lucius!
> Good boy, in Virgo's lap! Give it Pallas.
>
> Publius, Publius, what hast thou done?
> See, see, thou hast shot off one of Taurus' horns.
>
> IV.iii.63, 68

As the Elizabethans regularly used the word *lap* to include the sense
vulva, the innuendo on the arrow's seeming to land in Virgo's lap is
sharply at variance with the picture of afflicted but unbending fatherhood
that Titus represents. Yet perhaps this very disparity is the real point of
the speech. The bizarre touch of eroticism is one of Shakespeare's indications that Titus's madness, like Hieronimo's, is not wholly feigned, but
in part genuine.

Despite its early date, then, *Titus Andronicus* reveals in its use of bawdy
a precision and economy that come unexpectedly from so lurid and
derivative a work. It provides yet another piece of evidence to show that
Shakespeare's use of such material, even amongst his earliest plays, was
discriminating as well as sparing. Shakespeare the Bawdy Bard is a myth,
wished into existence by broadly-winking, rib-nudging middlebrows.

This chapter's examples of Shakespeare's use of ribaldry as an element in
characterisation could be duplicated repeatedly from the later plays.
Many such instances would be too obvious to be worth labouring.
Nobody needs to be told that people like Falstaff or Parolles, Thersites
or Pandarus, Pompey or Lucio, Boult or his employers—nobody needs
to be told that these are bawdy. Strip them of indecency, and they will
virtually cease to exist. Rather less obvious, but still significant to dramatic
structure, is the occasional touch of ribaldry from some more serious
character in whom we would not expect to find it. The Duchess of York
in *Richard II* exemplifies this during the excitement over her son Aumerle's
share in the plot to assassinate Bolingbroke:

YORK
Away, fond woman. Were he twenty times my son
I would appeach him.
DUCHESS OF YORK
Hadst thou groaned for him as I have done
Thou wouldst be more pitiful.
But now I know thy mind. Thou dost suspect
That I have been disloyal to thy bed,
And that he is a bastard, not thy son.
Sweet York, sweet husband, be not of that mind.
He is as like thee as a man may be;
Not like to me, or any of my kin,
And yet I love him.

V.ii.101

This odd mixture of sense and foolishness gets some of its queerness from
the juxtaposition of genuine emotion with vulgar thinking. It becomes
part of the complex of divided loyalties which Bolingbroke, as king,
shows himself fully capable of appreciating and handling.

Another unlikely figure to have her moment of bawdy—again it is
at a point of intense emotional crisis—is the Portia of *Julius Caesar*:

Dwell I but in the suburbs
Of your good pleasure? If it be no more,
Portia is Brutus' harlot, not his wife.

II.i.285

Sir Thomas North's version of Plutarch supplied Shakespeare with the
basic idea for these lines, and even with the word *harlot*; but in adding the
connotations of *suburbs*, associated with brothelry, the dramatist is in-
tensifying Portia's sarcasm to a degree which is fully characteristic of her
as she appears in the play.

Again, Helena, in *All's Well*, is saved from priggishness partly by her
ready tolerance of Parolles' sexual levities; and the same kind of thing
might be said of Rosalind or Perdita. Characterisation, however, is very
far from being the end-product of Shakespeare's artistry, and as character
itself becomes increasingly subsumed in the larger concerns of atmosphere
and theme, metaphor and myth, so too does bawdy. It is into these wider
areas that the next few chapters follow it.

NOTES

1. Although, to put latterday disintegrators at their ease, I have tried to be sparing
in my use of the name Shakespeare for the author(s) of *1 Henry VI*, the questioning of Shakespeare's authorship is a highly specialised matter lying outside the
scope of this book. With serious reservations in the cases of *Pericles* and *Henry*

VIII only, I have worked throughout on the basis of the Shakespearean canon as given in the standard modern editions.

2. Ben Jonson, *Poems*, ed. G. B. Johnston (Routledge, 1954), p. 180.

3. A. S. Cairncross, ed., *1 Henry VI* (New Arden edn, 1962), p. xxxviii.

4. J. R. Tanner, ed., *Tudor Constitutional Documents* (2nd edn, Cambridge University Press 1930), p. 195.

5. Bullough, *Narrative and Dramatic Sources*, iii, 77.

6. *Ibid.*, 61.

7. *Ibid.*, 56.

8. *Ibid.*, 77.

9. Is the name Horner one of Shakespeare's little jokes? In both Hall's and Fabyan's chronicles the armourer is unnamed, so this seems to be Shakespeare's casual invention. And while it lacks the sexual context of Wycherley's more famous Horner in *The Country Wife* (1675), it does have an ironic appropriateness as a name for Hall's 'tall and . . . hardye personage' whose strength and wits failed him when he became 'overladed with hote drynkes' (Bullough, iii, 105). Shakespeare's nicely esoteric naming of minor characters may be noticed in *Romeo and Juliet*, IV.iv.5, where it is probably the Nurse who is 'good Angelica'. As T. J. B. Spencer notes in his New Penguin edition of the play, Angelica is the name of the 'pagan princess of exquisite beauty and heartless coquetry' in Ariosto's *Orlando Furioso*. See also glossary, at *stock-fish*.

10. *The First Part of the Contention* (Q 1594), which is almost universally accepted as a Bad Quarto of *2 Henry VI*, spells out the name Basimecu more explicitly as 'bus mine cue'. In his *Shakespeare Glossary* (2nd edn, 1919), Onions adds, 'Still applied to Italian organ-grinders, with the pronunciation "bozzimacu", in some parts of Warwickshire'; cf. *Twelfth Night* II.iii.22, where Sir Andrew Aguecheek quotes Feste on 'the Vapians passing the equinoctial of Queubus'.

11. Harold C. Goddard, *The Meaning of Shakespeare* (2 vols, 1951), i. 29.

11. Goddard, *The Meaning of Shakespeare*, i, 29.

12. Bullough, iii, 188. Edward IV's amorous proclivities are also prominent in *The Mirror for Magistrates*, ed. Lily B. Campbell, pp. 236ff. and 373ff. See also, of course, Thomas Heywood's *1 and 2 Edward IV* (1600).

13. A. R. Myers, *England in the Late Middle Ages* (8th edn) Penguin Books, 1971), p. 129.

14. E. A. J. Honigmann, ed., *Richard III* (New Penguin edn, 1968), p. 41.

15. See Eugene M. Waith, 'The metamorphosis of violence in *Titus Andronicus*', *SS* 10 (1957), 39–49.

16. Eldred Jones, *Othello's Countrymen* (1955), pp. 57–9, 71.

5

Combination and Contrast

... showing how great machinations and slender designs may promote
or obviate one another, and the high and the low co-operate in the general
system by unavoidable concatenation.

Samuel Johnson, *Preface*

As Shakespeare moves on from the early plays to write the second series
of histories and the mature comedies it becomes easier to see his use of
indecency taking on a definite shape. It forms what might be thought of
as fields of magnetic force, not simply round particular characters, but in
relation to points of thematic energy. Bawdy takes special prominence
in what have come to be called mirror-scenes: scenes which implicitly
comment on the main matter of a play, anticipating or re-enacting the
content of other scenes in a changed idiom. Perhaps the best-known single
example is the playlet in which Falstaff mimics King Henry IV, his
burlesque studded with salacious jokes from both the Prince and himself.
Some critics have rightly stressed that not all such interludes in Shakespeare are necessarily reductive or deflating in their effect.[1] One of their
possible functions as parody is to forestall the adoption of a cynical or
dismissive attitude towards serious people or events. That mock inter-
view in *1 Henry IV*, culminating in a sobering switch of tone—

> FALSTAFF   ... old Jack Falstaff—banish not him thy Harry's company,
> banish not him thy Harry's company. Banish plump Jack, and banish
> all the world.
> PRINCE HAL   I do, I will
>
> II.iv.463

—guards an audience against misapprehensions. The Prince's reconciliation with the King, in the next scene but one, will be sincere, and we
can be in no doubt about that once we have weighed the implication of
'I do, I will.' Similarly, it is critically naïve to assume (as A. P. Rossiter

surprisingly did with *Romeo and Juliet*) that the bawdy account of a love-affair is automatically 'truer' or more realistic than the partly idealised account with which Shakespeare contrasts it. Of course indecency can be used as a means to reductive realism, and very decisively too, as I hope to show later; but to suppose that bubble-pricking must always be its effect would be to read *As You Like It* through the distorting spectacles of Touchstone, *Troilus and Cressida* through those of Thersites, and so on.

It seems sensible, then, before considering those plays that use indecency mainly as ironic parody, to look at some others in which it helps to place major issues in perspective, but does so without arrogating the role of ultimate truth-teller.

First, *Romeo and Juliet*. It has often been remarked that *Romeo* tacks back and forth between tragic and comic feeling a great deal more than Shakespeare's later tragedies. Much of the play imitates in its structure the serio-comic, seesaw pattern of those verbal antitheses which its dialogue so uncomfortably bristles with. In particular, readers encountering the text for the first time tend to find its long first act disconcerting. Only the rather heavyhanded guidance of the prologue, they point out, saves them from mistaking the exposition for that of a comedy based on some Rosaline–Romeo–Juliet love intrigue. It even opens with a whole series of lubricious jokes from Gregory and Sampson, who quibble for twenty-odd lines on such words as *stand, stir, thrust, weapon, tool, maid*. All this 'wit', however, cannot properly be read or acted at its face value as comedy. Its sharp contrast with the formality and impressive tone of the prologue sonnet has to be recognised *as* contrast, and it is important that the two idle servingmen are not only joking but are also daring one another into starting a street brawl as soon as opportunity offers. Sex, at this gutter level, is obscurely but intimately mingled with the urge to violence. It is a theme that will loom large in several of Shakespeare's later plays, whether through obsessive eruption (in Hamlet, Othello, Lear, Timon, Leontes) or through the plotting of villains (Regan, Cloten, Caliban). At the moment, in the opening scene of *Romeo and Juliet*, it creates the atmosphere in which the hero and heroine will have to struggle for breath: an atmosphere at once threatening and sleazily comic. Violence is about to invade the early morning with the same pointless ferocity as it will show again on the hot afternoon following the marriage. Its world is one that Romeo and Juliet would seem to have no connection with, but from the very start of the play it is lying in wait for them as surely as Macbeth's witches lie in wait for him. *Macbeth*-like ironies lurk beneath the conversational surface, too. It is not Sampson but Romeo who, in due course, will 'cut off' the maidenhead of a hostile family's maiden.

More immediately, from Romeo's point of view, his highflown senti-
ments for Rosaline and his subsequent love for Juliet have to reckon with
insistent mockery from Mercutio. Shakespeare's comic method with
Mercutio is to have him always on the alert to translate any sexual
emotion into strictly physical terms. It is a process that neutralises in
advance any tendency we in the audience might otherwise feel towards
poking fun at Romeo's intensity. Extravagant Romeo may be, particularly in his Rosaline phase, but, given a Mercutio as commentator, the
play has acknowledged the extravagance and allowed for it. Far from its
being the case that, as some critics have maintained, Mercutio has to be
killed off because he threatens our confidence in the hero, it would be
truer to say that if Mercutio did not exist it would be necessary for
Shakespeare to invent him.[2] Matters are so arranged that every time
Mercutio tries to undercut Romeo's emotion, he fails. Sometimes this is
because the mockery is so gross as to be self-defeating:

> Now will he sit under a medlar tree
> And wish his mistress were that kind of fruit
> As maids call medlars when they laugh alone.
> O, Romeo, that she were, O that she were
> An open-arse and thou a poppering pear![3]

II.i.34

It is unlikely that Mercutios of Shakespeare's own day spoke the term
'open-arse' here, as both the Bad and Good quartos of *Romeo and Juliet*
suppress it, and some such action as Benvolio's clapping his hand over
Mercutio's mouth seems called for; but with the quite common *medlar/
meddler* pun to herald it, the first half of the medlar's slang name of open-
arse would not go unnoticed. Clearly, all that Romeo needs to do about
so broad a sally is to keep out of the way and flatly disregard it: 'He jests
at scars that never felt a wound.' At other times he can be seen taking
Mercutio in his stride, countering quip with quip on the level of inconsequential banter:

ROMEO   . . . What counterfeit did I give you?
MERCUTIO   The slip, sir, the slip. Can you not conceive?
ROMEO   Pardon, good Mercutio. My business was great, and in such a
case as mine a man may strain courtesy.
MERCUTIO   That's as much as to say, such a case as yours constrains a
man to bow in the hams.
ROMEO   Meaning, to curtsy.
MERCUTIO   Thou hast most kindly hit it.
ROMEO   A most courteous exposition.

II.iv.46

Most of the bawdy in this exchange is of the volatile, undemonstrable kind discussed in chapter 1, but Mercutio's juxtaposition of 'a case' and 'bow in the hams' points to a sexual joke. Evidence suggesting that *case* can mean the male sex organs is assembled in the glossary, and the association of bowed thighs with sexual excess is quite common. Once again, however, our primary attention in reading or watching the play is not on the ribaldry itself, but on Romeo's refusal to be in any way ruffled by it.

Not even while the young men are trying on their masks for the Capulets' feast—a time when Romeo, still sighing over Rosaline, might be thought to be at his most vulnerable—not even then does Mercutio's attempt to 'cure' the lover succeed. As his weird, fast-flowing current of indecent humour and extravagant fancy sweeps him along, Mercutio here becomes that uneasy figure, the satirist who is himself a part of what he aims to satirise. It is typical of his role in the play that the immediate dramatic outcome of his long 'Queen Mab' speech is a sense of discomfort which seems to unnerve Mercutio himself no less than the others. 'This wind you talk of blows us from ourselves,' says Benvolio, speaking out of the dispirited atmosphere that Mercutio's outburst has created. Dramatically, it is then an easy step to Romeo's quasi-choric monologue 'my mind misgives ...'. Despite extensive cutting, the dark conclusion of the Queen Mab speech was well caught in Franco Zeffirelli's film version of *Romeo* (1968). Zeffirelli's whole reading of Mercutio made excellent sense of the role: Mercutio as an ageing manic-depressive, idling his time away in the company of men half his own age. And the harder such a friend tries to make fun of Romeo, the more fully he succeeds in placing beyond doubt Romeo's capacity for total commitment in love.

As Mercutio is to Romeo, so the Nurse is to Juliet. Essentially, the Nurse views all sexual activity from farmyard level, and there is at least a measure of truth in Mercutio's impolite assumption that she is a bawd. A consistent line can be traced from I.iii, with its garrulous reminiscence of her husband's smutty joke about Juliet falling backward, to III.v, where the Nurse blandly recommends bigamy. The mature scorn with which Juliet then rejects her provides another indication of the emotional depth in the lovers that renders their ultimate fate tragic rather than just pathetic.

It is perhaps a measure of Shakespeare's relative inexperience at the time of writing *Romeo and Juliet* that his contrasting of the old and the young gives rise to some blurred emotional focus in the third act. In III.ii, we find him using the Nurse as a means of dramatising the gap between the sensitive and the insensitive woman's response to an apparent betrayal:

JULIET
... O, that deceit should dwell
In such a gorgeous palace!
NURSE   There's no trust,
No faith, no honesty in men; all perjured,
All forsworn, all naught, all dissemblers.
Ah, where's my man? Give me some aqua vitae.

III.ii.84

The following scene, III.iii, is a parallel episode, in which Romeo in turn hears the news of his being banished, and his despair is given much the same comic treatment as Juliet's. But the juxtaposition of bawdy and serious feeling is startling. The Nurse arrives at Friar Lawrence's cell to find the young man 'There on the ground, with his own tears made drunk' —this tart description from the Friar is perhaps the clearest guide to the scene's particular quality. Since Romeo's situation is not hopeless, his paroxysm of woe is unjustified, and the Nurse's speeches, like some of the Friar's, place it at ironic distance.

O, he is even in my mistress' case,
Just in her case! O woeful sympathy!
Piteous predicament! Even so lies she,
Blubbering and weeping, weeping and blubbering.
Stand up, stand up! Stand, an you be a man.
For Juliet's sake, for her sake, rise and stand!
Why should you fall into so deep an O?

III.iii.85

This offers the usual sexual *double entendre* in the much-repeated *stand*, and probably also in the once-repeated *case*. The phrase 'fall into so deep an O' extends the innuendo: the letter O, like *nought* and *nothing*, served as a ready carrier of sexual associations for Elizabethans, and it would seem to have *vulva* as its secondary sense here (as also, perhaps, for Mercutio in the lines from II.i quoted on page 69). All in all, then, the Nurse's exclamations over Romeo represent a bold stroke, dramaturgically speaking, though to my mind an unsuccessful one. In so far as the indecencies make us laugh, our laughter is largely at Romeo's expense, and one senses in the writing much the same kind of insecurity of tone as in the strained oxymorons of these lamentation scenes—'Beautiful tyrant! fiend angelical! / Dove-feathered raven! Wolvish-ravening lamb!', and so on. Perhaps it is symptomatic of Shakespeare's difficulties here that he is leaning particularly heavily on the corresponding passages in the source poem, Arthur Brooke's *Romeus and Juliet* (1562). The dramatist might well have been better to keep his prostrate hero and quibbling heroine off-stage between about the middle of III.ii and the start of the great wedding-morning scene, III.v. Yet it must at least be acknowledged that the Nurse's bawdy combines with the Friar's gruff advice to gain vivid expression for the 'plain folks' ' view of the lovers in their new predicament.

A further possibility is that in the lamentation scenes Shakespeare may have been striving after the odd kind of tension that he achieves (again with the help of mild indecency) in IV.v, when the Nurse tries to rouse Juliet from unconsciousness:

> Why, love, I say! Madam! Sweetheart! Why, bride!
> What, not a word? You take your pennyworths now.
> Sleep for a week. For the next night, I warrant,
> The County Paris hath set up his rest
> That you shall rest but little. God forgive me!
> Marry, and amen! How sound is she asleep!
> I needs must wake her. Madam, madam, madam!
> Ay, let the County take you in your bed.
> He'll fright you up, i'faith.
>
> IV.v.3

Even though the theatre audience knows well enough that Juliet is not really dead, there is suspense in awaiting discovery of the *supposed* death, and this is heightened by the protracted sense of the ordinary, the humdrum, that the Nurse's prurience maintains. It is a Chekhovian effect, and one that will recur in starker forms later in Shakespeare's career. Macbeth's Porter creates it when he first identifies himself as a symbolic keeper of hell-gate, then goes on to greet Macduff and Lennox with a flow of Rabelaisian chat. The absurd irrelevance of his prattle is its dramatic point. While in a limited sense it provides 'comic relief' after the taut emotions of the murder scene, it also adds to the feeling of nightmare which the killing of Duncan has induced. Along the edge of the Porter's firmset territory of crude physical facts (drink, lechery, nosepainting, sleep and urine) there stretches the moral, spiritual and political morass that Macbeth and his wife have set quaking; and the longer Shakespeare extends the Porter's monologue, the more time there is for the audience to ponder what Macduff and Lennox are stepping into. Elsewhere, Cleopatra's conversation with the clown who brings the asps has something of the same quality, as also have the scenes in *Pericles* showing Marina in the brothel and, in *The Winter's Tale*, Paulina handing the infant Perdita to Leontes. These emotionally complex episodes in the late plays outgo the *Romeo* example in both scale and subtlety, yet *Romeo and Juliet* at least indicates how far comic indecency can be pushed in what is basically an unfunny context. The Nurse's speech as she tries to waken Juliet forms a small but typical part of the world of accident, muddle and human mediocrity to which the lovers fall victim.

Should the musicians' scene (IV.v.96–144) be read or acted as another interlude of the suspenseful kind I have been describing? H. T. Price, in an influential essay,[4] argued that it should be.

> The main action shows Romeo and Juliet being carried swiftly to destruction, and then Shakespeare holds up the plot for a while to give us a vignette of quite commonplace musicians, making bad jokes, careless and unconcerned as they pack up their music. In the theatre it seems incredible that the world of disaster should exist with a world of such security. At a good performance we get the feeling that we are viewing hell from a ringside seat.

This account is open to several objections. In this particular phase of the play, Romeo and Juliet are not being carried to destruction as swiftly as all that. They will be, in Act V; but not yet. The musicians' scene also differs importantly from the attempt to waken Juliet, or from the *Macbeth* Porter's scene, in that it gets much further away from the main plot. There may be some relevance to Juliet in the Nurse's two lines of possible bawdy, 'Honest good fellows, ah, put up, put up! / For well you know this is a pitiful case' (IV.v.97), but, if there is, it is quickly lost from sight on the arrival of Peter immediately afterwards. Peter's wit contest with the musicians has an engaging quality which Price seemed to acknowledge when he called it a vignette, but the result is that for these three or four minutes we all but *forget* Romeo and Juliet. The theatrical effect seems to me much less that of 'viewing hell from a ringside seat' than one of genuine, old-fashioned comic relief—something well within the range of Will Kempe as comedian.

More generally, in observing the contrast between the love-affair and its spasmodically bawdy surroundings, it is important not to etherealise Romeo and Juliet. They would never be proof against Mercutio's mockery if they themselves failed to acknowledge the physical basis of their love, and when they make this acknowledgement it is sometimes in terms that disregard polite convention. Romeo's wish that Juliet cast off the 'vestal livery' of the moon, Juliet's sensual longings in her prothalamion soliloquy, the agonised parting in the second balcony scene—all these have moments that could conceivably be called indecent. But no indecencies could be less flippant than these. Their cumulative effect is to add to the paradoxical double quality of solidity and buoyancy that characterises the lovers' relationship even to the point of death:

> I am no pilot; yet, wert thou as far
> As that vast shore washed with the farthest sea,
> I should adventure for such merchandise.
>
> II.ii.82

> O churl! drunk all, and left no friendly drop
> To help me after? I will kiss thy lips.
> Haply some poison yet doth hang on them
> To make me die with a restorative.
>
> V.iii.163

Shakespeare never lets Romeo or Juliet float off to a remote idealistic plane, 'Too flattering-sweet to be substantial'. It is partly by insisting on the simple human reality of their passion that he creates out of their destruction the first great love tragedy of English dramatic literature.

Some two or three years after *Romeo and Juliet*—the dates are uncertain—came *The Merchant of Venice*, another play in which sexual indecency has a significant role as ironic parody though not necessarily as 'realism'. Here, instead of helping to contrast the shallowness of minor figures with the deeper emotions of main protagonists, bawdy works in almost the opposite way, as part of the bright, humane side of a Shylock-darkened world. In saying this, I am not, of course, trying to relegate Shylock to some oversimplified, pre-Romantic role as mere predatory villain. Modern criticism of the play rightly insists on the ambivalence in Shakespear's handling of Shylock as both ogre and victim. But there is far less ambivalence surrounding his 'Christian' opponents (for all their truculence), and any reading or production that underrates the zest, colour, and decorous ceremonial of Venice and Belmont will misrepresent the comedy as a whole. It may be no accident that the play's bawdy is almost invariably lighthearted, and that roughly half of the indecent lines are concentrated in the last act, where they become part of the orchestration of a gentle postlude to the trial scene.

In the earlier acts it is, not surprisingly, Launcelot Gobbo who has the lion's share of ribaldry. Most of his quibbles are the normal stock-in-trade of the stage fool, and they can be paralleled in any other Shakespearean play where a clown or fool earns his keep, as Gobbo latterly does, by means of his verbal wit. Yet it is interesting to notice how closely his commercial preoccupations match the play's broader motif of cash and merchandise. While Antonio gambles with his own flesh to obtain money for his friend, and while Portia's suitors risk lifelong celibacy if the hazard of the metal caskets fails them, Launcelot tells his own fortune at a humbler social level:

> Go to, here's a simple line of life. Here's a small trifle of wives! Alas, fifteen wives is nothing; eleven widows and nine maids is a simple coming-in for one man. And then to scape drowning thrice, and to be

in peril of my life with the edge of a feather-bed! Here are simple scapes. Well, if Fortune be a woman, she's a good wench for this gear.

II.ii.148

In particular, the quibble on *coming-in* glancingly reflects Bassanio's enterprise, since the girl he hopes to marry is desirable not only sexually but also—and Bassanio is frank about it—for her wealth. So it is, too, with Lorenzo and Jessica. Their torchlight elopement is a youthful adventure inspired by genuine affection, yet it also offers cash rewards, immediately in the contents of Jessica's heavily laden box—

Here, catch this casket; it is worth the pains

II.vi.33

Why there, there, there, there! A diamond gone cost me two thousand ducats in Frankfurt!

III.i.76

—and later, as things turn out, in the full inheritance of Shylock's estate.

The bawdy touches in Launcelot's fortune-telling are thus less irrelevant than might at first appear, given a play so intricately concerned with risk and escape, love and hate. Appropriately, Launcelot too escapes from Shylock and successfully enrols for service at Belmont—despite his misdemeanour in 'the getting up of the negro's belly' (III.v.34). Lorenzo's sudden accusation, 'The Moor is with child by you, Launcelot', has puzzled many commentators, but this again provides a stroke of lubricious counterpart for other parts of the plot. By the end of this play, Shakespeare will leave nobody wholly blameless: if Shylock becomes Portia's victim at courtroom level, the anonymous Moor is left as Launcelot's below stairs.

Once again, though, it needs to be stressed that the notion of Shylock as victim is no clear or simple one for Shakespeare, and sexual indecency has a share in the qualifications that surround it. Solanio, as one of the play's leading Jew-baiters, narrates with evident satisfaction Shylock's loud bewailing of Jessica's flight:

> I never heard a passion so confused,
> So strange, outrageous, and so variable
> As the dog Jew did utter in the streets:
> 'My daughter! O my ducats! O my daughter!
> Fled with a Christian! O my Christian ducats!
> Justice! The law! My ducats and my daughter!
> A sealed bag, two sealed bags of ducats,
> Of double ducats, stol'n from me by my daughter!
> And jewels, two stones, two rich and precious stones,
> Stol'n by my daughter! Justice! Find the girl!
> She hath the stones upon her, and the ducats!'

II.viii.12

The particular emphasis on *two* stones suggests a bawdy allusion to testicles. The Elizabethans commonly used the word *stones* in that sense in relation to men as we still use it of horses, and its repetition by Salerio a few lines later increases the probability that Shakespeare intends a quibble. This joke, in both its timing and its taste, is fully in character for Solanio, to judge by some of his repartee in a later scene:

> SHYLOCK   My own flesh and blood to rebel!
> SOLANIO   Out upon it, old carrion! Rebels it at these years?
>
> III.i.31

The jibe about rebellion of the flesh is too cheap and slight to influence an audience's attitude to Shylock one way or another, but not so with the one about the two stones. It hints at the escape of Jessica from Shylock as a symbolic father-castration: the more so since Shylock's intermingling of *ducats* and *daughter* has already suggested another Elizabethan commonplace, that of the miser's paternal attitude to his wealth. (Autolycus, in *The Winter's Tale*, offers the merrymakers a ballad 'to a very doleful tune, how a usurer's wife was brought to bed of twenty money-bags at a burden'.)

Thus the bawdy-bizarre juxtapositions of 'his stones, his daughter, and his ducats' contribute to the farcical side of Shylock's presentation. It is typical of the play that this kind of heartless farce is left to co-exist as best it may with the moving pleas of III.i and IV.i: 'Hath not a Jew eyes? . . . I stand for judgement. Answer; shall I have it?'

Apart from Launcelot Gobbo and Solanio, most of the ribald or salacious lines in *The Merchant of Venice* cluster round the betrothal, and later the reunion, of Bassanio and Portia, Gratiano and Nerissa. The likemindedness of the latter couple and the ebullient happiness of the betrothal scene are neatly displayed in the gambling joke,

> GRATIANO   We'll play with them, the first boy for a thousand ducats.
> NERISSA   What, and stake down?
> GRATIANO   No, we shall ne'er win at that sport, and stake down.
>   But who comes here?
>
> III.ii.213

Once again a link with the dominant theme of hazard is noticeable; and before the laughter has ended, Salerio is here with a letter bringing the news of Antonio's danger.

The bawdy content of *The Merchant* culminates in the last two hundred lines of the play, where the squabble over the rings admits a series of *double entendres*.[5] This maintains the general tendency of Act V as a whole: whatever unease we have felt over the Christians' final treatment of

Shylock, Shakespeare is making sure that the play will at least end as 'Happy Comedy'. Quite apart from the flirtatiousness with which Portia and Nerissa spring their trap—

PORTIA

    Let not that doctor e'er come near my house.

    .   .   .   .

    I will become as liberal as you,
    I'll not deny him anything I have,
    No, not my body nor my husband's bed.

    .   .   .   .

    Now by mine honour which is yet mine own,
    I'll have that doctor for my bedfellow.

NERISSA

    And I his clerk. Therefore be well advised
    How you do leave me to mine own protection

                                          V.i.223

—it would be a moralistic audience indeed that could withhold its laughter from Gratiano's counterthreat to 'mar the young clerk's pen' or from his parting sally:

        Well, while I live I'll fear no other thing
        So sore as keeping safe Nerissa's ring.

                                        V.i.306

This last couplet is nicely pointed. *Thing*, placed at the end of a line, has the chance to reverberate with its anatomical senses, while jokes equating a ring with the female pudendum are fairly numerous in Renaissance literature. Rabelais provides a colourful pre-Shakespearean instance in Friar John's story of Hans Carvel, jeweller to the King of Melinda:

> In his old age he married the daughter of the bailiff in chancery, who was young, pretty, frisky, flirtatious, oncoming, and a good deal too charming to his neighbours and his servants. And so it came about at the end of a few weeks that he became as jealous as a tiger; and grew suspicious that she was getting her buttocks bumped elsewhere. . . . One night, in particular, as he lay beside her in this state, he dreamt that he talked to the devil and told him his grievances. The devil comforted him, and put a ring on his middle finger, saying: 'I will give you this ring. Whilst you wear it on your finger your wife will not be carnally known by any man without your knowledge and consent.' . . . The devil vanished, and Hans Carvel awoke quite delighted to find that he had his finger in his wife's what's-its-name.[6]

Logan Pearsall Smith once remarked that the first words of the fifth act of *The Merchant of Venice* put a kind of magic on him. Unfortunately he does not seem to have recorded whether he found the magic of the last words of the same act a few shades blacker. Yet that final couplet supplies a crisp and appropriate tag-line for a play that is concerned, not solely with a Jew among Christians, but also with the awkward fact that the human anatomy and objects of material wealth are difficult to keep apart.

'*The Merry Wives of Windsor* lies as an incongruity on any chart of Shakespeare's progress.' In making this remark, Philip Edwards was recording his general concurrence with a long line of critics who have stressed the weaknesses of this comedy.[7] A study of the play's bawdy certainly cannot provide the kind of appraisal that would console either those who regret the preponderance of its prose over its verse or those who sigh after the Falstaff of *Henry IV*; but such a study does bring into focus a quite intricate pattern of dramatic contrasts which may help to account for the continued popularity of *The Merry Wives* as a stage piece.

Falstaff, as the central figure and a would-be seducer into the bargain, has a surprisingly small share of the bawdy lines in the earlier scenes. This may be because his plans to subvert the two wives are at this stage less lustful than financially interested: he spies *entertainment* (which means employment as well as sexual amusement), and he proposes to *trade* (sexually, but also for profit). In the middle of the play, Shakespeare does allow him a couple of casually indecent ripostes:

> FALSTAFF   Take away these chalices. Go, brew me a pottle of sack finely.
> BARDOLPH   With eggs, sir?
> FALSTAFF   Simple of itself; I'll no pullet-sperm in my brewage. . . .
>   How now!
> QUICKLY   Marry, sir, I come to your worship from Mistress Ford. . . .
>   She does so take on with her men; they mistook their erection.
> FALSTAFF   So did I mine. . . .
>
>   III.v.24

If these two small jokes can be said to have dramatic significance, it lies in their indicating Falstaff's resilience. His spirits are already on the mend after his ducking. The speed of his recovery is something that directors of the play need to observe: I recall an unconvincing production (on tour in Glasgow in 1950) in which Wolfit began III.v with his feet in a mustard bath, thereby placing his performance squarely in a 'fat buffoon' tradition that seems to me to do the whole play less than justice.

It is not until Act V, when repeated frustrations have pushed out of sight any hope for cash gains, that Falstaff's talk becomes more insistently bawdy. The change comes quite suddenly.

> The Windsor bell hath struck twelve; the minute draws on. Now the hot-blooded gods assist me! Rember, Jove, thou wast a bull for thy Europa; love set on thy horns. O powerful love! that in some respects makes a

beast a man; in some other a man a beast. You were also, Jupiter, a
swan, for the love of Leda. O omnipotent love! how near the god drew to
the complexion of a goose! A fault done first in the form of a beast
—O Jove, a beastly fault!—and then another fault in the semblance of a
fowl—think on't, Jove, a foul fault! When gods have hot backs what
shall poor men do? For me, I am here a Windsor stag; and the fattest,
I think, i'th'forest. Send me a cool rut-time, Jove, or who can blame
me to piss my tallow?

V.v.1

Being more genuinely libidinous than anything we have heard from
Falstaff earlier in the piece, his prayer to the hot-blodded gods makes
articulate the vice for which he is about to be ritually punished. Volpone-
like, he goes on to construct an elaborate aphrodisiac fantasy involving
sweet-potatoes, eringoes and the supposedly wanton tune 'Greensleeves'.
But Falstaff's seduction scene is not destined for melodramatic interrup-
tion by any sword-waving Bonario. On the contrary, its atmosphere of
fantasy intensifies with the arrival of the 'fairies': '*Enter Sir Hugh Evans
like a satyr, Anne Page as a fairy, and others as the Fairy Queen, fairies, and
Hobgoblin; all with tapers.*' The fact that we know these sprites to be
Windsor townsfolk in disguise barely takes away anything from the
theatrical magicality of the scene. In a setting that resounds with fey
overtones recalling *A Midsummer Night's Dream*, Falstaff appears less
and less like the mere butt of a practical joke. Indeed, looked at from the
point of view of dramatic construction, this final scene of *The Merry
Wives* bears some resemblance to its counterpart in *The Merchant of
Venice*. Just as the music, moonlight, lovers, and even the jokes, of
Belmont cast a softening haze round that play's harsher episodes, so too
in Windsor Forest at midnight a typically Shakespearean ambivalence
turns the defeat of Falstaff to something rich and strange. His initial
appeal to Jove has set the tone and established a link between the man and
the god. Falstaff as near-aristocrat (at least by the standards of Windsor
town) has shreds of Olympian grandeur, even when bent on seduction—
which again recalls Jupiter. Here he sits, jovial, grandly antlered, at the
base of Herne's Oak, with a woman on each 'haunch'. When they run
off and he turns his face to the ground to be tormented, benign authority
is accepting ritual suffering. It is the dual role of a god in almost any
culture. To push this further and claim that Falstaff is taking upon him
the guilt of all the lecherous and all the greedy would be far-fetched, yet
the scene, as it goes on, becomes increasingly reminiscent of rural customs
we might still encounter, and which anthropologists since Frazer have
recorded with some precision. Readers of *The Golden Bough* will recall
sections on the ancient sacrifice of human victims, sometimes at the roots

of sacred trees, and an account of the relics of tree worship in modern Europe. Frazer traced connections between revered trees—including oaks —and those human embodiments of the tree spirit that figure prominently in many European spring festivals. Most of these popular festivals take place on May Day or the night before it, but some come a week earlier on 23 April—a key date for everyone who accepts the well supported theory that *The Merry Wives of Windsor* was first performed during celebrations associated with the Feast of St George in April 1597.

We must be careful here not to use one hypothesised circumstance to prop up another: we do not *know* that this comedy was written for the Garter festivities in 1597. But even without that, Northrop Frye's claims for a mythopoeic 'backbone' in the play carry some conviction:

> In *The Merry Wives* there is an elaborate ritual of the defeat of winter known to folklorists as 'carrying out Death,' of which Falstaff is the victim; and Falstaff must have felt that, after being thrown into the water, dressed up as a witch and beaten out of a house with curses, and finally supplied with a beast's head and singed with candles, he had done all that could reasonably be asked of any fertility spirit.[8]

There may even be a link between the pretended burning of Falstaff and the curious fact that, at least as late as the 1940s, the vegetation spirit known as Jack-in-the-Green was still being led about by *the chimney-sweeps* of some English localities. As Frazer long ago suggested, we can reasonably regard the pretence of burning people as a mitigated survival of an older custom of actually burning them.[9] And from the leaf-clad figure of Jack-in-the-Green, the Green Man or the Green Knight, it is also a small step—via the best known of all the Kings of the May, Robin of the Wood or Robin Hood—to Herne the Hunter, who was, it seems, another scapegoat:

> There seems to be a tradition that Herne was a keeper in Windsor Forest in the reign of Richard II. He kept two black St Hubert hounds and was held in esteem for his woodcraft. The other keepers were jealous of his repute and plotted his destruction. Herne rescued the King from a maddened stag, but was nearly slain himself by the beast. Suddenly there appeared a tall dark man, who gave his name as Philip Urswick, who declared he could cure Herne of his wounds. He proceeded to do so by cutting off the head of the stag and binding it to the head of Herne, who was then conveyed to Urswick's hut on Bagshot Heath. The act seems to identify Herne not only with the animal, but with Cernunnos, the god of horned creatures. The King announced his intention of making Herne his chief keeper, should he survive his injuries, and Urswick promised to tend him faithfully. But he offered Herne's rivals the chance of revenge against him ... and assured them that though Herne would survive, he would lose all his skill in woodcraft.

Urswick's promise held good and in time the King, irritated by his
chief warden's maladroit behaviour, cancelled his appointment,
whereupon Herne, in despair, hanged himself upon an oak, from which,
however, his body mysteriously disappeared.[10]

The further one traces the play's allusions, the more insistent its folklore
becomes: female disguise, a ducking, a haunted oak, ritual purification
by fire, the antlered man as scapegoat for a king and as the victim of
jealousy .... Let us admit, of course, that a great deal of what is said and
done in *The Merry Wives of Windsor* does *not* suggest folk ritual. It would
be rash to suppose that Shakespeare was consciously basing the comedy
on English popular customs. It is far more likely that he was, in his usual
way, welding together compatible incidents and ideas from other plays
that he had seen or read or heard about—the Robin Hood plays are the
most obvious possibilities, just as the stag's head could be that of any
Warwickshire or Berkshire mummer. Even after making such reservations,
however, we still find that, specifically in the last scene of *The Merry
Wives*, a resonant folk element works in harmony with Falstaff's bawdy
to enlarge the whole play excitingly. Only now does the full complexity
of Falstaff's role become apparent. He remains—to the distress of generations of critics—the central gull; but, as in *Henry IV*, he also supplies a
kind of life force, a source of vitality that both inspires the action of the
piece and invigorates its atmosphere. Enduring his successive indignities,
he can almost be said to preside over Windsor.

The incidence of ribaldry among the other characters of *The Merry
Wives* can be analysed more briefly. Mistress Quickly's is the most
extensive, partly because of her employment as a go-between (as Pistol
unchivalrously puts it, 'This punk is one of Cupid's carriers'), and partly
because her gift for malapropism lends itself to Freudian error:

FALSTAFF   Good morrow, good wife.
QUICKLY   Not so, an't please your worship.
FALSTAFF   Good maid, then.
QUICKLY   I'll be sworn; as my mother was, the first hour I was born.
FALSTAFF   I do believe the swearer.

II.ii.30

In what Dr Johnson called, not unjustly, 'a very trifling scene', Shakespeare brings Mistress Quickly into collision with a side of life in Windsor
that irresistibly suggests the grammar school, Stratford-upon-Avon,
circa 1572:

EVANS   ... What is 'fair', William?
WILLIAM Pulcher.
QUICKLY Polecats! There are fairer things than polecats, sure.

EVANS   Leave your prabbles, oman. What is the focative case, William?
WILLIAM   O—vocativo, O.
EVANS   Remember, William: focative is caret.
QUICKLY   And that's a good root.

IV.i.23, 45

The *focative-O-vocativo* joke depends on three interlocking sets of implications. First there is Mistress Quickly's interjection with 'Polecats!'—
meaning, almost certainly, prostitutes, since this is the sense in which it
recurs at IV.ii.162. (*Fitchew* is used in the same way in *Othello* IV.i.146.)
Secondly there is the jingle *focative/fuck*, arising through Evan's Welshi-
fied pronunciation. And thirdly there is the coital suggestion, in such a
context, of *case* (as meaning vagina) and of the repeated *O* sound, which
can be thought of as either a pudendal symbol or the echo of an orgasmic
cry. Given all these preliminaries, Farmer and Henley were probably
right to take Mistress Quickly's *good root* as implying *penis* besides just a
carrot.[11] But the sexual punning has still further labyrinths to thread:

EVANS   Oman, forbear.
MISTRESS PAGE   Peace.
EVANS   What is your genitive case plural, William?
WILLIAM   Genitive case?
EVANS   Ay.
WILLIAM   Genitive: horum, harum, horum.
QUICKLY   Vengeance of Jenny's case; fie on her! Never name her,
   child, if she be a whore.
EVANS   For shame, oman.
QUICKLY   You do ill to teach the child such words. He teaches him to
   hick and to hack, which they'll do fast enough of themselves; and
   to call 'horum'; fie upon you!
EVANS   Oman, art thou lunatics? Hast thou no understandings for thy
   cases, and the numbers of the genders? Thou art as foolish Christian
   creatures as I would desires.

IV.i.50

The puns *genitive case/Jenny's case* and *horum/whore* are straightforward
enough. Less obvious to the modern ear is what may also be a pun
harum/hare—assuming, that is, that in Shakespeare's own day the Latin
word would have been given the pronunciation ['hɛərəm]. From classical
times, and very extensively in medieval art, both the hare and the rabbit
have enjoyed associations with lust and fecundity, and if a director of
The Merry Wives were to ask his Mistress Quickly to register indignation
over William's *harum* he could quote in support Mercutio's 'old hare
hoar' jingle:

MERCUTIO   A bawd, a bawd, a bawd! So ho!
ROMEO   What hast thou found?

MERCUTIO   No hare, sir; unless a hare, sir, in a lenten pie, that is
something stale and hoar ere it be spent.
He walks by them and sings
>   An old hare hoar,
>   And an old hare hoar,
>   Is very good meat in Lent.
>   But a hare that is hoar
>   Is too much for a score
>   When it hoars ere it be spent.

II.iv.127

Apart from the obvious puns, here, on *stale* and *hoar*, it is perhaps not
entirely irrelevant that in a number of medieval paintings a *white* hare
appears beneath the feet of the Virgin Mary, signifying her victory over
lust.[12]

Parson Evans continues his string of unconscious innuendos with the
closely juxtaposed *understandings*, *cases*, *genders* and *desires*, and perhaps also
with further puns on *case* and *cods* when he warns William, a few lines
later, not to forget 'your qui's, your quae's, and your quod's'.[13] Although
we are nowadays at too many removes from Lily's Latin Grammar to
enjoy Sir Hugh Evans and Mistress Quickly to the full, it is easy to
imagine that some word-conscious theatregoers of 1597 or 1598 would
have found them funny. If, also, we bear in mind that the audience at any
court performance—during a Feast of the Garter, for example—would
have had a great deal more than 'small Latine', it becomes easy to envisage Shakespeare's indulging himself and them by returning, at least
for one short scene, to bawdy for simple laughter's sake.

The same simplicity, though in quite a different style of indecency,
surrounds the Host of the Garter Inn. His speciality is non-sexual coprology, and he shows in his way as much consistency as Mistress Quickly.
Her malapropisms are unconscious, undirected: his obscenities are thrown
off with evident enjoyment, and are almost all aimed at Doctor Caius,
his 'bully stale ... Castalion-King-Urinal ... Mounseur Mockwater',
but respected, it turns out, as a giver of 'the potions and the motions'.
Caius himself, making fritters of English no less expertly than his Welsh
rival, contributes to this fund of humour with the mispronunciation
turd for *third*, besides enriching the language of Shakespearean comedy
with the unforgettable threat, 'By gar, I will cut all his two stones; by
gar, he shall not have a stone to throw at his dog' (I.iv.101). Perhaps
Shakespeare was unconsciously sharpening his anti-French claws in
readiness for *Henry V*.

Ribaldry of yet another kind, and of a kind quite new to Shakespeare
if we accept the date of *The Merry Wives* as 1597, comes from Ford. Like

so many other self-envisaged cuckolds in Elizabethan comedy, Ford is
obsessed with horns—'Buck? I would I could wash myself of the buck!
Buck, buck, buck! ay, buck! I warrant you, buck; and of the season, too,
it shall appear' (III.iii.138)—and rage carries him to a fine pitch of eloquence when he hears that the maid's 'aunt of Brainford' is upstairs: 'A
witch, a quean, an old cozening quean! Have I not forbid her my house?
. . . I'll prat her. . . . Out of my door, you witch, you hag, you baggage,
you polecat, you ronyon!' (IV.ii.151). While the total effect is still farcical,
we can catch another glimpse here of the art that will later create Shakespeare's serious bawdy—the lewd, self-lacerating imaginings of Hamlet
and Othello, Posthumus and Leontes.

In broad outline, then, the use of bawdy in *The Merry Wives of Windsor*
comes to look like this: Falstaff speaks commercially at the start, erotically
near the end, thus providing some immediate pretext for his ill-treatment,
but also, paradoxically, increasing the kind of authority with which the
play endows him; the Host speaks with coprological mockery of the
French physician, who in turn helps Sir Hugh Evans and Mistress Quickly
to mangle and confuse the language of everyday middle-class life. Ford,
lonely in his supposed cuckoldom, mutters and shouts jealously, obsessed
by the thing he fears. The bourgeois wives, although 'merry' enough for
an occasional vulgar quip, are essentially too prim to be outspoken on
sexual matters. Slender, for all his awkwardness, only once blunders into
impropriety—'three veneys for a dish of stewed prunes'; whereas his
contrasting rival, the courtly young Fenton, never sullies his elegant
blank verse with anything indecent.

In 1602 the First Quarto promised on its title-page 'A Most pleasaunt
and excellent conceited Comedie'. If some loose ends in the plot and an
air of hurry in the writing somewhat limit the excellence of its 'conceit',
this is still a viable farce that has stood the searching test of the stage.
Where the study of Shakespeare's developing use of bawdy is concerned,
we should note that the indecencies here are more varied in tone and effect
than in any other play so far. *The Merry Wives* can be regarded as a
signpost to the increasingly specialised types of bawdy that are to operate
in the plays Shakespeare writes after the turn of the century.

Bawdy feels most at home in prose. If the generous lading of indecency
in *Much Ado* and *The Merry Wives* first prompts this generalisation, the
uneven distribution of bawdy between the verse and prose scenes of
Twelfth Night gives it firm support. This comedy has room for sexual
humour in one of its main plots but not the other: bawdy clings to the
province of cakes and ale.

Sir Andrew Aguecheek, as resident gull, misses the point of Sir Toby
Belch's more intricate jokes, but unconsciously creates others by imagin-
ing *double entendres* where none have been made.

> SIR ANDREW   Good Mistress Mary Accost—
> SIR TOBY (*aside*)   You mistake, knight. 'Accost' is front her, board her,
> woo her, assail her.
> SIR ANDREW (*aside*)   By my troth, I would not undertake her in this
> company. Is that the meaning of 'accost'?
>
> I.iii.52

If we except Feste, indeed, unconscious ribaldry is almost the standard
variety in *Twelfth Night*. Sir Toby and his collaborators specialise in
ambush, and their victims are all given equivocal lines as, one by one,
they fall into prepared traps. Malvolio, reading Maria's forged letter,
exhibits his special gullibility with the wholly unselfconscious indecencies
of 'By my life, this is my lady's hand. These be her very C's, her U's and
her T's; and thus makes she her great P's. It is, in contempt of question,
her hand' (II.v.86). Helge Kökeritz in *Shakespeare's Pronunciation* (1953),
p. 133, explained this C-U-T not as a jingle on *cunt* but as *cut* itself, a
word which, I am told, still occurs in English as a slang term for *vulva*.
Kökeritz also proposed that, following this, Malvolio's phrase 'her great
P's' implies urination; and Shakespeare, as if unwilling to let such neat
quibbles go to waste by passing unnoticed, alerts the audience through
Sir Andrew's characteristically naïve enquiry, 'Her C's, her U's and her
T's? Why that?'

Like Malvolio in the letter scene, Viola is in no mood for deliberate
joking when she finds herself trembling at the thought of an imminent
duel, so that Shakespeare is speaking past her, and direct to the audience,
when he lets the equivocal word *thing* catch the light:

> VIOLA (*aside*)   Pray God defend me! A little thing would make me
> tell them how much I lack of a man.
>
> III.iv.293

Even the poised Olivia gives occasion for this kind of laughter in the
theatre when the Malvolio plot encircles her:

> OLIVIA   Wilt thou go to bed, Malvolio?
> MALVOLIO   To bed! 'Ay, sweetheart, and I'll come to thee!'
>
> III.iv.28

Such moments are, of course, exceptional for Viola and Olivia, and it is
noticeable that Orsino, who comes much less into contact with the revellers, has no bawdy lines whatever. Once again, as in *The Two Gentlemen*

of Verona and *As You Like It,* Shakespeare has preserved the full charm of
his heroine by keeping tight control over the lubricious possibilities of
girl-boy disguise. Some scurrility from Sir Toby is allowed to enrich
the ironies of the duel scene—'Therefore on, or strip your sword stark
naked; for meddle you must, that's certain'—but the gossamer complexities of Viola's relationships with Orsino and Olivia never once
become coarsened with ribaldry. If they did, the play would lose its
emotional hold. *Twelfth Night* depends on vulnerability: the vulnerability
of Olivia, a countess in love with a page-boy who is not even a real page-
boy, and the vulnerability of Viola, trapped behind the mask. Both of
them live moment by moment at the risk of humiliation, and both are
saved by the apparent miracle of Sebastian's arrival. Lightning-flickers of
Lesbianism play round the two young women in their private conversations together (in I.v and III.i), yet even this belongs at another
extreme from bawdy.

The distinctive tonal finesse of the lovers' scenes in *Twelfth Night* can
be the more sharply identified if we compare the play with any of its
probable sources. The anonymous comedy *Gl'Ingannati* (acted 1531,
printed 1537), which is given in a lively translation (*The Deceived*) by
Geoffrey Bullough in his *Narrative and Dramatic Sources of Shakespeare,* ii,
286–339, is an altogether coarser-grained piece of work. It is characterised
by the pert improprieties of its heroine Lelia, who has, amongst other
things, been raped by Spanish soldiers before the action of the play begins.
More in the background, but still quite striking, are the disillusioned
bluntnesses of Clemenzia the nurse and Pasquella the maid, plus bedroom
sounds naively described by Clemenzia's daughter Gittina. Shakespeare's
other most likely source, Barnaby Riche's story of Apolonius and Silla,[14]
is closer to *Twelfth Night* in general feeling, yet even there the lady
Julina, the corresponding figure to Shakespeare's Olivia, finds herself
pregnant some months before her lover Silvio returns from his travels
to marry her. By omitting such strands from his love plot—just as he did
earlier, in converting Gascoigne's *Supposes* into the Bianca plot of *The
Taming of the Shrew*—Shakespeare is able to base his comedy squarely on
the contrast in values between the Viola–Olivia–Orsino group of
characters and the Belch–Maria–Malvolio group. It is a contrast in which
bawdy has its due place—on the revellers' side.

There is confirmation of all this in the epilogue, Feste's ballad 'When
that I was and a little tiny boy'. Encouraged, perhaps, by its brief re-
appearance at a crisis point in *Lear* (III.ii.74–7), many of the more recent
directors of *Twelfth Night* have had this sung with considerable pathos.
Its shaping narrative, after all, is a kind of rake's progress, and more than

once it offers what we might see as a slightly sour reflection on the past
and future of such a one as Toby Belch:

> But when I came, alas, to wive,
>   With hey-ho, the wind and the rain;
> By swaggering could I never thrive,
>   For the rain it raineth every day.

> But when I came unto my beds,
>   With hey-ho, the wind and the rain;
> With tosspots still had drunken heads,
>   For the rain it raineth every day.

The decline and fall sketched in these third and fourth stanzas become all
the more dispiriting if we accept the bawdy interpretation of stanzas 1
and 2 which was first put forward, as far as I have been able to ascertain,
by Leslie Hotson in *The First Night of 'Twelfth Night'* (1954), pp. 168–70:

> Historically, the Fool and indecency cannot be parted. To make up for
> his mental shortcomings, Nature was commonly believed to have
> endowed the Fool with an excess of virility, symbolized by his *bauble*.
> 'Fools please women best.' 'A fool's bauble is a lady's playfellow.' 'A
> foolish bed-mate, why, he hath no peer.' Priapus used to be described as
> *that foolish god*; and Mercutio's cynical notion of Love is a *great natural*
> with his *bauble*. . . . *Thing* in its 'bauble' sense is the key word . . . in the
> first stanza of Feste's song. In the Fool's childish state as a little tiny boy,
> a *foolish thing* was no more than a harmless trifle. Far otherwise, however,
> when he was grown 'fit for breed'—a lecherous knave and thief of love,
> on the prowl after other men's wives: ' 'Gainst knaves and thieves men
> shut their gate.' . . . Feste has already given us his exquisite love songs;
> now we are to be sent away with 'a song of good life'. What he trolls
> out is a Drunkard's Progress, an Elizabethan forerunner of such bibulous
> confessions as *I'm a rambling wreck of poverty* and *I've been a moonshiner
> for seventeen long years*: a moral and musical reminder that the wassailing
> of the Twelfth Night saturnalia had better not be followed as a way of
> life. That is the road to 'wet damnation'.

The crux of this interpretation is its acceptance of the phallic sense for
thing in this particular context, and on that I find Dr Hotson's argument
wholly persuasive. A more nebulous but lingering worry is that so
moralistic an interpretation may be forcing an undue 'relevance' onto the
little song—which is, after all, taking the place of a jig to round off the
performance. But then again, that substitution may in itself be significant.
As we know from other plays, Shakespeare was not always too with-
drawn to point a moral, and a song can do that when a jig cannot. For all
the final shoulder-shrugging of 'that's all one, our play is done', Feste's

chilling little epilogue reinforces doubts about the satisfactions of licentiousness.

Logically as well as chronologically, it seems appropriate to go straight from the shifting colours of *Twelfth Night* to the mingled yarn of *All's Well That Ends Well*. Here again bawdy is put to work as part of an intricate thematic combination.

Now, it goes without saying that a salacious remark coming from one speaker might, if transferred to another, be entirely serious and even innocent. If, say, we took some of the improprieties of the Courtesan in *The Comedy of Errors* or Margaret in *Much Ado* and re-allocated them to Luciana or Hero, the indecent implications could easily vanish, so remote is the cast of mind of these characters from the lubricious. What is less obvious, perhaps, is that much the same is true of entire plays. In *All's Well*, lines that in any of Shakespeare's early comedies would have been bawdy jokes find themselves now in a serious sexual context, and they take on a correspondingly serious tone. The business with the rings illustrates this. So also does the bed trick: as will happen again in *Measure for Measure*, a basically farcical device is rendered entirely non-farcical by the nature and purposes of the characters who employ it.

This does not mean that *All's Well* is sparing of indecencies. The Clown and Parolles see to that. But the play as a whole provides another illustration of Shakespeare's growing tendency to hold his bawdy characters apart from, and in sharp contrast with, a group of speakers who are rarely if ever bawdy. In transforming the 'Clever Wench' of his source—Boccaccio's story of Giletta of Narbona[15]—into the chaste Helena, aided in her plans by a significantly-named Diana, Shakespeare was advancing along the kind of path he had chosen in *Twelfth Night*. It was soon to lead him through the murkier corners of *Lear* and *Timon* and towards the chiaroscuro of the late plays. In remarking the close and serious attention paid to human sexuality in these Jacobean plays we do not need to construct surmises about changes in Shakespeare's attitude either to the sexual instinct in general or to venereal disease in particular. C. J. Sisson disposed of all that with deft irony many years ago in his British Academy lecture *The Mythical Sorrows of Shakespeare*. But it is necessary to keep in sight the dramatist's progression, however unsteady and unsystematic, into the ever deeper investigation of moral questions.

I stress this aspect of *All's Well* because one has to allow for it if one is to avoid misinterpreting Helena's share in the play's bawdy—a share that seems at first to contradict the principle of separation of character groups. Only a bare hundred lines of the play have been spoken before the heroine, with no apparent unwillingness, becomes engaged in a lengthy and half-jocular disquisition on virginity. The sexual-military quibbles of its opening exchanges are sufficiently important to merit quotation in full.

> PAROLLES Are you meditating on virginity?
> HELENA Ay. You have some stain of soldier in you: let me ask you a
>   question. Man is enemy to virginity; how may we barricado it against
>   him?
> PAROLLES Keep him out.
> HELENA But he assails, and our virginity, though valiant, in the defence
>   yet is weak. Unfold to us some warlike resistance.
> PAROLLES There is none. Man setting down before you will undermine
>   you and blow you up.
> HELENA Bless our poor virginity from underminers and blowers-up!
>   Is there no military policy how virgins might blow up men?
> PAROLLES Virginity being blown down, man will quicklier be blown
>   up; marry, in blowing him down again, with the breach yourselves
>   made you lose your city. It is not politic in the commonwealth of
>   nature to preserve virginity. Loss of virginity is rational increase, and
>   there was never virgin got till virginity was first lost.
>
> I.i.109

This turns out to have a close bearing on both the main plots of *All's Well*, one of them revolving round Helena's calculated loss of virginity, the other round Parolles's being deprived of his assumed soldiership. Through each of these plots the play throws a questioning light on conventional ideas about honour. Bertram, unlike Parolles, can exhibit real courage and a real soldierly dignity among other men. But is this enough for us to deem a man 'honourable'?[16] The answer has to be no, when we see Bertram playing fast and loose with the obligations that he has incurred (however unwillingly) in marriage. And complementarily: is a woman's chastity, often quite literally identified with her honour in seventeenth-century usage, in fact the be-all and end-all of her respectability? Again the play says no. Helena, having indeed meditated on virginity while Parolles joked about it, accepts and acts upon the truth that 'loss of virginity is natural increase'.

More parallelism through which the bawdy of *All's Well* works thematically may be seen in the role of the Clown. Lavatch, like Feste before him, is every inch a professional, and some of his bawdy is only joke-book material, the kind of thing that we can imagine Robert Armin playing straight to the audience:

> As fit as ten groats is for the hand of an attorney, as your French crown
> for your taffety punk, as Tib's rush for Tom's forefinger, as a pancake
> for Shrove Tuesday, a morris for May-day, as the nail to his hole, the

cuckold to his horn, as a scolding quean to a wrangling knave, as the
nun's lip to the friar's mouth; nay, as the pudding to his skin.

II.ii.20

So far as this kind of fun has dramatic function at all, it is perhaps to
elicit from the Countess that graceful and uncondescending tolerance
which also embraces Helena and which Bertram signally lacks. But
much of Lavatch's other extemporising—on marriage, on adultery, on
the simperings of courtiers—is a great deal more to the point. In I.iii he
persuades the Countess to grant him a hearing, just as Helena will persuade
the King in a later scene.

> CLOWN   I do beg your good will in this case.
> COUNTESS   In what case?
> CLOWN   In Isbel's case and mine own. Service is no heritage, and I
> think I shall never have the blessing of God till I have issue o'my
> body; for they say barnes are blessings.
> COUNTESS   Tell me thy reason why thou wilt marry.
> CLOWN   My poor body, madam, requires it. I am driven on by the
> flesh, and he must needs go that the devil drives.

I.iii.21

With Bertram-like cynicism, however, Lavatch now blunders on into a
defence of adulterers—

> for the knaves come to do that for me which I am aweary of. He that
> ears my land spares my team, and gives me leave to in the crop. If I be
> his cuckold, he's my drudge. He that comforts my wife is the cherisher
> of my flesh and blood; ... *ergo*, he that kisses my wife is my friend.

I.iii.42

This is antithetical clowning: it becomes a broadened, low-life version
of incidents from the main plot, and its effect, whether consciously
planned by Shakespeare or not, is to alert us to ethical issues. Helena, like
Lavatch, will ask approval for her marriage, and she will also, in due
course, take advantage of what Bertram thinks to have been an act of
adultery. 'He that ears my land ... gives me leave to in the crop.'

Another comic-salacious reflection of events in the main plot occurs
when the Clown returns from court bringing Bertram's letter to the
Countess. She is pathetically eager to learn her son's news—'Let me see
what he writes, and when he means to come'—but as she silently reads
the letter, Lavatch tells the audience that life at court has made him
changeable.

> I have no mind to Isbel since I was at court. Our old lings and our
> Isbels o'th'country are nothing like your old ling and your Isbels
> o'th'court. The brains of my Cupid's knocked out, and I begin to love
> as an old man loves money, with no stomach.

III.ii.12

Placed as it is, immediately before the theatre audience hears part of Bertram's letter read aloud, Lavatch's monologue shows up as a burlesque of instability. When there follows, a few moments later, his fumbling attempt to make jokes to the Countess about Bertram's defection—'your son will not be killed so soon as I thought he would . . . if he run away, as I hear he does. The danger is in standing to't; that's the loss of men, though it be the getting of children' (III.ii.36)—the result is a heightening of emotional tension. Far from giving the Countess any relief from the pain of learning Bertram's news, the fooling can only add to her distress, and hence to the reader's or audience's sense of her helplessness in this situation. Shakespeare is developing the complex technique with which he will later employ bawdy humour for the Fool's part in *King Lear*.

The one other important use of bawdy in *All's Well* comes with the interrogation of Parolles in IV.iii. Characteristically, he lets his 'betrayal' of the French officers take a scabrous turn, and Bertram, knowing himself to be vulnerable if questions of sexual behaviour are examined, tries to cut short the whole inquisition:

> FIRST SOLDIER   Do you know this Captain Dumaine?
> PAROLLES   I know him: 'a was a botcher's prentice in Paris, from
>   whence he was whipped for getting the shrieve's fool with child, a
>   dumb innocent that could not say him nay.
> BERTRAM   Nay, by your leave, hold your hands—though I know his
>   brains are forfeit to the next tile that falls.
>
> IV.iii.181

Sure enough, Bertram's own seduction of innocents soon figures prominently.

> PAROLLES   My meaning in't, I protest, was very honest in the behalf of
>   the maid; for I knew the young Count to be a dangerous and
>   lascivious boy, who is a whale to virginity, and devours up all the fry
>   it finds.
>
> IV.iii.213

Parolles's half-truths about Bertram's sexual misdemeanours are images in a distorting mirror—exaggerated, grotesque, yet sufficiently like the originals to have an essential, almost allegoric, validity. They provide an anticipatory glimpse of the relentless exposure of Bertram's hypocrisy which will follow when he too comes to be unmasked. Once again it has become the dramatic function of bawdy to direct the audience's attention to questions of value underlying the drama. Again, too, the technique is one that will be fully exploited in other plays.

*   *   *

In order to gauge the full extent to which Shakespeare can make scurrility serve both as truth drug and as scourge, we shall need to examine *Hamlet*, *Troilus and Cressida*, *Othello*, *King Lear* and *Timon of Athens*. But before doing so, it is necessary to retrace some chronological steps and note the use of bawdy as a realistic base, or, in the scientific sense, a 'control', in *King John*, *Henry IV*, *Henry V* and *As You Like It*.

NOTES

1. For example A. P. Rossiter in his lecture on 'Comic relief' in *Angel with Horns*, pp. 274–92; Dean Frye, 'The question of Shakespearean "parody" ', *EC*, xv (1965), 22–6; Richard Levin, 'Elizabethan "clown" subplots', *EC*, xvi (1966), 84–91.
2. The Mercutio of the play, as it happens, very nearly *is* Shakespeare's invention. In the two known English sources for *Romeo and Juliet*—Arthur Brooke's *Tragical History of Romeus and Juliet* (London, 1562) and the second volume of William Painter's collection *The Palace of Pleasure* (London, 1567)—Mercutio remains a background figure. His only function is the very limited one of seizing Juliet's hand in a friendly but icy grip during the Capulets' feast.
3. As given here, the last line of this quotation shows editorial emendation. In Q2 (the Good Quarto, 1599), the line reads, 'An open, or thou a Poprin Peare.' Q1 (the Bad Quarto, 1597) has the reading, 'An open *Etcætera*', which does at least make sense if, as elsewhere, *&c.* denotes vulva (see glossary). But this is not an area of the *Romeo and Juliet* text where Q1 has textual authority.
4. H. T. Price, 'Mirror-scenes in Shakespeare', in James G. McManaway *et al.*, *Joseph Quincy Adams Memorial Studies* (1948), pp. 101–13.
5. The battle of the rings is both longer and funnier in Shakespeare than in his probable source, the first story of the fourth day of Giovanni Fiorentino's *Il Pecorone* (*The Simpleton*). A translation is given in Bullough, i, 475–6.
6. François Rabelais, *Gargantua and Pantagruel*, trans. J. M. Cohen (1955), p. 368.
7. Philip Edwards, *Shakespeare and the Confines of Art* (1968), p. 71.
8. Northrop Frye, *Anatomy of Criticism* (1957), p. 183.
9. Sir James George Frazer, *The Golden Bough* (abridged end, 1922), p. 652.
10. Lewis Spence, *The Minor Traditions of British Mythology* (1948), p. 157. After giving details of the various Herne-the-Hunter myths, Spence adds: 'If this characteristically garbled account be of the nature of genuine folk-tale—and I cannot vouch for its authenticity as I am unaware of its original source—it would appear to point to a rivalry between the deity or genius of a beech-tree and that of an oak-tree.'
11. J. S. Farmer and W. E. Henley, *A Dictionary of Slang and its Analogues* (7 vols, New York, 1890–1903), vi 51.
12. For the sexual significance of hares and rabbits in medieval art, see D. W Robertson, *A Preface to Chaucer* (1962), pp. 113 and 128; and George Ferguson, *Signs and Symbols in Christian Art* (2nd edn, 1959), p. 20.
13. Helge Kökeritz, *Shakespeare's Pronunciation* (1953), p. 119, draws special attention to the qui's-quae's-quod's speech. He claims *qui's* (F1 *Quies*) as a pun on *keys*, but

I am unconvinced that *key* as a slang term for *penis* was ever as common as this assumes.

14. From Barnaby Riche, *Farewell to Military Profession* (London, 1581). The story is given in modern spelling in T. J. B. Spencer, ed., *Elizabethan Love Stories* (1968), pp. 97–117; see also Bullough, ii, 344–63.
15. *The Decameron*, iii, 9. Shakespeare probably used William Painter's translation, *The Palace of Pleasure* (edn of 1575), i, Novel 38. See Spencer, *op. cit.*, pp. 41–50; Bullough, ii, 389–96. On Boccaccio's use of the motif of the Clever Wench from earlier medieval narratives, see W. W. Lawrence, *Shakespeare's Problem Comedies* (Penguin edn, 1969), pp. 50–8.
16. I am indebted hereabouts to G. Wilson Knight, *The Sovereign Flower* (1958), especially p. 106.

6

Indecency as Realism

KING JOHN
   Doth not the crown of England prove the King?
   And if not that, I bring you witnesses:
   Twice fifteen thousand hearts of England's breed—
BASTARD
   Bastards and else.

King John II.i.273

As the foregoing chapter went some way to show, the use of bawdy to counterpoint serious situations or themes becomes normal practice in the drama of Shakespeare's maturity. So commonly does he do it, indeed, that it is no simple matter to pick out plays in which the indecencies can be said to present a consistently satiric or realist view of affairs. Yet there is a real sense in which, for example, the Bastard in *King John* or Falstaff in *Henry IV* is telling more of the truth about things than are the surrounding kings and princes. The share that bawdy takes in this demands investigation. So too with *Henry V*, where the indecencies of minor characters help to cast slight shadows across a bright chivalric picture, but eventually work more in support of the royal hero than against him. A quite similar process occurs in *As You Like It*, where Arcadian prettiness gains an enduring solidity from a very Shakespearean measure of sexual realism.

Of all Shakespeare's history plays, *King John* has been the one most often and most fiercely attacked for incoherence. Part of the critics' dissatisfaction is related, I suspect, to the surprisingly late date that many of them have accorded to the play. Sir Edmund Chambers suggested 1596–97, thus making it roughly contemporary with *The Merchant of Venice* and probably later than *Richard II*, and some later commentators eager to detect topical allusions to events of the 1590s naturally tended to corroborate this.[1] The New Cambridge and New Arden editors, however, despite having sharply divergent views on the relationship between this play and the anonymous *Troublesome Reign of John, King of England* (two parts, Qq 1591), both argued for an earlier date, in the region of 1590–91.[2] Seen with the kind of tolerance we should customarily extend to so early a play—to *The Gentlemen of Verona*, perhaps, or the three parts of *Henry VI*—*King John's* disparate construction and scrappy ending are not too worrying. What has to be accepted is that the play consists of three loosely connected movements or phases. The first of these, going up to and including III.iii, concerns itself with the English succession. Emphasis then shifts abruptly to John's struggle against the Pope; but this in turn becomes little more than a background to the story of Arthur's death and the temporary defection of the English nobles. These three phases are not unified tonally, and sexual indecency remains wholly confined to the first of them.

It is natural that Act I, being largely concerned with the disputed inheritance of the Faulconbridge brothers, should have a good deal to say about bastardy. The topic is not in itself bawdy, but Shakespeare goes out of his way to have Philip Faulconbridge treat his own illegitimacy with, alternately, bluff hilarity and arch innuendo. From the 200-odd lines that follow his first entry one could extract a miniature glossary of Elizabethan bawdy.

> Your tale must be how he employed my mother. . . . I would not be
> Sir Nob in any case. . . . Philip, good old Sir Robert's wife's eldest son.
> . . . In at the window, or else o'er the hatch . . . . What woman-post is
> this? Hath she no husband / That will take pains to blow a horn before
> her? . . . Sir Robert could do: well—marry, to confess— / Could he get
> me? Sir Robert could not do it . . . .
>
> I.i.98–236

Interweaving with all this, not only in the Bastard's own speeches but also in one of King John's (lines 116–20), there runs the standard joke about uncertain parentage:

> Most certain of one mother, mighty king—
> That is well known—and, as I think, one father;
> But for the certain knowledge of that truth
> I put you o'er to heaven and to my mother.
> Of that I doubt, as all men's children may.
>
> I.i.59

Philip Faulconbridge is, as King John says, a good blunt fellow—a great deal blunter than his pale namesake in *The Troublesome Reign*. This difference is so marked that one wonders why it should be that, at the

price of a clumsy disruption of courtly decorum, Shakespeare insistently
reiterates the bawdy aspect of the Bastard's bastardy. One answer is that
he is deliberately counterpointing affairs of state with the uncompromising
physicalities of private life. John's dispute with the King of France has
opened the play on a note of 'high' policy, but we may well be struck
by a likeness between that kingly quarrel and the wrangling of the
Faulconbridge brothers. In both conflicts the stake is feudal power.
Because the inheritance of land goes strictly by lineal descent, Philip
Faulconbridge, on admitting his bastardy, loses the family estate, while
as the recognised son of Cœur-de-Lion he gains an intangible authority,
formalised in the award of knighthood. King John, on the other hand,
keeps *his* lands, despite the weakness of his lineal right to them. He is a
king and no king, and as the play goes on Shakespeare unobtrusively
strengthens the moral position of the counter-claimant, Arthur, by
encouraging us to think of him as the son, rather than the nephew, of
the previous king. At the same time, John finds himself increasingly devoid
of true authority: there is no intangible dignity for him. Thus the two
situations, the king's and the knight's, are in a way complementary, and
across both of them there falls a faint shadow of absurdity, cast by the
fact that resolution of the Faulconbridge dispute depended on a question
of who slept with Lady Faulconbridge in a particular month many years
earlier. When the Bastard, after being installed at court, proceeds to
subject political events to an outsider's quizzical scrutiny, the shadow of
absurdity lengthens.

To stress this influence from the opening scene is not, I hope, to claim
the play as outright comicall satyre. Indeed, one of its disconcerting
characteristics is that it vacillates between an ironic mocking of embattled
rulers and a quite unironic celebration of their rhetorical grandeur. But
the prevailing effect in Act II is certainly the ironic one. The contestants
before Angiers are made to satirise themselves by self-caricature:

> KING JOHN
>   . . . I like it well. France, shall we knit our powers
>   And lay this Angiers even with the ground;
>   Then after fight who shall be king of it?
>
> II.i.398

—while the flippant commentator Faulconbridge undermines their
dignity with bawdy asides and interruptions:

> KING PHILIP
>   As many and as well-born bloods as those—
> BASTARD
>   Some bastards too.

KING PHILIP
    Stand in his face to contradict his claim.

   ·   ·   ·

BASTARD (*to Austria*)
           ... Sirrah, were I at home,
At your den, sirrah, with your lioness,
I would set an ox-head to your lion's hide,
And make a monster of you.

II.i.278, 290

As editors have pointed out, the Bastard's threat to cuckold Austria
makes poor sense in these circumstances, whereas in *The Troublesome
Reign* the threat is made to the Dauphin, Faulconbridge's successful rival
for the hand of Blanch. But, silly though it is, the threat is none the less
typical of that randy style of criticism of the kings and statesmen which
culminates in the Bastard's great soliloquy on Commodity. 'That smooth-
faced gentleman, tickling commodity' is vividly pictured as an ever-
successful seducer

        Of kings, of beggars, old men, young men, maids,
        Who having no external thing to lose
        But the word 'maid', cheats the poor maid of that.

II.i.570

    This turns out to be the last we see of Faulconbridge in his ebulliently
sardonic vein. As the play moves into its second and third phases the tone
becomes consistently serious, and although the Bastard returns from time
to time to his role of commentator he does so in a manner much less satiric
or detached than before, and entirely free of bawdy. Indeed, by the time
he reaches the monologue that ends Act IV—

        I am amazed, methinks, and lose my way
        Among the thorns and dangers of this world

IV.iii.140

—he is more deeply and concernedly involved in the action than one
might have supposed would be possible. What became of the cynical,
swashbuckling Faulconbridge of the first two acts? Part of the answer lies
in the fact that he was, even then, less cynical than he was pretending to
be, or thought himself to be. 'Gain, be my lord' is a sentiment flatly
contradicted by its speaker when, in the opening scene, he opts for
honour instead of land. (Faulconbridge is *Lear's* Edmund in reverse.)
But that provides only part of a solution to the change-of-tone puzzle,
and the sudden disappearance of bawdy from the play suggests an answer
of quite a different kind. Shakespeare may have switched his intention. He
seems to have begun with the idea of using a bluff comedian to provide
the audience, throughout, with detached, deflative comment on the

political chicanery that makes up so much of the King John story. This
commentator would have been a kind of proto-Falstaff, probably based
on the Philip Faulconbridge of *The Troublesome Reign* in his abbey-
ransacking mood (assuming that that play did precede Shakespeare's).
But it is hard to see how such a conception could have been satisfactorily
worked out, given plot material like the death of Arthur and the growing
vulnerability of John. The Bastard therefore has to take on a dual role, as
it were combining a Falstaff's jesting with the very different function of a
Prince Henry, effective defender of his father's dynasty against rebels. It
all makes for an awkward splice.

Of course this is mere speculation, and neither provable nor dis-
provable; yet it does help to account for the unease that *King John* has
created among critics and theatre audiences, particularly in the present
century. It also points to the tricky problem in dramaturgy that Shakespeare needed to solve before he could progress further with the kind of
history-play that was destined to become characteristically his own—a
drama combining affairs of state with the comically intransigent facts of
human appetite, sexual and otherwise. Such is *Henry IV*.

The 'organic' structure of each of the two parts of *Henry IV* has been
explored fully enough in recent years not to require exposition here.
Shakespeare, balancing the formalities of politics with comic interplay,
arranges his material in such a way that scene after scene comments on,
and adjusts our estimation of, what has gone before. It is typical of the
whole method that in Part 1 the dramatist should chop twenty-one years
off the historical age of Henry Percy to make him directly comparable
with Prince Henry. Hotspur's reckless pursuit of honour is pointedly
contrasted with the Prince's more coolly calculated progress towards it.
Falstaff casts a sardonic light on them both, but there can be no doubting
the decisiveness with which the Prince renounces him: when Falstaff's
bottle of sack is thrown at him across the stage, the symbolism shines
just as clear as it will in the other, parallel, rejection, at the end of Part 2.
Part 2 is essentially a re-enactment of Part 1 with changes of emphasis.
The battle of Shrewsbury demonstrates the Prince's public acceptance of a
chivalric code of behaviour in the military sphere, and this acceptance is
being paralleled in Part 2 when he formally confirms the rule of law in the
civil domain.

If this much may be regarded as being beyond critical dispute, at least
in broad outline, we can go on to ask where and how bawdy contributes
to that dramatic pattern.

The first point to note is that Shakespeare uses bawdy much more sparingly in the first part of the play than in the second. Part 1 runs to 2993 lines, of which only about twenty-one are demonstrably indecent. Part 2, a longer piece by nearly 10 per cent (3229 lines[3]), has some seventy-four instances of bawdy. In both parts, as one would expect, most of the indecency accumulates round Falstaff, who is bawdy in himself and the cause that bawdy is in other men. In *some* other men: not—significantly —in the Prince. In the course of Part 1's exposition, Prince Henry describes Falstaff in terms that supply the audience with an appropriately licentious frame of reference:

> What a devil hast thou to do with the time of the day? Unless hours were cups of sack, and minutes capons, and clocks the tongues of bawds, and dials the signs of leaping-houses, and the blessed sun himself a fair hot wench in flame-coloured taffeta, I see no reason why thou shouldst be so superfluous to demand the time of the day.
>
> I.ii.6

But when Falstaff later tries to draw the Prince into this ambience of easy sexual living, it is without success. Trying to turn the conversation away from the disquieting topics of gallows and buff jerkins, Falstaff demands to know whether the Hostess of the tavern is not 'a most sweet wench?' Henry brusquely refuses comment—'Why, what a pox have I to do with my Hostess of the tavern?'—and it remains true, throughout both plays, that this Prince Henry does not include women in his much-discussed 'loose behaviour'. It is far otherwise with Bolingbroke's 'un-thrifty son' as described and reported in *Richard II* (V.iii.22); but it would be no more reasonable to demand absolute consistency between the successive parts of the historical tetralogy than to require that the Falstaff of *The Merry Wives* should exactly match the Falstaff of *Henry IV*. In depicting a chaster Prince in *Henry IV* than he had described in *Richard II*, Shakespeare diverged from the chroniclers but may have been following the lead of *The Famous Victories of Henry V* (registered 1594, printed 1598). However it came about, this aspect of the characterisation of Prince Henry is important in maintaining, from the very start, one of those contrasts between him and Falstaff that make the knight's ultimate banishment quite unsurprising.

Falstaff himself, on the other hand, has the lion's share of the bawdy lines all through *Henry IV*, and his amatory involvement with the Hostess, Doll Tearsheet and others unnamed becomes part of the physicality in which he so firmly anchors the play. It has often been remarked how the inconsequential chatter in Part 2—about William the cook's difficulties over young pigeons for the dinner, about bills from the blacksmith for shoeing and plough-irons, about the price of bullocks or ewes—has the effect of providing solidity. Undemonstratively, but with cumulative importance, it all evokes that earth, that realm, that England which Henry IV and his rebellious peers are disputing. What is less often commented on is that Part 1 offers much of the same kind of realism. The carriers on the Dover road 'leak in your chimney' for want of a jordan and are too experienced to lend a lantern to the likes of Gadshill. The same tough knowingness underlies such things as Falstaff's guileful mistreatment of the Hostess:

FALSTAFF   There's no more faith in thee than in a stewed prune, nor no
            more truth in thee than in a drawn fox—and for womanhood, Maid
            Marian may be the deputy's wife of the ward to thee. Go, you thing, go!
HOSTESS   Say, what thing, what thing?
FALSTAFF   What thing? Why, a thing to thank God on.
HOSTESS   I am no thing to thank God on, I would thou shouldst know
            it, I am an honest man's wife, and setting thy knighthood aside, thou
            art a knave to call me so.
FALSTAFF   Setting thy womanhood aside, thou art a beast to say
            otherwise.
HOSTESS   Say, what beast, thou knave, thou?
FALSTAFF   What beast? Why—an otter.
PRINCE HAL An otter, Sir John? Why an otter?
FALSTAFF   Why? She's neither fish nor flesh, a man knows not where
            to have her.
HOSTESS   Thou art an unjust man in saying so, thou or any man knows
            where to have me, thou knave, thou.
PRINCE HAL Thou sayest true, Hostess, and he slanders thee most
            grossly.

                                                                III.iii.111

If, as seems probable, Falstaff's 'neither fish nor flesh' implies 'neither male nor female', then the corollary 'a man knows not where to have her' becomes one of Shakespeare's very few references to anal intercourse. As a jibe at the Hostess it seems bizarrely chosen, but like so many of Falstaff's wilder sallies it proves effective as bait for a conversational trap. Poor Mistress Quickly is always a ready victim for his glib tongue, and can be tricked in argument or wheeled into acquiescence as easily as Hotspur's Kate. These two, the Hostess and Lady Percy, may even be seen as the ultimate victims of Part 1 in much the same sense as Feeble is an ultimate victim in Part 2, last in the pecking-order. 'No man's too good to serve's Prince,' says the woman's tailor, leaving home for what could, for all he knows, be the last time. Mistress Quickly might well be saying, 'No woman's too good to serve Sir John.'

Among the aristocrats in *1 Henry IV*, the only speaker apart from Prince Henry to be found with any bawdy at all is Hotspur. Following the

hard bargaining of the rebels' conference in III.i, he works off nervous
tensions in foolery:

> HOTSPUR   Come, Kate, thou art perfect in lying down. Come, quick,
>   quick, that I may lay my head in thy lap.
> LADY PERCY   Go, ye giddy goose. . . . Wouldst thou have thy head
>   broken?
> HOTSPUR   No.
> LADY PERCY   Then be still.
> HOTSPUR   Neither, 'tis a woman's fault.
> LADY PERCY   Now, God help thee!
> HOTSPUR   To the Welsh lady's bed.
> LADY PERCY   What's that?
> HOTSPUR   Peace, she sings.
>
> III.i.221, 231

The courtly life, with musicians playing and a lady singing, would be too
leisured for Hotspur's eager temperament at the best of times, and when
the singing is in Welsh it makes him more impatient still. His cheeky
asides with Lady Percy are also, perhaps, giving further expression to his
low opinion of the ridiculous Glendower. In immediate social attitude
as well as in point of detail ('my head in thy lap'), this fidgeting and
clowning anticipates the fiercer spasm of publicly displayed bawdy that
will shake Hamlet in the court of Denmark.

The bawdy of *The Second Part of King Henry IV* differs from that of
Part 1 not only in extent but also in kind. It takes on a Hogarthian quality
which, as A. R. Humphreys has put it, includes irresistible *appreciation* of
human beings, however coarse or absurd they are.[4] Yet Hogarth's touches
of desperation can be seen here too. Much of the bawdy in *2 Henry IV*
echoes, in its own strident way, the still, sad music of some of the play's
monologues.

> Well, thus we play the fools with the time, and the spirits of the wise
> sit in the clouds and mock us.
>
> II.ii.135

> O God! that one might read the book of fate,
> And see the revolution of the times
> Make mountains level, and the continent,
> Weary of solid firmness, melt itself
> Into the sea . . .
>
> III.i.45

Falstaff would seem to be the breathing antithesis of such melancholy
thoughts, but he now begins to appear consistently in a light that is less
than rosy. Mistress Quickly, being as gullible as ever, can be easily foiled
in her attempt to have him arrested for debt, yet his governing motive in
soothing her is sheer rapacity. 'Go, with her, with her,' he urges Bardolph;

'hook on, hook on!' (II.i.155). His liaison with Doll Tearsheet also falls short of being any carefree frolic. As the Prince forewarns us, Doll is to Falstaff 'Even such kin as the parish heifers are to the town bull'. Now, prostitutes as the mythical heroines of anecdote are one thing, prostitutes in person on the stage quite another. While the commercial traveller's stories lightly entertain—

> 'How did an educated girl like you land up in a joint like this?'
> 'Luck!'

—the haggard face of many a real-life streetwalker presents a different picture. Shakespeare writes just this ambivalence into Doll Tearsheet. Doll is undeniably funny—in her sentimentality ('Come, I'll be friends with thee, Jack. Thou art going to the wars'); in her professional pride ('Away, you mouldy rogue, away! I am meat for your master') and professional guile (she is pregnant with a cushion when arrested); above all, in her flow of backyard eloquence: 'What! you poor, base, rascally, cheating, lack-linen mate! ... Away, you bottle-ale rascal! you basket-hilt stale juggler, you!' On the other hand, when we first encounter this 'road' she is drunk, tousled and feeling sick; and our last glimpse of her comes as they drag her off to whipping or worse. We may even be left wondering whether that pregnancy really should be taken as faked or as actual. A dark undertone can also be heard in much of the bawdy dialogue connected with her. Disease looms large, and Falstaff's efforts to laugh it aside become more gross than witty:

> FALSTAFF   If the cook help to make the gluttony, you help to make
> the diseases, Doll. We catch of you, Doll, we catch of you; grant that,
> my poor virtue, grant that.
> DOLL   Yea, joy, our chains and our jewels.
> FALSTAFF   'Your brooches, pearls and ouches.' For to serve bravely is to
> come halting off; you know, to come off the breach with his pike bent
> bravely, and to surgery bravely; to venture upon the charged chambers
> bravely—
> DOLL   Hang yourself, you muddy conger, hang yourself!
> HOSTESS   By my troth, this is the old fashion. You two never meet but
> you fall to some discord.
>
>   II.iv.44

An equally mottled effect, though from a markedly different style of bawdy, comes into the play with Justic Shallow. Looking back with inane nostalgia on his years as a law student, he intensifies our sense of a world in which many people are losing the fight against eroding time:[5]

> SHALLOW   ... And is Jane Nightwork alive?
> FALSTAFF   She lives, Master Shallow.

SHALLOW   She never could away with me.

FALSTAFF   Never, never; she would always say she could not abide
Master Shallow.

SHALLOW   By the mass, I could anger her to th'heart. She was
then a bona-roba. Doth she hold her own well?

FALSTAFF   Old, old, Master Shallow.

SHALLOW   Nay, she must be old; she cannot choose but be old; certain
she's old; and had Robin Nightwork, by old Nightwork, before I
came to Clement's Inn.

SILENCE   That's fifty-five year ago.

III.ii.192

Again, if we suspect a touch of sarcasm in Falstaff's 'We have heard the
chimes at midnight, Master Shallow', the suspicion hardens when we
learn more of the facts about the youth of Robert Shallow.

> This same starved justice hath done nothing but prate to me of the
> wildness of his youth and the feats he hath done about Turnbull Street;
> and every third word a lie, duer paid to the hearer than the Turk's
> tribute. I do remember him at Clement's Inn, like a man made after
> supper of a cheese-paring. When 'a was naked, he was for all the world like
> a forked radish, with a head fantastically carved upon it with a knife. 'A
> was so forlorn that his dimensions to any thick sight were invisible. 'A was
> the very genius of famine; yet lecherous as a monkey, and the whores
> called him mandrake.

III.ii.295

So even Shallow's bawdy has been shallow. His vision of himself as a
gay young blade has no more substance than Pistol's liquor-hazed mental
realm of histrionics. Far from recapturing a wild youth after he comes
with Falstaff to London, he is brought face to face with bleak realities:
Henry V has been crowned, the rule of law confirmed, the Hostess
arrested, and Falstaff and all his company are to be carried to the Fleet.

FALSTAFF   Master Shallow, I owe you a thousand pounds.

SHALLOW   Yea, marry, Sir John; which I beseech you to let me have
home with me.

FALSTAFF   That can hardly be, Master Shallow.

V.v.74

All in all, then, the bawdy of *2 Henry IV* makes a contribution that
may well cause the modern reader of Shakespeare to range this history
alongside the darker dramas of the 1600s rather than with its actual contemporaries around 1597. To find any similar set of lower-life characters
acting out, at their humdrum level, a ruler's vision of human ineffectuality,
one has to look ahead to *Measure for Measure* or *The Tempest*.

*   *   *

In *Henry V* bawdy plays a much less important role than in either part of *Henry IV*, and on the whole it is less firmly integrated thematically with the political material. Falstaff disappears, leaving what might otherwise have been his share of the action to Pistol, and leaving to the very different figure of Chorus the task of providing a commentary on events. Through the choruses almost as much as through Henry's own speeches, the play works solidly in support of the popular sixteenth-century view of Henry V—as deserving victor against overwhelming odds at Agincourt, as 'the mirror of all Christian kings ... this grace of kings ... This star of England'. There are marginal reservations. The walls of Harfleur, assaulted under the sweeping rhetoric of a gallant royal captain, fall to an army which also provides employment for argumentative theorisers like Macmorris and scurrilous thieves like Bardolph and Nym. Similarly, the obstinate questionings of Williams need to be answered, or at least talked down, before the king can go on to defend his conquest with an eased conscience. Yet Shakespeare admits the various qualifications without letting them much impede the thrust of the main nationalistic action, and critics who labour to represent this as an anti-war play are guilty of wilful distortion.

Nevertheless, some of the melancholy of *2 Henry IV* spills over to the new play. At the dawn of Crispin's Day, Henry V's responsibilities weigh on him scarcely less heavily than did his father's on him. And just as before, we also find dejection modifying the nature and functions of bawdy passages. The Hostess's description of the death of Falstaff—probably the most moving episode in this whole play—has its sadness accentuated rather than lessened by the grudging admission that her hero 'did in some sort, indeed, handle women' in the days before he became rheumatic. Doll Tearsheet, too, is mentioned in much the same context of venereal infection as was created by Falstaff during her first scene in *2 Henry IV*. Then it was 'We catch of you, Doll, we catch of you'; now it is Pistol's rather less playful jibe at Nym—

> No, to the spital go,
> And from the powdering tub of infamy
> Fetch forth the lazar kite of Cressid's kind,
> Doll Tearsheet she by name, and her espouse.
>
> II.i.71

The point is carried to a chill conclusion when we learn, near the end of the play, that either Doll herself or Nell Quickly[6] has actually died of syphilis:

PISTOL
  Doth Fortune play the housewife with me now?
  News have I that my Doll is dead i'th'spital
  Of malady of France,
  And there my rendezvous is quite cut off.

V.i.76

Even allowing for the possibility that *Henry V* may have been finished
hurriedly (as the last act's heavy reliance on some version of *The Famous
Victories* would suggest), this makes a lonely and pitiful note on which to
hear the last of Falstaff's ragamuffins. Their gradual elimination from the
play helps to emphasise the lonely glory of the king: 'Banish plump
Jack, and banish all the world.' But there is grim irony at their own
expense, too, if we happen to recall Pistol's prelude to the death of
Falstaff: 'Let us condole the knight; for, lambkins, we will live.'

  Two other eruptions of bawdy into *Henry V* demand comment, one
in III.iv, the scene of the Princess Katherine's English lesson, and the
other in V.ii, where forty-odd lines of sexual innuendo separate Henry's
wooing of Katherine from the formal betrothal.

  Besides filling psychic time between the capture of Harfleur and the
news of Henry's having crossed the Somme, Katherine's language lesson
establishes her as a character, and does so in a way that will pay dividends
in the bilingual wooing scene. Shakespeare exhibits his usual skill in
combining near-opposites when he blends her cool charm with the kind
of fun that can be extracted from the misinterpretation of unfamiliar
language. Thus, we might almost imagine ourselves back in the Windsor
household of Dr Caius and Mistress Quickly when, towards the end of
Katherine's lesson, we encounter two obscene puns, *foot/foutre* and
count/cunt. At the lowest level, these quibbles would please the more
stridently anti-French section of a popular Elizabethan audience. For the
more sophisticated, Katherine's embarrassment would foreshadow the
engaging modesty with which she later meets the advances of King
Henry. With the Princess, just as with Bardolph and Nym and Pistol at
the opposite end of the social scale, Shakespeare is bringing home to us
some of the human implications of international politics as he sees them.

  Could the same be said of the bawdy exchange that immediately
follows the wooing itself?

BURGUNDY   ... If you would conjure in her, you must make a circle;
  if conjure up love in her in his true likeness, he must appear naked
  and blind. Can you blame her, then, being a maid yet rosed over with
  the virgin crimson of modesty, if she deny the appearance of a naked
  blind boy in her naked seeing self? It were, my lord, a hard condition
  for a maid to consign to.

KING HENRY   Yet they do wink and yield, as love is blind and enforces.
BURGUNDY   They are then excused, my lord, when they see not what
they do.
KING HENRY   Then, good my lord, teach your cousin to consent winking.
BURGUNDY   I will wink on her to consent, my lord, if you will teach
her to know my meaning: for maids, well summered and warm kept,
are like flies at Bartholomew-tide, blind, though they have their eyes,
and then they will endure handling, which before would not abide
looking on.
KING HENRY   This moral ties me over to time and a hot summer; and
so I shall catch the fly, your cousin, in the latter end, and she must
be blind too.
BURGUNDY   As love is, my lord, before it loves.
KING HENRY   It is so; and you may, some of you, thank love for my
blindness, who cannot see many a fair French city for one fair French
maid that stands in my way.
FRENCH KING   Yes, my lord, you see them perspectively, the cities
turned into a maid; for they are all girdled with maiden walls, that
war hath never entered.
KING HENRY   Shall Kate be my wife?
FRENCH KING   So please you.

                                                              V.ii.288

Like Katherine's English lesson, this has no counterpart in *The Famous Victories* or, of course, in the chronicles, yet Shakespeare devotes some forty lines to it, and at a point where his play is clearly drawing to a close, too. Producers often cut it, either because of its obscurity for non-academic audiences or simply because it slows down the whole dénouement. But it has its own dramatic contribution to make. Within Burgundy's officers'-mess banter lies a core of resentment at Henry's ruthlessness. The Princess symbolically *is* France, 'the cities turned into a maid', and conquest by Henry is a hard condition not only in the jocular priapic sense but in the sphere of politics also. King Henry, for all his acting the blunt English soldier, is quite acute enough to perceive Burgundy's nuance—and tough enough to maintain, even in flyting, the unyielding attitude that he has taken towards the French from the very start: 'love is blind and enforces . . . so I shall catch the fly, your cousin'. When the French King joins in the game to urge the negotiating value of his unoccupied territories, there is a trace of conqueror's impatience in the five monosyllables with which Henry closes the wit combat: 'Shall Kate be my wife?' And even then, with all the circumspect care we saw in 'Hal' before Gad's Hill, in Prince Henry before his coronation, and recently in King Henry fooling cautiously with Williams and Fluellen, he still takes the trouble to insist on the French King's agreeing to the style *Praeclarissimus filius noster Henricus, Rex Angliae et Haeres Franciae.* The

English possessions in France will eventually be lost, as oft our stage hath shown'; but they will not be lost by this monarch.

Henry's bawdy-match with Burgundy is thus something more than the trivial embellishment it may at first appear to be. It is yet another of the many bawdy conversations in Shakespeare which, when examined closely, can be seen to be working significantly on the atmosphere or the thematic implications of their scenes. Such passages are usually dispensable in performance, but dispensable only in the limited sense that no obvious damage will be done to the plots of their plays if they are omitted. They operate on the stuff of drama, on its texture, its tone, its rhythms, its implications. Above all, in the particular case of the Henry IV and Henry V plays, these conversations help to root the political history in the soil of personal life.

Not long before or after *Henry V*, Shakespeare was at work on a comedy that stood in need of a very similar kind of rootedness. 'There has to be someone in Arden to remind us of the indispensable flesh.' In a sentence, Harold Jenkins puts his finger on the essential difference between *As You Like It* and its main source, Thomas Lodge's romance *Rosalynde* (1590).[7] Lodge presents a whole array of formalised Dresden china figures with scarcely a word of anything indecorous to disturb their conversational poise. There are, admittedly, outright bursts of violence—at the wrestling match (with deaths), in the incident with the lion, in the fight between Rosader and the supporters of Saladyne, in the attempt to abduct Aliena, and in the final battle—but Lodge presents none of these episodes in such a way as to suggest that the pretty display of life in the forest could easily be upset. Shakespeare cuts back the element of physical conflict, reducing it to the wrestling match, a brief tussle between Orlando and Oliver, and a few scattered threats; but he brings 'the indispensable flesh' into bold prominence. Professor Jenkins, in the essay from which I have quoted, sees Touchstone as *the* vehicle of the play's realism, 'the obvious choice for the sensual lover who will burlesque the romantic dream'. Burlesque it he certainly does, both in his mating with Audrey and in his re-collections of Jane Smile:

> I remember when I was in love I broke my sword upon a stone and bid him take that for coming a-night to Jane Smile, ... and I remember the wooing of a peascod instead of her, from whom I took two cods and, giving her them again, said with weeping tears, 'Wear these for my sake.'
> II.iv.42

Yet Touchstone is by no means alone in sounding the note of frank sensuality in *As You Like It*. Celia will turn a candid phrase when she thinks it needful—

> So you may put a man in your belly.
>
> III.ii.197

> You have simply misused our sex in your love-prate. We must have your doublet and hose plucked over your head, and show the world what the bird hath done to her own nest.
>
> IV.i.186

And for level-headed realism in the contemplation of love, Touchstone and Celia are both outdone by Rosalind herself. Coleridge, like many of the play's editors, was startled by Rosalind's admission that some of her early moodiness is not for her father but for her child's father (I.iii.11), but if S.T.C. had been less disconcerted by this firm stroke of Shakespeare's brush he might have gone on to reflect on the consistency with which Rosalind continues to speak 'indelicately'. Like her prototype in Lodge's romance, she selects for her disguised self the name Ganymede: 'Jove's own page', with all his ancient associations of pederasty, provides an apt identity for an adventuresome girl-boy. In the forest, however, on hearing that Orlando is nearby, her first thought is entirely practical— how to become unambiguously female again, and quickly: 'Alas the day, what shall I do with my doublet and hose?' The same practicality is brought to bear on poor comical-pastoral Phebe and Silvius:

> 'Tis such fools as you
> That makes the world full of ill-favoured children.
>
> III.v.52

There are moments of blunt physicality, too, in Rosalind's flirtation with Orlando in the 'wooing' scenes. Spermal fluid and digital stimulation may well be implied when she advises that 'for lovers lacking—God warn us!—matter, the cleanliest shift is to kiss' (IV.i.69). Nor is there anything abstract in her interpretation of Orlando's 'love me, Rosalind' a few lines later: 'Yes, faith will I, Fridays and Saturdays and all.' Then again, a young woman so clear about her own intentions will not mince matters when describing her cousin's:

> in these degrees have they made a pair of stairs to marriage which they
> will climb incontinent or else be incontinent before marriage. They are
> in the very wrath of love and they will together; clubs cannot part them.
>
> V.ii.35

By running such quotations together, one inevitably gives the wrong impression. There is nothing brazen about Rosalind—that is easily seen if we put these extracts back into their various contexts. But her kind of modesty, like Juliet's, admits neither coyness nor self-deception. This is what makes her proof against the frigid pride of a Phebe on the one hand and, on the other, against Touchstone's insolent suggestion that she is a tart:

> If the cat will after kind,
> So be sure will Rosalind.
> Wintered garments must be lined,
> So must slender Rosalind.
> They that reap must sheaf and bind,
> Then to cart with Rosalind.
>
> .   .   .   .   .
>
> He that sweetest rose will find,
> Must find love's prick and Rosalind.
>
> III.ii.99

Rosalind takes this rhyme at its proper value, as a parody of Orlando's bad verses and the dead conventions that prop them up. Touchstone's real impertinence lies in his telling her what she already knows (and what Shakespeare knows we know she knows): that love is as much a physiological as a spiritual phenomenon. Ripeness is all, and in Orlando's clumsy attempts at poetry Rosalind can detect his progress towards ripeness. So when Touchstone meddles he is being less realistic than he thinks, and he deserves his scolding for cynicism:

TOUCHSTONE   . . . This is the very false gallop of verses. Why do you infect yourself with them?
ROSALIND   Peace, you dull fool, I found them on a tree.
TOUCHSTONE   Truly, the tree yields bad fruit.
ROSALIND   I'll graff it with you, and then I shall graff it with a medlar; then it will be the earliest fruit i'th'country: for you'll be rotten ere you be half ripe, and that's the right virtue of the medlar.

III.ii.109

With Touchstone, in fact, Shakespeare is once again employing the safety mechanism that could be noticed long ago in Speed and later in Mercutio. The cynic attacks lovers with the dry wit of would-be realism, but the lovers too are realistic, and more capaciously so than the cynic. Consequently, while his cynicism saves *the play* from cloudy idealism, it falls far short of debunking the lovers who stand at the play's emotional centre.[8]

Much the same is true of Shakespeare's one other important addition to Lodge's selection of characters, Jaques. Jaques, however, is involved in scarcely any of the sexual jokes of *As You Like It*. His name yields a famous coprological pun, on *jakes*, but the dramatic exploitation of this comes primarily in his melancholy, a malady associated in some minds with the solitude of the close-stool. (Sir John Harington's *Metamorphosis of Ajax* might be said to have tiled the way for such modern works as James Joyce's *Ulysses*, John Osborne's *Luther* or Philip Roth's *Portnoy's Complaint*.) Jaques is said to have been sexually dissolute in his past life, 'a libertine / As sensual as the brutish sting itself', but he speaks little bawdy now: a sardonic mention of goldsmiths' wives at III.ii.264, and a couple of puns on *hour* and *tail* which he claims to be quoting from Touchstone:

> '... And so from hour to hour we ripe, and ripe,
> And then from hour to hour we rot, and rot,
> And thereby hangs a tale.'

II.vii.26

Helge Kökeritz (*Shakespeare's Pronunciation*, p. 117) noted the *hour/whore* and *tale/tail* puns, but surprisingly made no comment on the quibble in *hangs*: where *tale* is implying *tail* and hence *penis*, and the context is one of hourly or whoremasterly rotting, then surely the tail hangs in diseased impotence? Be that as it may, the whole homily does sound like genuine Touchstone rather than anything we need associate closely with Jaques.

That being the case, the bawdy of *As You Like It* becomes virtually a monopoly for Rosalind, Celia and Touchstone, with the two girls as the true sexual realists and Touchstone—despite his name—only a pretender to realism. All three combine, nevertheless, in as much as their bawdy works parallel with Jaques' satirical thrusts to give the play a dimension that is non-Arcadian without being destructively anti-Arcadian. This is an aspect of that relativism or complementarity which is fundamentally characteristic of the piece, and of so much else in Shakespeare. By keeping the talk and events in firm relation to life outside the charmed circle of the Forest of Arden, bawdy helps to maintain a 'fully lived' quality that recalls Falstaff while at the same time anticipating *Twelfth Night*, *Measure for Measure* and the last plays.

But before the final blessings of *The Tempest* or *Henry VIII*, Shakespeare was to turn sexual indecency to quite another purpose. Its function in his tragic and tragi-comic explorations of the black possibilities in human appetite will concern us next.

NOTES

1. E. K. Chambers, *William Shakespeare: A Study of Facts and Problems* (2 vols, 1930), i, 366. Cf., for example, G. B. Harrison reviewing the New Cambridge *King John* in *MLR*, xxxii (1937), 455–6.

2. J. Dover Wilson, ed., New Cambridge *King John* (Cambridge University Press, 1936), pp. lv–lvii; E. A. J. Honigmann, ed., New Arden *King John* (1954), pp. xliii–lviii. For *The Troublesome Reign*, see Bullough, iv, 72–151.

3. These totals, based on lineation in *The Cambridge Shakespeare* of 1891, are taken from Peter Alexander, *Shakespeare's Life and Art* (1939), Appendix, Table F.

4. A. R. Humphreys in New Arden *2 Henry IV* (1966), p. 62.

5. On the importance of Time in *2 Henry IV*, see especially L. C. Knights, *Some Shakespearean Themes* (2nd edn, 1966), pp. 46–56.

6. Both F1 and the 'bad' Q1 of *Henry V* read *Doll* in V.i.77. Many editors have changed this to *Nell*, since it is Mrs Pistol, 'the quondam Quickly', whom Pistol would call his and think of as his 'rendezvous', not his old enemy Doll Tearsheet. It is not unusual for Shakespeare to prove forgetful over the occasional character's name. Another possibility, explored by J. H. Walter in his New Arden *Henry V* (1954), pp. xli–xliii, is that this farewell speech may originally have been conceived as Falstaff's, not Pistol's: Doll would then have fitted. But again, assuming that Shakespeare meant to name the Hostess here, one could agree with William Empson that 'there is a deserved irony if Pistol, who talked brutally about Doll's trouble at the beginning of the play, finds at the end that the same applies to his Nell' (*The Kenyon Review*, xv (1953), 216).

7. Harold Jenkins, *'As You Like It'*, SS 8 (1955), 48. Lodge's *Rosalynde: Euphues golden legacie* is given in full by Bullough, ii, 158–256.

8. 'The result of including in Touchstone a representative of what in love is un-romantic is not ... to undercut the play's romance: on the contrary, the fool's cynicism, or one-sided realism, forestalls the cynicism with which the audience might greet a play where his sort of realism had been ignored. ... Romantic commentators construed him as "Hamlet in motley," a devastating critic. They forgot, characteristically, that he is ridiculous: he makes his attitudes pre-posterous when he values rank and comfort above humility, or follows biology rather than beauty. In laughing at him, we reject the tendency in ourselves which he for the moment represents. The net effect of the fool's part is thus to consolidate the hold of the serious themes by exorcising opposition' (Barber, *Shakespeare's Festive Comedy*, p. 232).

7

The Language of
Sexual Revulsion

Yes. Some things you must always be unable to bear. Some things you
must never stop refusing to bear. Injustice and outrage and dishonour
and shame. No matter how young you are or how old you have got.
William Faulkner, *Intruder in the Dust*

For Shakespeare, as for so many of his contemporaries, the early Jacobean
years are characterised by serious indecency. Bawdy wit hardens to ice,
bawdy humour turns grotesque. Coleridge's dictum, that by a law of the
human mind the terrible always touches on the verge of the ludicrous,
now shows its converse: the ludicrous becomes part of the terrible when
the Shakespearean heroes of the early 1600s contemplate sexual love as
seen in the distorting mirrors of their initial tragic experience. It is not
that they lack ideals. On the contrary, such men as Hamlet, Troilus,
Othello or Timon are idealistic to a fault. But as long as they remain
afflicted by the contagious breath of human depravity, the idealism only
makes their sense of corruption all the fuller; and they find that the
sexual fidelity they long for is being mocked by a seemingly invincible
opposition. To the audience, though not, usually, to the hero himself,
his sense of overwhelming defilement becomes one measure of the grand
ideals that lie at the roots of his struggle.

An assessment of this process as it goes on in *Hamlet*, *Othello*, *King Lear*
and *Timon of Athens* is the main business of this chapter, but three tragi-
comedies also find their place here. *Troilus and Cressida* (*c.* 1602), *Pericles* (*c.*
1607/8)[1] and *Cymbeline* (*c.* 1608/9) all use bawdy as a medium of disgust
or aggression rather than fun, and although, in *Troilus*, the whimsical
lubricities of Pandarus may seem harmless, his dejected mein at the end
of the play tells its own tale of corruption and failure. *Measure for Measure*,

on the other hand, is not included in this chapter, even though its likely date of composition, 1604, falls almost in the middle of the decade being reviewed. I prefer to discuss it later, because its use of bawdy differs strikingly from that of the plays closest to it in time of writing. Despite an emphasis on corruption, *Measure for Measure* carries its sexuality more lightly than would at first appear: so much so, that from the specialised point of view of this book it belongs with *Antony and Cleopatra* and the finely-balanced late comedies to be considered in chapter 8.

To begin, then, with *Hamlet*. He would be a bold critic who would maintain that *Hamlet* stands in need of radical reinterpretation, yet with the coming of modern psychology this tragedy stood to gain more than any of the others. Dover Wilson fought a doomed rearguard action against the massed armour of post-Freudian literary study: it was mis-leading, he said, to try to describe Hamlet's state of mind in terms of modern psychology, both because 'Shakespeare did not think in these terms' and because Hamlet was a character in a play, not in history.[2] As a warning against some of Ernest Jones's (or Andrew Bradley's) less scrupu-lous critical procedures, Dover Wilson's protest was valid and timely in 1935, but it needed to be modified first by the fact that Sophocles, for example, clearly did think in psychological terms when he wrote *Oedipus Tyrannus*, and secondly by the reflection that Shakespeare too was well equipped to anticipate Freud imaginatively, even though psychoanalysis was not his intent. Recognising this, most twentieth-century critics have taken care to give full weight to Hamlet's disgust at the hasty and inces-tuous remarriage of his mother. Out of his overwhelming disillusion come the two main eruptions of bawdy into the tragedy, one in the play scene and the other in the closet scene.

The immediate victim of Hamlet's sexual jokes at the start of the play scene (III.ii.108–16) is of course Ophelia, whose innocent maladroitness when used as a decoy in III.i has made it seem to the Prince that she is criminally implicated with her father and Claudius. It now becomes Hamlet's turn to use her as a decoy, embarrassing her with coarse witti-cisms that prove to be the opening moves in an attack on his mother. 'What should a man do but be merry? For look you how cheerfully my mother looks, and my father died within's two hours' (III.ii.120). The same process is repeated, with heightened tension, just before Lucianus's murder-speech:

HAMLET   ... This is one Lucianus, nephew to the King.
OPHELIA   You are as good as a chorus, my lord.

HAMLET   I could interpret between you and your love, if I could see
the puppets dallying.
OPHELIA   You are keen, my lord, you are keen.
HAMLET   It would cost you a groaning to take off mine edge.
OPHELIA   Still better, and worse.
HAMLET   So you mis-take your husbands.—Begin, murderer . . . .

                                                                III.ii.238

The firmly placed plural *husbands* once again focuses attention on Gertrude
and Claudius—all the more appropriately as Hamlet goes on to call for
what proves to be the decisive speech of 'The Mousetrap'.

So far, the Prince's bawdy has been tactical. At the risk of resurrecting
Salvador de Madariaga's back-stabbing Hamlet[3] one might even call it
Machiavellian. In the closet scene, however, the circumstance of a private
conversation with Gertrude releases Hamlet's full torrent of sexual
revulsion, and his self-restraint disappears.

> Rebellious hell,
> If thou canst mutine in a matron's bones,
> To flaming youth let virtue be as wax
> And melt in her own fire; proclaim no shame
> When the compulsive ardour gives the charge,
> Since frost itself as actively doth burn,
> And reason panders will.
>
> .   .   .   .
>   Nay, but to live
> In the rank sweat of an enseamed bed,
> Stewed in corruption, honeying and making love
> Over the nasty sty!

                                                                III.iv.82, 91

The Ghost's reproof brings this neurotic rush of words under partial
control, but even in the steadier second half of the scene Hamlet still
shows a morbid preoccupation with the physical details of his mother's
incest. His ambivalence of attitude gains clearest expression of all in the
queer, convoluted double negative of his final injunction:

> Not this, by no means, that I bid you do:
> Let the bloat King tempt you again to bed;
> Pinch wanton on your cheek; call you his mouse;
> And let him, for a pair of reechy kisses,
> Or paddling in your neck with his damned fingers,
> Make you to ravel all this matter out,
> That I essentially am not in madness,
> But mad in craft.

                                                                III.iv.181

These strangely lascivious outbursts from Hamlet go far towards
justifying Ernest Jones's view that what Shakespeare depicts is a Prince

whose desperate sense of betrayal stems ultimately from repressed sexual jealousy centred on his mother.[4] The lewd imaginings are a sign of panic, and a sign that the evil that Hamlet has watched spreading round him like a stain is now penetrating his own mind, producing an ugly fascination with what he most fears and hates. His refusal to murder Claudius 'pat', in cold blood, commands our respect; but the scene with Gertrude brings a counterbalancing realisation that even in Hamlet himself 'rank corruption, mining all within', could yet infect unseen. To such a process the killing of Claudius would be almost irrelevant. And it is the irrelevance of vengeance, rather than any simple reinstatement of princely idealism, that brings the play to its eventual resolution. In the graveyard scene Hamlet broods on death, as he has brooded so often before, but there is now a significant shift in his viewpoint. That corruption of the living which has obsessed him in the past now fades into comparative insignificance beside the physical corruption of the dead. His new concern is less for life's squalor than for its pathetic smallness in relation to death. As he talks with Horatio and the gravedigger, we can see him acquiring a new objectivity, a new power to accept things as they are. One might guess, hereabouts, that there will be no more anguished bawdy from this fifth-act Hamlet, and not much more talk of revenge. He still envisages killing Claudius, but his attitude to the killing has become passive rather than active: he can feel an unseen universal noose tightening about them both. Whether an act of vengeance takes place or not, Claudius—like Alexander the Great, or imperious Caesar, or even just Yorick—is under sentence of death in any case. Seen from the long perspective of the graveyard, the villain has shrunk; so also has my lady who paints an inch thick, the play's recurrent image for female duplicity.[5] Hamlet has blood on his hands and will soon be murdered, but at least he has conquered his own sense of uncontainable repugnance.

Outside its main spasms, Hamlet's bawdy calls for little comment. Before his suspicions harden towards Rosencrantz and Guildenstern he is willing to join them in casual, undergraduate humour:

GUILDENSTERN   . . . On fortune's cap we are not the very button.
HAMLET   Nor the soles of her shoe?
ROSENCRANTZ   Neither, my lord.
HAMLET   Then you live about her waist, or in the middle of her favours?
GUILDENSTERN   Faith, her privates we.
HAMLET   In the secret parts of Fortune? O, most true; she is a strumpet.

                                                                 II.ii.228

But only eighty lines later he has 'an eye of' the two spies, and will joke with them no more:

HAMLET   . . . Man delights not me—no, nor woman neither, though by
    your smiling you seem to say so.
ROSENCRANTZ   My lord, there was no such stuff in my thoughts.
HAMLET   Why did ye laugh, then, when I said 'Man delights not me'?

                                                                              II.ii.308

Only one other character in *Hamlet* has any considerable number of
indecent lines, and it seems paradoxical that this should be the innocent
young Ophelia. The fact that her presumed original in Belleforest's
Amleth story[6] is somewhat less innocent makes little difference. The
paradox disappears in any case when one recollects that Ophelia's bawdy
results from madness, besides being further distanced from the girl herself
by occurring in song.

> Tomorrow is Saint Valentine's day,
>   All in the morning betime,
> And I a maid at your window,
>   To be your Valentine.
> Then up he rose and donned his clothes,
>   And dupped the chamber-door;
> Let in the maid, that out a maid
>   Never departed more.
>
> .   .   .   .   .
>
> By Gis and by Saint Charity,
>   Alack, and fie for shame!
> Young men will do't, if they come to't;
>   By Cock, they are to blame.
> Quoth she, 'Before you tumbled me,
>   You promised me to wed.'
>
> .   .   .   .   .
>
> 'So would I 'a done, by yonder sun,
> An thou hadst not come to my bed.'
>
>   IV.v.46, 56, 63

The vulgarity of this ballad, so completely uncharacteristic of Ophelia
when sane, creates strong pathos not only through that contrast but also
by glancing back to Hamlet's cruel public jibes in the play scene. Further-
more, this is a song about seduction, about the very thing that her
devious father and brother had once warned Ophelia to fear. ' 'Tis in
my memory locked. . . .' Hamlet himself had later inveighed against the
notion of a love-affair—'Get thee to a nunnery. Why wouldst thou be a
breeder of sinners?' Small wonder that Ophelia, having lost her wits,
should now be depicted as dwelling obsessively on the sexual aspects of a
lost innocence.[7] In this, she obliquely resembles Hamlet himself, thought-
sick at the acts of his mother. Ophelia is again like Hamlet in being left

isolated at the Danish court, but with the important difference that her isolation—in schizophrenia—is total and final.

Behind the bawdy of disillusion and insanity in Hamlet and Ophelia, it has been fairly easy to keep in sight an ideal of love. When we turn from *Hamlet* to *Troilus and Cressida*, however, things are very different. Only a determinedly optimistic interpretation could find this play going beyond mockery of the ideal to necessary affirmation of it. As Peter Alexander once remarked, *Troilus* is to the great tragedies something like the antimasque to the masque[8]—not, of course, in any sequential or chronological way, but in the sense that it sardonically reverses their more heroic assertions. It reduces epic chivalry to the fruitless intrigues and cold-blooded treacheries of 'those that war for a placket'. It presents love as something so elusive and fragile as to be scarcely worth seeking at all. If there is hope or reassurance in the play, it is of a kind that borders on cynicism, drawing what nourishment it can from the bland realism of a Ulysses:

> TROILUS
> Let it not be believed for womanhood.
> Think, we had mothers; do not give advantage
> To stubborn critics, apt, without a theme,
> For depravation, to square the general sex
> By Cressid's rule. Rather think this not Cressid.
> ULYSSES
> What hath she done, Prince, that can soil our mothers?
>
> V.ii.127

Throughout *Troilus and Cressida* the function of bawdy is to act as a belittling agent. Again and again we see Troilus trying to escape its influence, only to find it waiting for him round the next corner. The personalities, even the very names, of Pandarus and Cressida undercut the prince's idealism with the deft scalpel of Shakespearean irony.

> I stalk about her door
> Like a strange soul upon the Stygian banks
> Staying for waftage. O, be thou my Charon,
> And give me swift transportation to these fields
> Where I may wallow in the lily beds
> Proposed for the deserver! O gentle Pandar . . . .
>
> III.ii.8

On its own small scale this speech typifies the kind of saturnine juxtaposition that recurs throughout the play. The more the lovers strain to make their actions transcendental, the more earthbound and physical the

office of a procurer shows them to be.[9] His ministrations never allow them
to escape from the comic plane for long at a time, and it is probably no
accident that this Pandarus, with his leering sensuality and clumsy wit,
becomes a great deal seedier than his original in Chaucer's *Troilus and
Criseyde*. Shakespeare also accords him the Vice's privilege of addressing
the audience directly, as his equals—

> And Cupid grant all tongue-tied maidens here,
> Bed, chamber, pander, to provide this gear!
>
> III.ii.206

> What a pair of spectacles is here!
>
> IV.iv.13

—with the result that even in their most deeply emotional scenes together
the lovers are made to look naive. Later, when Cressida has left Troy
and the play is moving towards its grey conclusion, the dispiriting quality
of her letter to Troilus ('Words, words, mere words, no matter from the
heart') is deepened by the go-between's accompanying recitation of what
the Elizabethans would have taken to be venereal symptoms:

> A whoreson tisick, a whoreson rascally tisick so troubles me, and the
> foolish fortune of this girl, and what with one thing, what another, that
> I shall leave you one o'th's days; and I have a rheum in mine eyes too,
> and such an ache in my bones that unless a man were cursed I cannot
> tell what to think on't.
>
> V.iii.101

The general malaise that Pandarus describes could in fact arise from
syphilis in its lengthy secondary phase, just as the watering eyes and
aching joints could be symptoms of the iritis and arthritis sometimes
associated with gonorrhoea in an advanced stage.[10] When Pandarus
again returns to the theme of his disease in speaking the play's epilogue,
he completes the flyblown frame in which Troilus and Cressida are
enclosed; and his farewell tag

> Full merrily the humble-bee doth sing
> Till he hath lost his honey and his sting

may well remind us of that sad observation from Troilus which could be
the motto for much of the play: 'This is the monstruosity in love, lady,
that the will is infinite, and the execution confined; that the desire is
boundless, and the act a slave to limit' (III.ii.78).

Shakespeare would not be Shakespeare, however, if he allowed
Troilus and Cressida simply to illustrate this aphorism straightforwardly,

without complications. One major source of complexity is the characterisation of Cressida. Like Chaucer before him Shakespeare avoids
putting himself in the position of having to defend easy virtue, but he
heaps up a generous measure of sympathy for Cressida by emphasising
her self-distrust. When we first meet her she sounds as randy as her
modern reputation would lead us to expect:

> CRESSIDA . . . If I cannot ward what I would not have hit, I can watch
> you for telling how I took the blow; unless it swell past hiding, and
> then it's past watching.
> PANDARUS   You are such another!
>
> I.ii.260

Yet when this same girl arrives at the moment of surrender to Troilus,
nothing could be further from the cool self-possession of a practised tart.

> CRESSIDA
> My lord, I do beseech you, pardon me;
> 'Twas not my purpose thus to beg a kiss.
> I am ashamed. O heavens! what have I done?
> For this time will I take my leave, my lord.
> TROILUS   Your leave, sweet Cressid!
> PANDARUS   Leave! An you take leave till tomorrow morning—
> CRESSIDA   Pray you, content you.
> TROILUS   What offends you, lady?
> CRESSIDA   Sir, mine own company.
> TROILUS   You cannot shun yourself.
> CRESSIDA   Let me go and try.
> I have a kind of self resides with you;
> But an unkind self, that it self will leave
> To be another's fool. I would be gone.
> Where is my wit? I know not what I speak.
> TROILUS
> Well know they what they speak that speak so wisely.
> CRESSIDA
> Perchance, my lord, I show more craft than love;
> And fell so roundly to a large confession
> To angle for your thoughts; but you are wise—
> Or else you love not; for to be wise and love
> Exceeds man's might; that dwells with gods above.
>
> III.ii.133

There is nothing to suggest that these hesitations are faked. On the contrary, they give expression to a kind of residual innocence, akin to that of
Dylan Thomas's Polly Garter; and the innocence shows up all the more
plainly because of its contrast with the undiscriminating seductiveness of
Helen in the immediately preceding scene. Shakespeare's whole treatment

of Cressida as a character is similar to his procedure with Julius Caesar. Inheriting both flattering and unflattering portraits of the one person, he embodies both of them in his play and then characterises other people— Troilus and Diomedes, for example—according to the partial views they select. Troilus sees in the girl nothing but perfection at first ('Her bed is India; there she lies, a pearl', I.i.99), and in the end nothing but perfidy ('This she? No, this is Diomed's Cressida', V.ii.135). Ulysses sees only the courtesan:

> Fie, fie upon her!
> There's language in her eye, her cheek, her lip;
> Nay, her foot speaks . . . .
>
> IV.v.54

For us in the audience she is all these Cressidas and more: a kaleidoscopic creation whose fine changes of emotion and perception make the blunt phrase 'As false as Cressid' sound almost tragically crude.

When it comes to blunt phrases, there can be no outdoing Thersites, whose tireless commentary emphasises a relationship between sexual appetite and the sordid, tired Trojan war. 'All the argument is a whore and a cuckold,' he declares, and the play's numerous jibes at Helen as adulteress and at Menelaus as cuckold give the line a measure of aphoristic truth. By the time one has watched Helen of Troy flirting with Pandarus, and Hector being butchered on the orders of the 'great' Achilles whose life he has just spared, it becomes easy to share the cynicism of Thersites's parrot-cry 'Lechery, lechery! Still wars and lechery!' Easy, yet not quite adequate. True to Homer's account of him—Chapman's translation calls him the filthiest Greek that came to Troy[11]— Thersites has a gift for nosing out all that is vicious or worthless, and it is typical of him that when Troilus, Cressida and Diomedes pass before him he registers only a gross, caricatured picture of their situation. On other matters too his railing becomes so monotonously shrill as to be self-defeating: after a time we automatically discount about three-quarters of what he says. This makes it peculiarly appropriate that Hector should not bother killing such a self-confessed knave: as a living symbol of depravity, Thersites is more a byproduct of the long war than a force in it. It also seems right that his scurrilities should in the end turn inwards upon himself: 'I am a bastard too; I love bastards. I am a bastard begot, bastard instructed, bastard in mind, bastard in valour, in everything illegitimate. . . . Farewell, bastard' (V.vii.16). Coming where it does, only a few minutes before Pandarus's venereal epilogue, this strikes what will prove to be the final note of the play—a tone not so much of total sexual revulsion as of just a sick futility. For some critics it represents the logical and inescapable outcome of the whole thing. In A. P. Rossiter's view, for example,[12]

> There is no such thing as true honour (based on genuine values) on either side, Trojan or Greek. All the high thinking comes to nothing: ceases to apply the moment men have to act. It is *doing* that counts . . . . Moreover, it is passion that leads to the act; and the impassioned will (lustful or furious) is impervious to right reason.

It seems to me, however, that this uncompromisingly nihilistic reading promotes Thersites, Pandarus and the disillusioned Troilus to positions of undue dominance. That these three combine to bring the tragi-comedy to its conclusion in a waste of shame cannot be denied, but to argue backwards from this, maintaining that simple lust was all that originally motivated Troilus and Cressida, is to oversimplify. What Shakespeare showed us in the first three acts was not the plain lechery that Thersites would allege, but love—albeit a love subject to circumstance and human limitations: 'The desire is boundless, and the act a slave to limit.' It is in defining that limit, rather than in trying to destroy the love-ideal itself, that bawdy plays a major part.

At first glance, the pattern of scurrility in *Othello* looks very like that of *Hamlet*. In both tragedies men of princely bearing and sensibility give vent to vicious obscenities, the outcome of disillusion over the supposed nature of women they love. Desdemona and Ophelia are innocent and chaste, yet both are spoken to as if they were prostitutes; and Hamlet's neurotic haranguing of his mother finds a parallel in Othello's accounts of Desdemona's 'crime':

> What committed!
> Committed? O, thou public commoner!
> I should make very forges of my cheeks,
> That would to cinders burn up modesty,
> Did I but speak thy deeds. What committed?
> Heaven stops the nose at it, and the moon winks;
> The bawdy wind, that kisses all it meets,
> Is hushed within the hollow mine of earth
> And will not hear it. What committed?
> Impudent strumpet!

IV.ii.71

There are major differences, however. Hamlet's bawdy is largely self-generating, whereas Othello's is artificially induced, caught, like jealousy itself, as a sickness from Iago. Along with Iago's susceptibility to sexual jealousy (revealed in his far-fetched suspicion of both Othello and Cassio with his 'night-cap') goes a readiness to envisage other people's sexual activities in salacious detail: 'Even now, now, very now, an old black ram / Is tupping your white ewe.' When this combines with the bawdy-monger's invariable gift for caricature—'you'll have your daughter covered with a Barbary horse; you'll have your nephews neigh to you'— it easily succeeds in unnerving Brabantio and stimulating the unimaginative Roderigo.

As the plot develops, Shakespeare uses Iago's lubricious turn of mind to establish salient facts about each of the other main characters. With Desdemona, for example, newly arrived in Cyprus and anxiously awaiting Othello, Iago takes on the temporary role of court jester:

> IAGO   Come on, come on: you are pictures out of doors, bells in your
>   parlours, wild-cats in your kitchens, . . . players in your housewifery,
>   and housewives in your beds.
> DESDEMONA
>   O, fie upon thee, slanderer!
> IAGO
>   Nay, it is true, or else I am a Turk:
>   You rise to play and go to bed to work.
>
> II.i.108

But the *risqué* chaff is wasted on Desdemona. Her main attention remains fixed on the harbour, alert for any sign of Othello's safety. There is a nice social nuance, too, in her turning away from Iago to listen instead to the more sympathetic and courtly Cassio. The 'daily beauty' in Cassio's life that helps to intensify the Ancient's envy becomes apparent here. It can be glimpsed again, just before the brawl, in another of Iago's rare conversational failures:

> IAGO   . . . Our General cast us thus early for the love of his Desdemona;
>   who let us not therefore blame. He hath not yet made wanton the
>   night with her; and she is sport for Jove.
> CASSIO   She is a most exquisite lady.
> IAGO   And, I'll warrant her, full of game.
> CASSIO   Indeed, she is a most fresh and delicate creature.
> IAGO   What an eye she has! Methinks it sounds a parley to provocation.
> CASSIO   An inviting eye, and yet methinks right modest.
> IAGO   And when she speaks, is it not an alarum to love?
> CASSIO   She is indeed perfection.
> IAGO   Well, happiness to their sheets! Come, Lieutenant, I have a stoup
>   of wine . . . .
>
> II.iii.14

Whether this represents an attempt to elicit some quotable indiscretion from Cassio, or merely a device to promote his sexual interest in Desdemona, Shakespeare does not specify. The passage could legitimately be acted in either way, and it would still serve to bring out the opposed cast of mind of the two speakers. The Lieutenant will not be drawn on such a topic, least of all by his social and military inferior. So with Cassio, just as with Desdemona, Iago's temporary rebuff illustrates a propriety that shows the victims' innocence but which also, in the long run, will increase their vulnerability.

No such defeats, small or large, can be recorded of Iago's machinations with Othello. It is typical of the villain's caution that in the early stages of the 'temptation' he speaks scarcely any bawdy at all. When he first risks the word *cuckold* it is only in the context of the warning, 'O, beware, my lord, of jealousy!' (III.iii.163–8). Similarly, the first references to horns— 'this forkèd plague . . . a pain upon my forehead here' (III.iii.273, 281)— come from Othello himself, while Iago is off-stage. Only when the Moor's passion has grown and he cries out for proof does Iago allow his side of the conversation to take a concupiscent turn:

> But how? How satisfied, my lord?
> Would you, the supervisor, grossly gape on?
> Behold her topped?
>
> .   .   .   .
> It is impossible you should see this,
> Were they as prime as goats, as hot as monkeys,
> As salt as wolves in pride, and fools as gross
> As ignorance made drunk.
>
> III.iii.391, 399

From this he moves on to his account of Cassio's alleged dream: a doubly bawdy piece of fiction, this, since it combines indefinite suggestions of sodomy with the most precise description of a coital act in the whole of Shakespeare. As a device for compelling Othello to think precisely on the event of adultery, it could scarcely be bettered.

It is interesting that the interlude in which Cassio asks Bianca to copy the handkerchief (III.iv.165–97) involves little ribaldry, despite Bianca's being a courtesan. The original reason for this may lie in Shakespeare's presumed source, Giambattista Giraldi Cinthio's story of Disdemona of Venice and the Moorish Captain, where the handkerchief-copier is not the same woman as the harlot.[18] But whatever the original cause of this scene's fairly low sexual temperature, one of its effects is to provide a cool contrast with the distracted fevers of Othello before and after it. No sooner are Iago and Othello back on stage than Iago has introduced the 'naked in bed' image that brings on Othello's fit. After that, the bawdy comes thick and fast, with Iago using every gratuitous detail that his libidinous imagination offers.

OTHELLO
  A hornèd man's a monster and a beast.
IAGO
  There's many a beast then in a populous city,
  And many a civil monster.
OTHELLO
  Did he confess it?
IAGO   Good sir, be a man.
  Think every bearded fellow that's but yoked
  May draw with you. There's millions now alive
  That nightly lie in those unproper beds
  Which they dare swear peculiar. Your case is better.
  O, 'tis the spite of hell, the fiend's arch-mock,
  To lip a wanton in a secure couch,
  And to suppose her chaste!

                                                    IV.i.62

Shakespeare so arranges matters that chance also lends a hand. Bianca, returning with the handkerchief, flies out at Cassio in jealousy, and the words reaching Othello bank the fires of his imagination still higher:

  A likely piece of work, that you should find it in your chamber,
  and not know who left it there! This is some minx's token, and
  I must take out the work? There, give it your hobby-horse,
  wheresoever you had it.

                                                    IV.i.151

This short scene, like almost all the verbal bawdy in *Othello*, is Shakespear's invention. In Cinthio, the Moor only sees the handkerchief from the street, while Cassio's servant is copying it. Shakespeare's handling of the episode, by contrast, makes bawdy as much a part of the plot machinery for a few moments as the handkerchief itself.

  Throughout the rest of the play a desperate form of bawdy serves as an indicator of Othello's fluctuating self-control. When most in command of himself—questioning Emilia at the start of IV.ii, for instance—he sounds almost as he used to: dignified, even austere. But the very sight of Desdemona stirs up in him grotesque imaginings, as in the 'brothel' scene, IV.ii.23–93. At the beginning of the murder scene (V.ii), the restraint in his monologue produces a conscious avoidance of obscenity:

            It is the cause, it is the cause, my soul:
            Let me not name it to you, you chaste stars!
            It is the cause.

Although Othello's tone is priestlike, obscurantist, the explicit acknowledgement of a sexual linguistic taboo at least shows him containing his feelings, after his fashion. Once Desdemona has wakened, however, he gradually gives way to fury, and the spectacle of her weeping for Cassio brings a return to brothel-talk, even as he reaches for the pillow to smother her:

DESDEMONA
  Alas, he is betrayed, and I undone.
OTHELLO
  Out, strumpet! Weep'st thou for him to my face?
DESDEMONA
  O banish me, my lord, but kill me not!
OTHELLO
  Down, strumpet!

V.ii.77

Fifty lines later, in much the same way, a reversion to bawdy articulates his rage at Emilia's plain speaking. 'She turned to folly; and she was a whore. . . . Cassio did top her: ask thy husband else.' This proves to be the last of these outbursts. Once the revelation of true facts has begun to cleanse Othello's imagination, indecency has no further place in the tragedy. 'Moor, she was chaste; she loved thee, cruel Moor.'

A word or two must be added regarding the willow song and the conversation in which it is set. The final verse of the ballad—

> I called my love false love, but what said he then?
>   Sing willow, willow, willow:
> If I court moe women, you'll couch with moe men

IV.iii.52

—serves much the same dramatic function as the bawdy in Ophelia's songs. Putting it in naturalistic terms one might say that by a Freudian error, Desdemona at first forgets about this verse, starting on another in its place:

DESDEMONA (*singing*)
  Let nobody blame him; his scorn I approve—
    (*She speaks*)
  Nay, that's not next. Hark, who is't that knocks?
EMILIA   It's the wind.

IV.iii.49

On recollecting the missing stanza, she can instantly see its macabre relevance to her own situation, as also can the audience. With a speed and force that are possible only in drama, the stanza reminds her of a whole bleak realm of human experience that she has never known at first hand until now. She asks Emilia about it.

> Dost thou in conscience think—tell me, Emilia—
> That there be women do abuse their husbands
> In such gross kind?

IV.iii.58

Emilia's lightly cynical, lightly ribald answers, slipping unobtrusively into blank verse as they gather momentum, do more for the play than merely re-emphasise Desdemona's innocence. They speak straight to the audience in support of what a later age was to call women's rights. Shakespeare has come a long way, ideologically, since the subservience of poor Katherina, the tamed shrew. Beyond that again, Emilia's apologia, even by its very pace and tone, establishes for *Othello* as a whole the feeling that reasonableness still exists, that despite all the perversions and furies an ordinary recognisable world will somehow prevail.

It may be that Shakespeare had a similar implicit reassurance in mind when he introduced the Clown into two earlier scenes, III.i.1–29 and III.iv.1–22. If so, those scenes fail to achieve it, and in my view the ingenious but strained interpretations of them that some recent critics have put forward only reinforce Shakespeare's own defeat.[14] But Emilia's speeches in the last pages of IV.iii succeed, to my mind unchallengeably, in providing the play with a norm of sanity just when it needs it most. Their touches of bawdy, coming within minutes of the most inflamed of Othello's outbursts, give a good indication of the skill and precision with which the Shakespeare of 1604, or a year or two earlier, has learned to use the bitter and lighthearted aspects of indecency in forceful combination.

William Hazlitt wrote of *King Lear*: 'It is then the best of all Shakespear's plays, for it is the one in which he was the most in earnest.' While that sweeping appraisal may raise a patronising smile in our more sophisticated but less self-confident critical age, *Lear* remains undisputedly a major document in what has been called the genre of wisdom literature. In the light of its general earnestness, the prominent place which this tragedy gives to bawdy might seem anomalous, were it not that *Hamlet* and *Othello* had already shown how much tragic power Shakespeare's use of sexual indecency could command.

Like *Romeo and Juliet*, *Lear* involves us in bawdy conversation almost as soon as it has begun.

> KENT   Is not this your son, my lord?
> GLOUCESTER   His breeding, sir, hath been at my charge. I have so often blushed to acknowledge him that now I am brazed to it.
> KENT   I cannot conceive you.
> GLOUCESTER   Sir, this young fellow's mother could; whereupon she grew round-wombed, and had indeed, sir, a son for her cradle ere she had a husband for her bed. Do you smell a fault?
> KENT   I cannot wish the fault undone, the issue of it being so proper.

GLOUCESTER ... Though this knave came something saucily to the
world, before he was sent for, yet was his mother fair; there was good
sport at his making, and the whoreson must be acknowledged.

I.i.7

This firm placing of Edmund's bastardy has obvious importance in a play
whose double plot will hinge on father-child relationships. Edmund,
deprived of legitimate claims to power and wealth, seeks to gain these
ends by Machiavellian means. In broad outline, Shakespeare's Gloucester
plot is following its apparent source, the story of the Paphlagonian King
and his two sons, in Sidney's *Arcadia*.[15] It makes an important difference,
however, that whereas Sidney plunged *in medias res* with an already
chastened father, one who had little to say about the concubine who bore
his bastard son, Shakespeare presents Gloucester as being quite ebullient
over the whole business. The hearty tone of Gloucester's 'confession' to
Kent is much like that of the later soliloquy (I.ii.2–15) in which Edmund
contrasts himself with 'honest madam's issue' and the tribe of fops created
within a dull, stale, tired bed. Father and son sound very much alike, and
before the end of the play both will have been forced out of their pro-
tective shells of flippancy. Edmund will try to defend his new-gained
honour on chivalric ground of Edgar's choosing, and will fail. Gloucester's sowing of wild oats will come under stricture—

> The gods are just, and of our pleasant vices
> Make instruments to plague us:
> The dark and vicious place where thee he got
> Cost him his eyes.

V.iii.168

Although this Calvinistic judgement is not fully endorsed by the play as a
whole, it adds its own wryness to our recollection of Gloucester's jocularity. Far from lightening the sombre shades of Sidney's Paphlagonian
story, the bawdy added by Shakespeare serves ultimately to darken the
picture still more.

The mild indecencies associated with Edmund's illegitimacy also have
a farther-reaching function: they join with certain of the Fool's jokes,
the ravings of 'Poor Tom', the sexy plottings of Gonerill and Regan
over Oswald and Edmund, and finally with Lear's own insights, to fill
out the play's vision of the sexual urge as a force in human destiny.
Edmund notes in his father

> the excellent foppery of the world, that when we are sick in fortune—
> often the surfeits of our own behaviour—we make guilty of our disasters
> the sun, the moon, and stars, as if we were villains on necessity, ...
> drunkards, liars, and adulterers by an enforced obedience of planetary

influence; and all that we are evil in, by a divine thrusting-on. An
admirable evasion of whoremaster man, to lay his goatish disposition to
the charge of a star.

I.ii.118

About his father, Edmund is largely right. As the play goes on, Gloucester
indeed barely rises beyond this level of thought; but it is far otherwise
with Lear. For a start he has the Fool to guide him, a commentator who is
always ready to call his master's bluff when Lear would deny any share in
the blame for his own sufferings. A good deal of the Fool's bawdy is
merely peripheral—casual odds and ends of popular material forming
part of his repertoire as a court jester.

> LEAR
> O me, my heart, my rising heart! But down!
> FOOL   Cry to it, nuncle, as the cockney did to the eels when she put
> 'em i' the paste alive. She knapped 'em o' the coxcombs with a stick
> and cried 'Down, wantons, down!'

II.iv.116

There are times, though, when this ribaldry strikes tangentially at the
ever-circling question of Lear's lack of foresight in giving all to his
hypocrite daughters.

> The cod-piece that will house
> Before the head has any,
> The head and he shall louse;
> So beggars marry many.

III.ii.27

Another effect of bawdy in the Fool's role is the creation around Lear
of a chilled pathos at moments of climax. For example, only a few
seconds after Lear's heart-rending plea 'O let me not be mad, not mad,
sweet heaven!' we hear from the Fool the surprising couplet

> She that's a maid now, and laughs at my departure,
> Shall not be a maid long, unless things be cut shorter.

I.v.48

This slight and bizarrely placed version of the *thing* joke suggests the
experienced clown who, on discovering some emotional situation that
he cannot deal with, falls back behind the defensive barrier of his professional routine. Like Chaplin or Archie Rice, Lear's Fool is squaring his
shoulders, switching on a grin and 'cracking a joke'—in this particular
instance a bawdy one. Much the same effect occurs at the end of III.ii:

> When priests are more in word than matter,
> When brewers mar their malt with water,
> When nobles are their tailors' tutors,
> No heretics burned, but wenches' suitors—

.   .   .   .   .

> When usurers tell their gold i' the field,
> And bawds and whores do churches build—
> Then comes the time, who lives to see't,
> That going shall be used with feet.
>
> III.ii.81, 91

At the end of the eighteenth century, George Steevens, who always had an eye for the salacious, observed that this piece of doggerel looked like a parody of some pseudo-Chaucerian lines to be found in Puttenham's *Art of English Poesy* (1589).[16] But the parody, if parody it is, quickly becomes a satiric turn in its own right—the staring-eyed vision of a court jester who is going mad along with his master. Just as with the 'She that's a maid now' couplet, the members of the theatre audience find the Fool suddenly stepping out of the fictional frame to address them in an absurdist way. So addressed, they become at once more sympathetic and more uneasy—uneasy, particularly, over any such concept as destiny or predetermination.

With so disconcerting a jester at his side, Lear is unlikely to remain satisfied with the fatalism and moral evasiveness of a Gloucester. Part of the 'physic' for his madness, consequently, is a long process of anatomising the more destructive human appetites. The assistance of Poor Tom in this process makes it inevitable that the sexual appetite will loom large among the rest, since the disguised Edgar harps insistently on the themes of fornication and adultery.

> LEAR   What hast thou been?
> EDGAR   A servingman, proud in heart and mind, that curled my hair,
> wore gloves in my cap, served the lust of my mistress' heart and did
> the act of darkness with her; ... one that slept in the contriving of
> lust and waked to do it. Wine loved I deeply, dice dearly, and in
> woman out-paramoured the Turk.... Keep thy foot out of brothels,
> thy hand out of plackets, thy pen from lenders' books, and defy the
> foul fiend.
>
> III.iv.81

A number of the freely associated images of concupiscence from the play's mad scenes find dramatic embodiment in the plots and counter-plots of Regan and Gonerill to get the 'love' of Edmund. (For Gonerill there is also Oswald, quite literally a serving-man proud in heart and mind.) Between them, these characters provide an active manifestation of the riotous appetite on which Lear harangues Gloucester:

> Adultery?
> Thou shalt not die. Die for adultery? No.
> The wren goes to't, and the small gilded fly
> Does lecher in my sight.

Let copulation thrive; for Gloucester's bastard son
Was kinder to his father than my daughters
Got 'tween the lawful sheets.
To't, luxury, pell-mell, for I lack soldiers.
Behold yon simpering dame
Whose face between her forks presages snow,
That minces virtue and does shake the head
To hear of pleasure's name—
The fitchew nor the soiled horse goes to't
With a more riotous appetite.
Down from the waist they are centaurs,
Though women all above;
But to the girdle do the gods inherit,
Beneath is all the fiends'—
There's hell, there's darkness, there is the sulphurous pit—
burning, scalding, stench, consumption!

IV.vi.110

Kenneth Muir[17] has pointed out resemblances between this speech and phrases in Samuel Harsnett's *Declaration of Egregious Popish Impostures*, (1603). It is typical of Shakespeare's deliberate way with bawdy, by the time he writes *Lear* in 1605 or 1606, that he should ignore the lightweight indecencies available to him in *The True Chronicle History of King Leir and his Three Daughters* (published in May 1605) and take up instead, for Edgar as well as the King, much more lurid sexual material from Harsnett's attack on Jesuit exorcists. The characteristic exaggerations of bawdy, as shown in the adultery monologue, are also central to *King Lear's* concern with the animal urges barely hidden beneath man's veneer of civilisation. Are these urges controllable? Vested authority tries to control them, just as Albany does his limited best to restrain Gonerill. But the authorities—kings, dukes, robed men of justice—are human too:

GLOUCESTER   O, let me kiss that hand!
LEAR   Let me wipe it first; it smells of mortality.

IV.vi.133

So it is that the great image of authority is a farmer's dog, a cur, chasing a beggar, or the beadle lashing a whore when 'Thou hotly lusts to use her in that kind / For which thou whipp'st her.' Once again Shakespeare is anticipating modern psychologists in defining an aspect of the earthly hell that has already found partial expression through the storm, through Edgar's wild chatter about animals, birds and devils,[18] and through the bestial cruelty of Regan and Cornwall.

We would look in vain to find in these middle scenes of the tragedy a powerful ideality established in the face of such images of universal corruption. But Cordelia is not far away, and when Lear awakens to see her as a soul in bliss she becomes the embodiment of an ideal—if not that of justice, then certainly that of forgiveness. Paradoxically, her power as a figure of love, sympathy and tolerance is not denied but confirmed when Shakespeare so manipulates his source material as to make the French army lose the battle in Act V. In Holinshed's *Chronicles* and again in Spenser (*The Faerie Queene*, II, x, 27–32), Regan and Gonorilla are beaten, and Cordeilla restores her father to the British throne. It is only some years after Leir's peaceful death that Cordeilla loses a battle against her sisters' sons, and in despair hangs herself. The *Chronicle History of King Leir* ends happily with Leir's restoration to the throne. When Shakespeare goes his own way by having Lear and Cordelia become Edmund's prisoners, he also has Lear transcend all the suffering and injustice in that great speech of resignation 'Come, let's away to prison' (V.iii.8–19). Later in the same scene, when Gonerill, having poisoned Regan, kills herself, the self-destroying nature of unrestrained appetite is exposed.

For a time it seems that the civilised order will gain a final triumph over Natural brutish man. Then Shakespeare throws everything open to doubt again with the killing of Cordelia. Her murder comes almost as much from sheer accident (Edmund's forgetfulness) as from vicious design, and this suggests the 'cheerless, dark, and deadly' insuperability of a random universe. If, on the other hand, Cordelia is still breathing as Lear lays her down, it will be a new miracle—as he puts it, 'a chance which does redeem all sorrows / That ever I have felt.' So the ultimate question of *King Lear*, the question of whether love and forgiveness can prevail against the combined assaults of human evildoing and inhuman chance, hangs on the stir of a feather. Shakespeare leaves the issue unresolved. Lear may die in hope, as has often been suggested, yet he does nevertheless die. The strength of the play lies not in its attempting to answer the great question but in its formulating it with superb fullness, clarity and vigour.

For some years now, critics of *Timon of Athens* have been in broad agreement that the play is unfinished and that it may even owe its inclusion in the First Folio to the temporary withdrawal of *Troilus and Cressida*.[19] This makes it unwise to draw any firm conclusions from its use of bawdy, as the internal proportions of the play might obviously have changed if Shakespeare had gone on working on it. In the text that has come down to us, the incidence of bawdy falls into something of the same shape as in *Othello*, though with important differences. The first three acts reveal comparatively little indecency, and what there is comes mainly from a self-evidently evil speaker, Apemantus. Act IV brings an explosion of bitter, impassioned obscenity from the play's hero. Timon's sexual revulsion is less solidly motivated than either Othello's or Lear's, since he suffers neither the apparent betrayal of a wife nor exposure to the ravings of a Poor Tom. Instead, only the arrival on the scene of Alcibiades and his two mistresses serves as immediate provocation for an elaborate fantasia on prostitution and sexual corruption in general. It is striking, too, that, unlike Othello and Lear, Timon never regains his sense of proportion. When he retreats into his cave to die, he does so in the unreconciled, irreconcilable spirit of an Apemantus, 'opposite to humanity'.

The scabrous wit of Apemantus as exhibited in the first two acts can be seen to stand squarely in the Thersites–Iago–Edmund tradition of black humour. Typically, Apemantus denies that human joy could ever have legitimate antecedents—'Ho, ho! I laugh to think that babe a bastard' (I.ii.109)—and the same ready-made cynicism informs all his sexual jokes. Timon is at first sane enough to reprove him:

TIMON   Wilt dine with me, Apemantus?
APEMANTUS   No. I eat not lords.
TIMON   An thou shouldst, thou'dst anger ladies.
APEMANTUS   O, they eat lords. So they come by great bellies.
TIMON   That's a lascivious apprehension.

                                                                          I.i.205

By the end of Act IV, however, Timon has ceased to disregard this self-confessed carper, and has instead become willing to argue with him on his characteristically brutish level.

Timon's own share of bawdy is wholly confined to Act IV, and it charts the final stages of his decline into nihilism. For a time it would pass for satire—

> Matrons, turn incontinent.
> Obedience, fail in children.
>   .   .   .   .   .
>   To general filths
> Convert o'th'instant, green virginity,
> Do't in your parents' eyes.
>   .   .   .   .   .
>   Maid, to thy master's bed;
> Thy mistress is o'th'brothel.

                                                                          IV.i.3

But as the soliloquy of IV.i rushes on, it becomes only a generalised and malevolent rant. The Timon who wishes cold sciatica upon senators, and who invites an engulfing riot of lust and liberty to 'Creep in the minds and marrows of our youth', with the whole process to culminate in itches, blains and general leprosy (here, as in *Henry V*, a venereal disease) —this Timon is not attacking things as they were, but rather indulging in a wild rhapsody of universal hate. That a large element of fear underlies the hatred may be deduced from the speaker's obsession with sexual disease, both in this monologue and in those of IV.iii. The arrival of Alcibiades with Phrynia and Timandra inspires in Timon a neurotic vision of all-consuming licentiousness. Though professionally greedy for gold, the two courtesans seem fairly harmless in themselves. The very fact that there are two of them rather than only one, as there was in Plutarch's account of Alcibiades' murder and burial,[20] makes their protector doubly debonair when he enters 'with drum and fife, in warlike manner'. To Timon, however, Phrynia is a fell whore—

> This fell whore of thine
> Hath in her more destruction than thy sword,
> For all her cherubin look.

IV.iii.62

Let us grant that Phrynia and Timandra are not Ophelia and Desdemona; but even the spuriousness of a courtesan's cherubin look gives little occasion for the pornographic caricature that Timon now goes on to draw:

> Be whores still.
> And he whose pious breath seeks to convert you—
> Be strong in whore, allure him, burn him up;
> Let your close fire predominate his smoke,
> And be no turncoats. Yet may your pains, six months,
> Be quite contrary; and thatch
> Your poor thin roofs with burdens of the dead—
> Some that were hanged. No matter.
> Wear them, betray with them, whore still.
> Paint till a horse may mire upon your face.
>
> .   .   .   .   .   .
>
> Consumptions sow
> In hollow bones of man; strike their sharp shins,
> And mar men's spurring. Crack the lawyer's voice,
> That he may never more false title plead,
> Nor sound his quillets shrilly. Hoar the flamen,
> That scolds against the quality of flesh
> And not believes himself. Down with the nose,
> Down with it flat, take the bridge quite away
> Of him that, his particular to foresee,
> Smells from the general weal. Make curled-pate ruffians bald,
> And let the unscarred braggarts of the war

> Derive some pain from you. Plague all,
> That your activity may defeat and quell
> The source of all erection.

IV.iii.140

So extreme and sustained is this diatribe of revulsion that it threatens to dislocate the whole fictional-historical framework of the play. One can hardly blame Shakespearean critics of ante-Sisson times for having sought some non-theatrical explanation of it all in the dramatist's biography. Yet Timon's fascinated loathing of the courtesans does make a kind of sense within the terms of reference fixed by the drama itself. In IV.iii the hero is scared, as he has always been scared. Only anxiety could account for the reckless lavishness of his generosity in the opening scenes, and the same personal insecurity now appears in paranoidal form:

> Let not the virgin's cheek
> Make soft thy trenchant sword; for those milk-paps
> That, through the window, bared, bore at men's eyes
> Are not within the leaf of pity writ,
> But set them down horrible traitors.

IV.iii.115

Timon's own shrillness confirms the truth of what Alcibiades observes— that the man is mad: 'Pardon him, sweet Timandra, for his wits / Are drowned and lost in his calamities.'

Unfortunately, this does not wholly dispose of the matter. Lear, too, is mad, but we do not for that reason disregard what he says about human depravity. If anything, the opposite is the case. With Timon, however, we have the odd situation that whereas Shakespeare presents the steward Flavius as a living contradiction of all the hero's *non*-sexual disillusion, he leaves the sexual revulsion to take care of itself. The calm normality of Alcibiades, for example, remains altogether too neutral to assert any opposing principle.[21] It might perhaps be argued that in a scene so roughly sketched as to include the Gilbertian repentances of the Bandits, the speeches of all minor characters, including Alcibiades, must be regarded as uncompleted; but such a claim belongs too firmly in the realm of conjecture to be critically helpful. If we take *Timon of Athens* as we find it. we have to acknowledge that most of its bawdy does indeed expose the mental world of one who never knew the middle of humanity but only 'the extremity of both ends'. That this extremist was not Shakespeare but Shakespeare's Timon, the other tragedies amply prove. And the unfinished *Timon* stands alone with *Troilus and Cressida* in allowing cynicism about sexual experience to be its last word on the subject.

*   *   *

From most critical viewpoints, *Cymbeline* fits tidily into the place that chronology gives it, among Shakespeare's last plays. Recent editors have hazarded guesses of 1608 or 1609 as its most probable time of composition,[22] and it has long been regarded as a companion piece to its close successor or contemporary, *The Winter's Tale*. Like both *The Winter's Tale* and *Pericles*, it has a plot that belongs in the romance genre, and many of its underlying concerns—loyalty, chastity, separation, remorse, reconciliation—are shared with *The Tempest* also. So far as its use of bawdy is concerned, however, *Cymbeline* belies this grouping. Its affinities are with *Othello*, *Lear* and *Timon*, plays in which the sexual elements are rarely funny and often sinister. Perhaps the dark implications of *Cymbeline's* bawdy can best be brought out by a survey of its functions for each of the three characters to whom most of it belongs—Iachimo, Posthumus and Cloten.

It has become a commonplace of *Cymbeline* criticism that Iachimo is no Iago. He has been said to lack both the sense of purpose and the steady malignity of the earlier villain: 'there is something fantastic about the fellow,' wrote Granville-Barker, 'and no tragically-potent scoundrel, we should be sure, will ever come out of a trunk.'[23] That is true so far as it goes. Iachimo does partake of the grotesque quality that characterises much of this whole play. But to stress his sub-tragic stature is beside the point. Like the Queen, the King's sons and Belarius, Iachimo *as a character* is a stock figure, yet his scheming comes close to being as vicious as Iago's, both in style and in result. When he sets out to incite jealousy, first in Posthumus and later in Imogen, his mode of suggestiveness is exactly Iago's: 'You may wear her in title yours; but you know strange fowl light upon neighbouring ponds. . . . If you buy ladies' flesh at a million a dram, you cannot preserve it from tainting' (I.iv.84, 130). And he uses another Iago-like technique when he makes sudden, unnerving lurches into bawdy exaggeration:

> O dearest soul, your cause doth strike my heart
> With pity that doth make me sick! A lady
> So fair, and fastened to an empery,
> Would make the great'st king double, to be partnered
> With tomboys hired with that self exhibition
> Which your own coffers yield! with diseased ventures
> That play with all infirmities for gold
> Which rottenness can lend nature! such boiled stuff
> As well might poison poison!

I.vi.117

The decisive difference, I would suggest, is not between Iachimo and Iago but between the royal Imogen and naive Desdemona. While both

heroines serve as the embodiment of wifely loyalty, Imogen's loyalty is
of a more mature order than Desdemona's. The effect of this difference
on the tonality of the entire play can be felt when Imogen rounds on
Iachimo to answer him with princely vigour.

So far so good, one might feel, were it not for the King's hostility to
his daughter. Clearsighted though she is, she cannot know what Shakespeare allows us in the audience to know—that she is already encircled by
people who are, in one way or another, her enemies. So the trunk plot
succeeds, and Imogen's next indirect assailant is Posthumus himself.

Posthumus speaks no bawdy lines in the play until after becoming
convinced that Imogen has committed adultery. He then falls victim to a
typically Jacobean sexual nausea.

> No, he hath enjoyed her.
> The cognizance of her incontinency
> Is this: she hath bought the name of whore thus dearly.
> .   .   .   .   .
> Never talk on't;
> She hath been colted by him.
>
> II.iv.126

The misogynous soliloquy that ends Act II has been censured as wild and
disintegrating.[24] Certainly the lines show bathos and a measure of incoherence, but it is a literal rather than emotional incoherence, and, as
with *Cymbeline* as a whole, the disparities and absurdities are part of the
point. Life is a disparate business, and Imogen's tough, resourceful struggle
with it forms an extended contrast with Posthumus's easy disillusion.
His rant is the outpouring of a mind temporarily unhinged by that
disillusion. Further, as we in the audience well know, Posthumus is
entirely wrong about Imogen, who still is 'As chaste as unsunned snow'.
Shakespeare accordingly lessens our empathy with the hero by making
his fulminations bawdily absurd.

> O, all the devils!
> This yellow Iachimo in an hour—was't not?
> Or less!—at first? Perchance he spoke not, but,
> Like a full-acorned boar, a German one,
> Cried 'O!' and mounted; found no opposition
> But what he looked for should oppose and she
> Should from encounter guard.
>
> II.v.13

The distancing of Posthumus can be seen on a larger scale in what seems
at first glance to be a major dislocation in the structure of the play: we
are not shown the hero's recovery from his Act II state of bitterness. He

simply disappears for two whole acts, and by the time we meet him again in V.i he is calm, repentant and on the point of seeking death as punishment for having had Imogen murdered. Yet in leaving a gap in Posthumus's story, Shakespeare has been less careless than he may seem. His primary interest—the play's primary interest—is in Imogen, and the progress of the action after Posthumus's second-act tirade encourages us to relate everything to her rather than to him. What we then see is resilient and chaste womanhood sustaining a long series of attacks—from Cymbeline and his Queen, from Cloten and Iachimo, from Posthumus, and from the deceptiveness and chanciness of life itself.

With Cloten, as with Iachimo, and even with Posthumus in his wager-taking, the threat is specifically directed against Imogen's chastity. Cloten makes an interesting comparison with one Armenio, his counterpart in *The Rare Triumphs of Love and Fortune*, a play of the early 1580s on which *Cymbeline* seems to be based. Of the two, Cloten has much the bawdier turn of mind, so that the total share of lubricity is altogether larger in the economy of Shakespeare's play than in *Love and Fortune*. This shambling lecher at court represents no less a danger to Imogen's safety than does Iachimo. So closely do their separate schemes interlock, indeed, that it often seems impossible that she can escape, despite the spasmodic hopes held out in some quasi-choric speeches from the Second Lord and Pisanio (II.i.54–63, III.v.157–62, IV.iii.36–46). Emblematically, Imogen's bedside reading is the story of Tereus, a tale of rape and mutilation: 'here the leaf's turned down,' notes Iachimo, 'Where Philomel gave up.' As he returns fearfully to his claustrophobic hiding-place he looks again towards Imogen and adds: 'Though this a heavenly angel, hell is here.' The words take on a double truth, because they have barely died away before Cloten arrives on stage, ready to reel off coarse jokes to his hired musicians.

> Come on, tune. If you can penetrate her with your fingering, so. We'll try with tongue too. . . . If this penetrate, I will consider your music the better; if it do not, it is a vice in her ears which horsehairs and calves' guts, nor the voice of unpaved eunuch to boot, can never amend.
>
> II.iii.13, 28

The peculiar vileness of Cloten's *double entendres* comes from their being delivered as monologues rather than in the course of any conversational cut and thrust. Shared between two or more speakers his innuendos would pass as harmless chatter. Flowing uninterruptedly from the black holes of a single mind, they acquire a quality of sniggering gaucheness. On the stage Cloten can take on a certain pathos, not unlike that of Middleton's somewhat similar creation The Ward in *Women Beware*

Women. But despite occasional flashes of authorial pity, neither Shakespeare nor Middleton leaves any doubt about the hideous threat that such a creature would represent in the role of lover. Cloten amounts to more than 'that harsh, noble, simple nothing' whom Imogen describes, and when he conceives his plan for raping her it becomes only too easy to imagine his being able to succeed. He is—to adapt another of Granville-Barker's phrases—an educated Caliban.

It is all the more disconcerting, consequently, when Imogen, reviving from deathly unconsciousness outside Belarius's cave, finds Cloten as her headless 'bedfellow' and mistakes him for Posthumus. This weird occurrence bears out in action Imogen's own aphorism, 'Our very eyes / Are sometimes, like our judgements, blind.' But if that were all, Shakespeare's far-fetched stage situation would be a crazily elaborate way of making so ordinary a point. What should be borne in mind as well is the lingering influence of the obsequies that so shortly preceded Imogen's awakening. When Belarius, Guiderius and Arviragus strewed their flowers over the pair of bodies, male and female, the funeral rites merged into marriage symbolism; and that makes it surprisingly easy to imagine now, with Imogen's help, that her pursuer Cloten and her husband Posthumus have mysteriously merged their identities. 'Thersites' body is as good as Ajax', / When neither are alive.' At the risk of over-schematising the play, one might envisage Cloten as a satanic 'shadow' of Posthumus in much the same way as Wagner in *The Ring* sees Alberich and Wotan as two aspects of the same power-figure.[25] In all superficial ways Cloten and Posthumus are utterly unlike, yet both have sought Imogen's love, only to turn on her in hate.

Happily this uncanny identification of hero and villain is no more than an illusion, a stage trick. Cloten will stay dead, while Posthumus—his name presages it—survives to be reunited with Imogen:

> Why did you throw your wedded lady from you?
> Think that you are upon a rock, and now
> Throw me again.

V.v.261

Our instinctual certainty that he will never again reject her represents a double victory for the wifely ideal that she embodies.[26] Like Lear, Posthumus has emerged from sick revulsion into a new world of sanity and forgiveness, and Imogen has at the same time escaped the clouds of hostile, bawdy sexuality that hung about her for so long. In the face of an opposite that was dangerous as well as mocking, ideality has been doubly affirmed.

*   *   *

As an end-note to this chapter, a word or two about *Pericles*, which comes strikingly close to *Cymbeline* in feeling and not far ahead of it in date (*c.* 1607/8). The widely held opinion that Shakespeare did not write the play's first two acts need not concern us here, since it happens that these acts, at least in the form in which they have reached us via the Quarto of 1608, introduce no bawdy. On discovering the incest between Antiochus and his daughter, Pericles shows disgust, but not the hysterical kind of disgust that finds expression in gross terms. The play then continues free of verbal indecency—even in II.i, the fishermen's scene—until IV.ii, by which time we are well inside the segment generally accepted as Shakespeare's.

The three brothel scenes, IV.ii, v and vi, have often been compared with the underworld scenes of *Measure for Measure*, but again *Cymbeline* makes the apter parallel. For Marina as for Imogen, the situation is one of virtue-in-danger, and it is presented here with an archetypal simplicity of outline. The physical and moral degradation threatening Marina is boldly dramatised in the utter dejection of the Pander and his troop when they first appear:

> BAWD   We were never so much out of creatures. We have but poor
> three, and they can do no more than they can do; and they with
> continual action are even as good as rotten. . . . The stuff we have, a
> strong wind will blow it to pieces, they are so pitifully sodden.
> PANDER   Thou sayest true; they are too unwholesome, o' conscience.
> The poor Transylvanian is dead that lay with the little baggage.
>
> IV.ii.7,18

Insistence on the deadly physical corruptiveness of the brothel can be heard again in the discussion of Monsieur Veroles, 'the French knight that cowers i'th'hams' (IV.ii.104), and yet again in the breezy arrival of Lysimachus:

> LYSIMACHUS   How now! How a dozen of virginities?
> BAWD   Now, the gods to bless your Honour!
> BOULT   I am glad to see your Honour in good health.
> LYSIMACHUS   You may so; 'tis the better for you that your resorters
> stand upon sound legs. How now! Wholesome iniquity have you,
> that a man may deal withal and defy the surgeon?
>
> IV.vi.19

Such an emphasis heightens suspense over Marina's fate, while at the same time eliminating even for the most hard-boiled of audiences any risk of her being thought priggish. Comparison between this part of the play and its source material, the thirteenth and fourteenth chapters of Lawrence Twyne's novel *The Pattern of Painful Adventures*,[27] shows the dramatist making the most of the brothel-keepers' cold-bloodedness but playing down Twyne's suggestion that their trade is rich. The new stress falls rather on their depraved lust.

> BAWD Boult, take her away; use her at thy pleasure. Crack the glass of her virginity, and make the rest malleable.
> BOULT An if she were a thornier piece of ground than she is, she shall be ploughed.
>
> IV.vi.141

Consequently when Lysimachus and the two Gentlemen of IV.v are brought 'out of the road of rutting' and even Boult has been won over to gentleness by Marina's persuasion, virtue has gained a multiple triumph. Marina's success is all the more important to the moral design of the play because it represents the outcome of a head-on collision of values, with the miseries and cruelties of the brothel neither evaded nor laughed aside. *Pericles*, for all its vagaries of structure and narrative line, can thus claim the merit of providing, in this fourth act, a convincing objective correlative for what in *Timon* was an arbitrary and weakly motivated disgust. It confirms Shakespeare as being firmly in command again of the measured idealism that had helped to shape the final dispensations of *Hamlet*, *Othello* and *Lear*. It focuses sharply on the fact that sex can be both shameful and ugly, but it also focuses on the kind of callousness that makes it so—a poison for which antidotes are possible. Finally, looked at from the point of view of Shakespeare's developing technique in the dramatic use of bawdy, *Pericles* shows the farthest swing of the pendulum away from the casual scurrilities of his very early comedies.

NOTES

1. On the question of shared authorship, see above, chapter 4, n.1, pp. 65–6.
2. J. Dover Wilson, *What Happens in 'Hamlet'* (3rd edn, 1951), p. 218.
3. Salvador de Madariaga, *On 'Hamlet'* (1948).
4. Ernest Jones, *Hamlet and Oedipus* (1949), pp. 81–8. Jones's interpretation is not invalidated by the fact that earlier versions of the Hamlet story had also told of Hamlet's railing against his mother's sexual laxity. Shakespeare puts the harangue to subtler and more extensive use than does either Saxo Grammaticus (*Historia Danica*, late twelfth century) or François de Belleforest, *Histoires Tragiques* (Paris, 1559–80). For translations of the relevant sections of these, see Joseph Satin, ed., *Shakespeare and his Sources* (1966), pp. 389–90 and 401–3.
5. Cf. *Hamlet* III.i.51–3, III.i.142–3 and V.i.187–9. M. C. Bradbrook has written vividly of the Elizabethan habit of painting the face to hide disease or dirt. She remarks: 'The ghost's description of his poisoning in *Hamlet* is in the same kind of language as Hamlet's attack on his mother for her lechery' (*Themes and Conventions of Elizabethan Tragedy* (1935), pp. 170–1).

6. Satin, *op. cit.*, pp. 399–400.

7. Peter J. Seng, in his excellent book *The Vocal Songs in the Plays of Shakespeare* (1967), p. 153, suggests that there could also be sexual implications in a later snatch of song, 'For bonny sweet Robin is all my joy' (IV.v.183), since this is likely to be from one of the Robin Hood ballads, now lost.

8. Alexander, *Shakespeare's Life and Art*, p. 197.

9. See D. R. C. Marsh, 'Interpretation and misinterpretation: the problem oʃ *Troilus and Cressida*', *Shakespeare Studies*, i (1965), 188.

10. Shakespeare again comes remarkably close to clinical accuracy when he has Thersites curse Patroclus with 'catarrhs, loads o' gravel in the back, lethargies, cold palsies, raw eyes, dirt-rotten livers, wheezing lungs, bladders full of imposthume, sciaticas, limekilns i'th'palm', etc. (V.i.17). Cf. Sir Stanley Davidson, ed., *The Principles and Practice of Medicine* (10th edn, 1971), pp. 62–4.

11. *The Seven Books of Homer's Iliads*, trans. George Chapman (London, 1598), ii: Bullough, vi, 120.

12. Rossiter, *Angel with Horns*, p. 146.

13. Cinthio, *Gli Hecatommithi* (2 vols, Venice, 1565), Década iii, Novella 7: trans. Spencer, *Elizabethan Love Stories*, pp. 197–210. No English source for *Othello* is known.

14. See Leonard Prager, 'The clown in *Othello*', *SQ*, xi (1960), 94–6; L. J. Ross, 'Shakespeare's "dull clown" and symbolic music', *SQ*, xvii (1966), 107–28; and R. A. Watts, 'The comic scenes in *Othello*', *SQ*, xix (1968), 349–54.

15. Sir Philip Sidney, *Prose Works*, ed. Albert Feuillerat (4 vols, 1912–26), i, 206–14.

16. Steevens's note (1793) is cited in H. H. Furness, ed., Variorum *King Lear* (Philadelphia, 1880), p. 179. The Fool's rhyme at the end of III.ii does not appear in the 1608 Quarto of *Lear*, but that does not necessarily throw doubt on Shakespeare's authorship of it.

17. Kenneth Muir, *Shakespeare's Sources*, i (1957), 160.

18. Knights, *Some Shakespearean Themes* (*ed. cit.*), p. 84, remarks aptly of one of Poor Tom's speeches, 'The effect is as though the evolutionary process had been reversed to show where man as mere earth-bred creature belongs.'

19. See introductions to *Timon of Athens* by J. C. Maxwell (New Cambridge edn, 1957) and H. J. Oliver (New Arden edn, 1959); also Charlton Hinman, *The Printing and Proof-Reading of the First Folio of Shakespeare* (2 vols, 1963), ii, 261, 526.

20. Bullough, vi, 262–3.

21. In calling Alcibiades neutral I am thinking specifically of the sexual context. On more general grounds I would not disagree with the view expressed by David Cook in *SS 16* (1963), 84: 'The burden of the play, positively expressed in Alcibiades, is the need to accept and love man as he is, and to acknowledge our human condition.'

22. J. M. Nosworthy in New Arden *Cymbeline* (1955), pp. xiv–xvii; and J. C. Maxwell in New Cambridge edn (1960), pp. xi–xii.

23. Harley Granville-Barker, *Prefaces to Shakespeare* (1963 edn, 4 vols), ii, 146.

24. By Nosworthy, *op. cit.*, p. lxvi.

25. Schwarz-Alberich and Licht-Alberich. See Ernest Newman, *The Wagner Operas* (2nd edn, 1961), p. 554; and Robert Donington, *Wagner's 'Ring' and its Symbols* (1963), p. 187.

26. I assume that marital rejection is what Imogen is talking about when she says, smilingly, 'Throw me again.' If, on the other hand, she meant 'throw me to the

floor' (as in wrestling)—a possibility that tempted Edward Dowden into conjectural emendation of F1's 'Rock' to 'lock'—she would be giving the play its last, and most domestic, bawdy joke.

27. An edition of *The Pattern of Painful Adventures* was published in London in 1607. An earlier edition, possibly *c.* 1594, is reprinted in Bullough, vi, 423–82.

8

The Life of a Man

When daffodils begin to peer,
  With heigh, the doxy over the dale,
Why, then comes in the sweet o'the year,
  For the red blood reigns in the winter's pale.
                                        The Winter's Tale IV.iii.1

We have seen that where the use of bawdy is concerned, Shakespeare's later plays stubbornly refuse to fall into any such tidy groupings as Problem Plays, Great Tragedies and Late Plays. The indecencies of *Pericles* and *Cymbeline*, though less distressing than those of *Othello* or *Lear*, far exceed, in their power to disturb, those of *Macbeth*, *Coriolanus* or even *Hamlet*; while as early as *Measure for Measure* (written not later than 1604), Shakespeare can be seen to be manipulating bawdy in a way that simultaneously acknowledges the corrupting power of the sexual urge and asserts its vital resilience. Much the same duality controls *Antony and Cleopatra*, where bawdy casts an enticing glow round the Alexandrian court but also lends destructive ferocity to Antony's rages in the third and fourth acts. Above all else, however, this tragedy's bawdy evokes a sense of tolerance, which is exactly what again characterises the last three plays, *The Winter's Tale*, *The Tempest* and *Henry VIII*. *The Tempest* and *Henry VIII* use ribaldry sparingly, but they use it in situations that force us into fresh recognition of both its nourishing and its vicious aspects, ineradicable elements of human existence. Our knowledge of history inclines us to share the gentle cynicism of the old lady who assumes that Anne Bullen would venture maidenhead to be a queen— despite the sunny innocence of Shakespeare–Fletcher's portrait of Anne. And the same essential fact of life looms out more blackly when Prospero shoulders responsibility for the lecherous Caliban: 'This thing of darkness I / Acknowledge mine.'

This spirit of wry acceptance contributes to the air of maturity in these late plays, a quality that has led some twentieth-century critics to luxuriate in the plays' profundity. With *The Winter's Tale* in particular, Shakespeare creates at least the illusion that the whole of human experience is on display. An exceptionally large (and exceptionally explicit) time-span, a wide range of emotion, heavy stress on the seasons' renewal, a pattern of separation and rediscovery—all this gives dramatic substance to the happy reassurance that, even in the face of folly and cruelty, life brings its own redemptions. The play's bawdy becomes closely relevant to this theme when the lurid indecencies that speak a wintry jealousy are unexpectedly complemented by countryfolks' jollity in summer. Together, the two kinds of bawdy work towards the type of completeness that Wolfgang Clemen[1] has pointed to in the imagery of this same text:

> *The Winter's Tale* reveals in several respects an essentially Shakespearian tendency which we can trace throughout his whole dramatic career and which becomes more and more conspicuous towards its end: the endeavour to establish a balance between opposites, never to give only one colour without supplementing it by a complementary colour, never to yield to one specific mood without contrasting it by other entirely different moods and spheres. This desire always to create a complex, round and full picture partly accounts for Shakespeare's masterly faculty to blend various genres, sources and elements into a new organic whole. It is not only brought out by his maturer technique of characterization but becomes evident in almost all aspects and features of his art ...

his use of bawdy being no exception. The tendency to discriminate in the dramatic placing of indecency now reaches culmination-point. Probably no other English play has ever used bawdy with greater finesse than *The Winter's Tale* or *Antony and Cleopatra*. To support this claim in more detail, I should like to approach these texts through their natural forerunner *Measure for Measure*.

The main tenor of bawdy in *Measure for Measure* is cheerful. That may seem an odd thing to say of so dark a comedy: the shadow of prison bars falls across many scenes, and the play as a whole keeps firmly to a limiting, tragi-comic view of man[2]—

man, proud man,
Dressed in a little brief authority,
Most ignorant of what he's most assured,
His glassy essence, like an angry ape
Plays such fantastic tricks before high heaven
As makes the angels weep; who, with our spleens,
Would all themselves laugh mortal.

II.ii.117

Yet even in presenting a wide range of different attitudes to fornication, *Measure for Measure* includes very little of the hysteria that gives rise to embittered bawdy. Isabella, once or twice, unknowingly admits to what we nowadays recognise as sexual inversion:

> Th'impression of keen whips I'd wear as rubies,
> And strip myself to death as to a bed
> That long I have been sick for, ere I'd yield
> My body up to shame
>
> II.iv.101

—but most of her condemnations of carnal sin are as conventional as the Duke's. She as a novice and he as a friar pass exactly the judgements we should expect of them in those roles. Claudio, for his part, is shown to be anything but bawdily disposed. He stands condemned for fornication, but it emerges that he was already betrothed to Juliet before the 'crime' took place, and against Angelo's puritanical judgement of the case Shakespeare balances the comments of such disinterested onlookers as the Provost:

> She is with child,
> And he that got it, sentenced: a young man
> More fit to do another such offence
> Than die for this.
>
> II.iii.12

Further, bringing Juliet herself on stage, the dramatist confirms through her demeanour the fully committed seriousness of her relationship with Claudio. All this eliminates the kind of irresponsibility with which Shakespeare's main source, George Whetstone's two-part play *Promos and Cassandra* (1578), had surrounded the love-affair: 'This severe lawe, by the favour of some merciful magistrate, became little regarded, untill the time of Lord *Promos* auctority: who convicting, a yong Gentleman named *Andrugio* of incontinency, condemned, both him, and his minion to the execution of this statute.'[3] Just as with *Twelfth Night* and certain of the earlier comedies, bawdy has been pruned out of the main plot in *Measure for Measure*: its place, almost exclusively, is in the brothel-keepers' sub-plot.

To call the brothel-keepers' part of the play a plot at all is perhaps to synthesise it unduly. It consists rather in a series of separate incidents interspersed among the main events of the play but involving a specific group of characters—Lucio the dissolute gentleman, Mistress Overdone and her man Pompey, Froth and two other (nameless) gentlemen, and their constabular opponent, Elbow. The manoeuvres and conversations of this group give dramatic body to the general licence that the Duke's

fourteen years of indulgent rule have fostered. 'Liberty plucks justice by
the nose,' explains the Duke to Friar Thomas, and that is indeed what
happens when, for example, Elbow fumbles the case against Froth and
Pompey in II.i.

Here again it is interesting to compare Shakespeare with Whetstone.
The sub-plot of *Promos and Cassandra*, which supplies the material for
Pompey's career, together with the closing down of the brothels and
(later) the arrest of Mistress Overdone, is much firmer in shape than the
low-life parts of *Measure for Measure*. The bawd Lamia seduces Phallax,
Lord Promos's officer, and thereby provides a parallel for the corrupt
behaviour of Promos in subverting Cassandra. Shakespeare dispenses
with this simple parallelism in the interests of more complex moral
situations—Escalus grappling honestly but at first unavailingly with
Pompey and Elbow; the whoremongers buying and selling men and
women as beasts (III.ii.2) yet escaping scot free when Claudio is condemned; Lucio and Pompey incorrigibly insisting on the power of lust
in the face of both law and disease. In so far as the widespread sexual
promiscuity in the play is seen as vicious, it makes a telling contrast with
Claudio's life-giving offence, and roughly corresponds to the tolerated
waste ground of Angelo's metaphor at II.ii.170:

> Having waste ground enough,
> Shall we desire to raze the sanctuary
> And pitch our evils there?

Much of Pompey's bawdy, however, is cheerfully buoyant. Although
he has to admit, under pressure from the Duke, that his trade as a pimp
'does stink in some sort' (III.ii.26), the admission is doubly offset—by
the fact that the Duke himself has just filled the role of pander in arrang-
ing the bed plot, and by Pompey's having the traditional clown's ability
to survive indignities and see a funny side in almost anything. Lucio
also, despicable though he is, has enough of this jack-in-the-box resilience
to serve as a likably amusing proponent of lechery: 'Why, what a
ruthless thing is this . . ., for the rebellion of a cod-piece to take away the
life of a man!'

The extensive bawdy dialogue in *Measure for Measure*, then, becomes
as ambivalent as anything in the play. On the one hand it gives dramatic
substance to what for the Duke, for Angelo, for Isabella, are 'filthy vices
. . . abominable and beastly touches' (II.iv.42 and III.ii.22). On the
other hand it contrasts with the dark secrecy and menace of the subtler
type of sexuality embodied in Angelo. The very openness with which
Pompey acknowledges his trade has something healthy about it. *Measure*

for Measure is pointing ahead to the complexities of *Antony and Cleopatra* and *The Winter's Tale*, where sex will more than ever be capable of shattering the social fabric, but where the earthbound limitations of man-as-animal will also prove to be a source of comfort and renewal.

> Shakespear's Antony and Cleopatra must needs be as intolerable to the true Puritan as it is vaguely distressing to the ordinary healthy citizen, because, after giving a faithful picture of the soldier broken down by debauchery, and the typical wanton in whose arms such men perish, Shakespear finally strains all his huge command of rhetoric and stage pathos to give a theatrical sublimity to the wretched end of the business, and to persuade foolish spectators that the world was well lost by the twain.

Theatre-going puritans are thinner on the ground than they were when Bernard Shaw wrote that tongue-in-cheek diatribe,[4] yet it is still worth quoting for its implicit tribute to Shakespeare as dramaturgical risk-taker. The play's earlier scenes certainly give full weight to the un-dignified aspects of the famous love-affair. A bawdy view is the first one put to us, by Philo: Antony's heart has become 'the bellows and the fan / To cool a gipsy's lust', and

> you shall see in him
> The triple pillar of the world transformed
> Into a strumpet's fool.
>
> I.i.9

When this is offset, a moment later, by Antony's own vision of the uncontainable grandeur of love, there begins yet another Shakespearean struggle between an idealised love and a mocking opposition. As a number of critics have made clear,[5] there is constant oscillation in the attitudes of audience or reader towards this play's two main characters. At one moment we are sharply aware of the transcendental lovers—

> Eternity was in our lips and eyes,
> Bliss in our brows' bent, none our parts so poor
> But was a race of heaven
>
> I.iii.35

—but at the next there can be no gainsaying the strictures of either their enemies or (more damagingly) their friends:

> POMPEY   ... But let us rear
> The higher our opinion, that our stirring
> Can from the lap of Egypt's widow pluck
> The ne'er-lust-wearied Antony.
>
> II.i.35

SCARUS   . . . Yon ribaudred nag of Egypt—
Whom leprosy o'ertake!

      .   .   .   .   .
                              She once being loofed,
The noble ruin of her magic, Antony,
Claps on his sea-wing . . . .

                                                        III.x.10, 18

Clearly, Shakespeare is not pushing towards any simple or moralistic
judgement of his hero and heroine. His task is to identify them, and to do
it as fully as dramatic poetry will allow; because only when we know as
nearly as possible the whole truth about them can we share the author's
insight into their predicament.

The primary function of bawdy in all this is obvious: it helps to
establish and maintain the play's balance between the transcendentalism
of the love-affair and the all-too-apparent sensuality. Cleopatra is both
'empress' and 'No more but e'en a woman', just as Antony's boisterous
delights show his back, dolphin-like, above the element they live in, yet
keep him destructively immersed in it nevertheless. The sensual element
makes its dramatic presence felt very early in the exposition, through the
randy chatter of Cleopatra's women.

IRAS   There's a palm presages chastity, if nothing else.
CHARMIAN   E'en as the o'erflowing Nilus presageth famine.
IRAS   Go, you wild bedfellow, you cannot soothsay.
CHARMIAN   Nay, if an oily palm be not a fruitful prognostication,
    I cannot scratch mine ear.

                                                        I.ii.45

Throughout the play, the imagery most insistently associated with Egypt
maintains this emphasis on wantonness, indulgence, fruitfulness.

There is, however, a second aspect of *Antony and Cleopatra's* bawdy
material, less often noticed by critics. This is its role in contrasting
Cleopatra temperamentally with Antony. In the queen, passion and
levity mingle easily, as her ready tolerance of the courtiers' gossip makes
clear. Her own half-bored, half-flirtatious conversations with the eunuch
Mardian blend easily with those between her women and Alexas. With
Antony, by contrast, the courtiers are altogether more reserved and
cautious. The giggles of I.ii end abruptly on a mistaken warning from
Enobarbus of Antony's approach. Later, when Enobarbus hears the news
of Fulvia's death, he seems to be suppressing a tempting series of bawdy
quibbles:

Why, sir, give the gods a thankful sacrifice. When it pleaseth their deities
to take the wife of a man from him, it shows to man the tailors of the
earth; comforting therein that when old robes are worn out there are

members to make new. If there were no more women but Fulvia, then
had you indeed a cut, and the case to be lamented. This grief is crowned
with consolation: your old smock brings forth a new petticoat; and
indeed the tears live in an onion that should water this sorrow.

I.ii.156

Antony recognises the levity but refuses to respond to it: 'No more
light answers.' Honour calls him back to Rome, and the erotic voice of
Egypt must for the time being be ignored. Stirred by Cleopatra, Antony
will always become 'himself'—or at any rate that part of himself com-
pounded of lover, roisterer, sensualist. But he has another self, as ruler of
armies and nations. His own awareness of this lends a fleeting sincerity
to his marriage with Octavia, just as it also prevents him from apologising
on occasions when apology would take away from his dignity. Bawdy
Egypt lays siege to this side of Antony's personality, and his ultimate
downfall comes largely from the conflict between the two. Since king-
doms are in fact more than just clay, his integrity as a statesman proves
incompatible with his integrity as lover of Cleopatra, yet to him either
is meaningless without the other. Hence the Antony of Act III—lurching
to different emotional extremes, most fiercely of all in the abuse of
Cleopatra when she has let Thidias kiss her hand:

> I found you as a morsel cold upon
> Dead Caesar's trencher. Nay, you were a fragment
> Of Cneius Pompey's, besides what hotter hours,
> Unregistered in vulgar fame, you have
> Luxuriously picked out . . . .

III.xiii.116

These are Antony's first bawdy lines in the play, and nothing could be
more different in tone or impulse from Cleopatra's absent-minded
flirtatiousness with Mardian. A resemblance sets in only when Antony's
fury comes to verge upon the ludicrous—

> O that I were
> Upon the hill of Basan to outroar
> The horned herd!

III.xiii.126

—and this is Antony at his most erratic. The reconciliation, towards the
end of the scene, leads him out of one ambivalent rhetoric into another.

> Come on, my queen,
> There's sap in't yet. The next time I do fight
> I'll make death love me, for I will contend
> Even with his pestilent scythe.

III.xiii.191

As Enobarbus points out in soliloquy, such shrillness reveals in Antony not renewed strength but imminent defeat. Sure enough, Antony's rage erupts again when he blames Cleopatra for the defection of his fleet ('Triple-turned whore! 'tis thou / Hast sold me to this novice'); but what Enobarbus could not have predicted is that final defeat, for Antony, comes with the story that the queen is dead. 'Unarm, Eros. The long day's task is done, / And we must sleep.' This, with its complement, the reunion in the monument at the point of *real* death, at last brings to an end the long conflict between Antony's competing freedoms, the freedom to love untrammelled and the freedom to rule untrammelled. The conflict is only brought to an end rather than resolved: the play will afford no resolution except in the strictly limited terms of Cleopatra's dream of an idealised Antony.

Since the temperamental differences between Antony and Cleopatra have been made so clear, the fifth act brings a new suspense. Cleopatra promised the dying Antony that she would commit suicide—'My resolution and my hands I'll trust; / None about Caesar'—but she now approaches her death in characteristically erratic fashion. For the audience, much of the tension of her political duel with Caesar arises from the possibility that she may again betray Antony in some way, presumably by preferring safety to honour as she did in both sea battles. If this were to happen again now, Antony's sense of his own dignity would be made to look totally absurd, and the play would indeed come to resemble the picture of self-delusion and wantonness that Bernard Shaw jokingly described. As it turns out, however, Cleopatra's loyalty not only proves lasting, but is strengthened by her repugnance at the thought of going as a prisoner to Rome:

> Rather on Nilus' mud
> Lay me stark naked, and let the water-flies
> Blow me into abhorring!
>
> V.ii.58

To Proculeius, such an image seems out of proportion to the actual situation, yet this is only because he is unable to enter Cleopatra's mental world. She knows that the degradation of being led in triumph would sully and despoil that magnificence which her attachment to Antony has come to represent. Her firm apprehension of such degradation goes along with the soaring flight into ideality which, in the 'Emperor Antony' and 'Immortal longings' monologues, becomes a final reassertion of freedom.

It is towards this kind of conclusion that the bawdy associated with Cleopatra may be seen to drive. On the 'factual' level it lampoons her, picturing her as trull, gipsy, mare, nag, whore and so on; but her personality withers such fact, shrivels it to nothing. What we see is not a trull but Antony's sinuous 'serpent of old Nile', complete with the endless, elemental, life-renewing connotations of Nile and snake alike. One can say this without, I think, claiming unreservedly that a transcendental Cleopatra carries the day. Such a view would underrate the play's anti-romantic touches, particularly in the last act, where Shakespeare holds open alternative perspectives through Caesar, Proculeius, Dolabella and the Clown ('I know that a woman is a dish for the gods, if the devil dress her not'). But the play's bawdy, like the play as a whole, asserts, much more than it questions, the ungovernable and illimitable in mankind. The act of sexual passion, far from being a slave to limit as it was for Troilus and Cressida, here rebels against constriction, and successfully commands admiration.

With the bawdy of the first half of *The Winter's Tale* we are in familiar territory. The fevered imaginings of Leontes recall similar outbursts from Othello and Posthumus, and if there is a discernible difference it lies chiefly in Leontes' being made more searingly articulate than those others.

> Inch-thick, knee-deep, o'er head and ears a forked one!
> Go play, boy, play: thy mother plays, and I
> Play too—but so disgraced a part, whose issue
> Will hiss me to my grave. Contempt and clamour
> Will be my knell. Go play, boy, play. There have been,
> Or I am much deceived, cuckolds ere now;
> And many a man there is, even at this present,
> Now, while I speak this, holds his wife by th'arm,
> That little thinks she has been sluiced in's absence,
> And his pond fished by his next neighbour, by
> Sir Smile, his neighbour.
>
>   I.ii.186

With the exception of one or two counter-indecencies from the bluff Antigonus, threatening to geld his daughters and himself (II.i.143–50), nothing in the Sicilian exposition suggests that any other style of bawdy will occur. But when the scene changes from court to country, the play's mode of ribaldry changes no less decisively:

> SHEPHERD   I would there were no age between ten and three-and-
> twenty, or that youth would sleep out the rest; for there is nothing in
> the between but getting wenches with child, wronging the ancientry,
> stealing, fighting. . . . Mercy on's, a barne! . . . A boy or a child, I wonder?
> A pretty one, a very pretty one. Sure, some scape. Though I am not

bookish, yet I can read waiting gentlewoman in the scape: this has
been some stair-work, some trunk-work, some behind-door-work.
They were warmer that got this than the poor thing is here.

III.iii.58

When it comes to jumping to false—and degrading—conclusions, king
and shepherd are as one, yet they differ as widely as could be in matters
of charity.[6]

A third type of bawdy is that of Autolycus, who energises all the more
boisterous episodes in and around the sheep-shearing festival. The
sometime servant of Prince Florizel has fallen on hard times ('With die
and drab I purchased this caparison'), but neither his cutpurse's quickness
nor his balladmonger's *élan* has deserted him.

> The white sheet bleaching on the hedge,
>> With heigh, the sweet birds O, how they sing!
> Doth set my pugging tooth an edge,
>> For a quart of ale is a dish for a king.
>
> The lark, that tirra-lyra chants,
>> With heigh, with heigh, the thrush and the jay,
> Are summer songs for me and my aunts
>> While we lie tumbling in the hay.

IV.iii.5

At the shearing-feast itself (IV.iv), the singing and joking associated with
such tumbling in the hay is first set against the social grace of Perdita:

CLOWN   Prithee bring him in, and let him approach singing.
PERDITA   Forewarn him that he use no scurrilous words in's tunes.
CLOWN   You have of these pedlars that have more in them than you'd
think, sister.
PERDITA   Ay, good brother, or go about to think.

IV.iv.213

Again, later, the songs and jokes separate the festival from the 'sad talk'
of the old Shepherd with his two gentlemen visitors, the disguised
Polixenes and Camillo. Yet Perdita does not share the aloofness of the
two Bunburyists. Her discussion with Polixenes about flowers is bawdy
enough to keep us mindful of her peasant upbringing, though at the
same time modest enough to be consistent with her distaste for being
'Most goddess-like pranked up' in her party clothes:

> the fairest flowers o'th'season
> Are our carnations and streaked gillyvors,
> Which some call Nature's bastards; of that kind
> Our rustic garden's barren, and I care not
> To get slips of them.

.   .   .   .   .

> I'll not put
> The dibble in earth to set one slip of them:
> No more than, were I painted, I would wish
> This youth should say 'twere well, and only therefore
> Desire to breed by me.
>
> IV.iv.81, 99

Obviously, too, she enjoys the fun over which she presides, including the dance of the twelve satyrs. In short, one of the things that this whole long scene makes clear is that Perdita, as romance princess, can move freely in both the courtly and the rustic worlds. As Florizel's eulogy would suggest, the ease of queenship is her birthright.

> Each your doing,
> So singular in each particular,
> Crowns what you are doing in the present deeds,
> That all your acts are queens.
>
> IV.iv.143

It is pre-eminently through this particular scene and this particular character that Shakespeare gives *The Winter's Tale* its quality of all-inclusiveness. Where Time is omnipotent, spring can be counted upon to repair the ravages of winter, and the life of men embraces 'delicate burdens of dildos and fadings, jump her and thump her' (IV.iv.196) as well as the spite and obscenities of a self-imagined royal cuckold. Time, bringer of death *and* blossom, of middle-aged jealousy *and* young love, remains in control. 'Welcome hither,' says Leontes when Florizel and Perdita reach his sad court, 'As is the spring to th'earth!' Rejecting the grey ending of Robert Greene's *Pandosto*, in which Bellaria stays dead and Pandosto kills himself, Shakespeare substitutes the near-miraculous resurrection of Hermione—

> PAULINA   ... Come,
> I'll fill your grave up. Stir; nay, come away.
> Bequeath to death your numbness, for from him
> Dear life redeems you.
>
> V.iii.100

And behind them all, insignificant to the plot but indispensable from the living world of the play,[7] lopes Autolycus, snapping up his unconsidered trifles. 'For the red blood reigns in the winter's pale.'

The Tempest takes up, through Miranda and Caliban, the theme of 'virtue endangered' that looms so large in the earlier romances, but it does so without any of the agonies that drew tortured indecencies from Posthumus and Leontes. It is typical of the new play's whole method

that Caliban's threat to Miranda's chastity should first be introduced as a
thing of the past, detected, forestalled, and now narrated, by Prospero.
But Caliban's delight in recollecting the incident helps to place him
morally—

> O ho, O ho! Would't had been done!
> Thou didst prevent me. I had peopled else
> This isle with Calibans
>
> I.ii.349

—and it combines with references to his mother's witchcraft to endow
him with lastingly sinister potential. The sexual violation of Miranda
remains prominent among his ambitions for revolt, even when Stephano,
not himself, is to be the rapist: 'Ay, lord. She will become thy bed, I
warrant, / And bring thee forth brave brood' (III.ii.105). This motif of
threat to Miranda gains full thematic force when Shakespeare depicts
her betrothal to Ferdinand in IV.i. Commentators have often remarked
on the weight and repetitiveness with which Prospero insists that the
couple must not 'give dalliance / Too much the reign'. This goes beyond
ordinary parental caution, and one suspects an authorial preoccupation
when the theme becomes prominent in the masque also:

> CERES   Tell me, heavenly bow,
> If Venus or her son, as thou dost know,
> Do now attend the queen? Since they did plot
> The means that dusky Dis my daughter got,
> Her and her blind boy's scandalled company
> I have forsworn.
> IRIS   Of her society
> Be not afraid. I met her deity
> Cutting the clouds towards Paphos, and her son
> Dove-drawn with her. Here thought they to have done
> Some wanton charm upon this man and maid,
> Whose vows are, that no bed-right shall be paid
> Till Hymen's torch be lighted: but in vain.
> Mars's hot minion is returned again . . . .
>
> IV.i.86

The mention of Dis, however, offers a pointer to the fundamental
contrast that Shakespeare is setting up. Here we have Ferdinand and
Miranda, prince and princess, ardently in love but pledged to that self-
control on which the ordered progression of most human society depends.
Not far away lurks Caliban, willing servant of the underworld and
embodiment of all the baser qualities of Dis, including an unbridled lust
that is the reverse of Ferdinand's honour. In the sphere of practical affairs,
attack and defence, Caliban and his drunken adopters can be fairly easily
foiled, especially by a ruler with magical powers at his command. Yet

the inherent qualities of the monster would be enough in themselves to cause Prospero to throw over the masque abruptly and fall into a passionate reverie. Anne Righter has remarked how *The Tempest*, an unusually short play by Elizabethan standards,

> continually gives the impression of being much bigger than it actually is. Like an iceberg, it conceals most of its bulk beneath the surface. The verse gestures repeatedly towards these hidden dimensions, towards a collection of submerged facts about characters and situations which Shakespeare seems to have worked out in his own mind, but which he did not choose to elucidate in the play as it stands.[8]

The Caliban—Ferdinand contrast is rich in this 'submerged' property, and when Prospero describes the price of pre-marital copulation as 'barren hate, / Sour-eyed disdain and discord' (IV.i.19), his words conjure up miseries strongly reminiscent of Leontes's. The offered alternative— and again we have already seen it, acted out in later scenes of *The Winter's Tale*—is the kind of ordered fertility over which Ceres presides.

Apart from this half-hidden struggle between licence and control as symbolised in Caliban and Ferdinand, bawdy has little to do in *The Tempest*. The atmosphere of II.i (the scene in which Antonio and Sebastian try to murder Alonso and Gonzalo) gains some of its sultriness from ill-natured sniggering over Gonzalo's naively conceived Utopia, but this is trivial. It becomes only one of many indications that the fleering Sebastian would have made a small-minded, as well as treacherous, king.

This, then, is yet another play in which Shakespeare uses bawdy sparingly, and always with precise dramatic point. If proof were still needed that he progressively lost interest in the use of lubricity as a simple laughter-raiser, his last comedy would provide its full share of evidence.

In *King Henry VIII* we find bawdy almost entirely relegated to the sidelines. Only once does it contribute to the main action, when Surrey includes venery among the charges brought against Wolsey (III.ii.295). Otherwise, the play's bawdy attaches to the lookers-on and to those who prepare for, but take small part in, glittering scenes of pleasure and pomp. As in *The Tempest*, some indecencies work towards contrast between unlike personalities. Lord Sandys and Sir Thomas Lovell are scathing about dandified courtiers—

LOVELL   . . . The sly whoresons
   Have got a speeding trick to lay down ladies.
   A French song and a fiddle has no fellow.
SANDYS   The devil fiddle 'em!

I.iii.39

—but quickly resort to bawdy small-talk themselves at Cardinal Wolsey's reception; and Sandys no sooner leaves the safety of the cosily ribald, all-male group, than he finds himself coolly snubbed by the dignified Anne Bullen:

SANDYS   . . . By your leave, sweet ladies.
  If I chance to talk a little wild, forgive me;
  I had it from my father.
ANNE   Was he mad, sir?

I.iv.25

This demure self-possession shows up again in Anne's scene with the old lady (II.iii.1–49). In recommending that the Maid of Honour should 'venture maidenhead . . . to queen it', the old lady has some startling quibbles ('In faith, for little England / You'd venture an emballing'), and their polite yet firm rebuttal by Anne brings out her contrasting purity of motive. For all its mid-Jacobean date—Elizabeth I had been dead for ten years by the time it was staged—the play is as cautiously respectful towards the old queen's mother as it is towards her father. Holinshed, in his wisdom, had been discreet about Anne Boleyn's qualities: Shakespeare and Fletcher are positively enthusiastic.

Elsewhere in the play, only the porter and his man holding the doors of the palace against their 'faithful friends o'th'suburbs' (in V.iv) fall naturally into libidinous talk. In reviving, for the nonce, the tradition of the Elizabethan chronicle play, Shakespeare or Fletcher has slipped easily into the uses for bawdy that we noted in such works as *Henry VI*, contributing to the characterisation of leading figures and to the vulgarisation of the vulgar. The 125-year-old argument over the authorship of *Henry VIII* is not strictly pertinent to this book, but one may observe, in passing, that if Fletcher had a hand in I.iii, II.iii or V.iv, he showed there a marked ability to imitate his master's long-practised ways with bawdy.

Assuming, though, that the touches of indecency in *Henry VIII* are Shakespeare's own, this final play in the canon shows something of that tolerant inclusiveness which characterises *Antony and Cleopatra* and *The Winter's Tale*. Around the sombre history of Wolsey and Queen Katherine there glitters the light of pageantry; and at the edges of that again, flickerings of comic bawdy signal a wayward, but indestructible, zest.

NOTES

1. W. H. Clemen, *The Development of Shakespeare's Imagery* (1951), p. 195.
2. Implications of the term *tragi-comic* as applied to a Brechtian, anti-heroic view of man are cogently explored by Rossiter in *Angel with Horns*, pp. 116–7.

3. George Whetstone, in 'The Argument of the Whole History (of Promos and Cassandra)', ed. J. W. Lever in New Arden *Measure for Measure* (1965), p. 166.

4. Bernard Shaw, Preface to *Three Plays for Puritans* (1901; Penguin Books edn, 1946), p. 29.

5. Notably Ernest Schanzer, in *The Problem Plays of Shakespeare* (1963), pp. 132–83, where he stresses the structural similarities between *Antony* and *Henry IV*; and A. P. Riemer, in *A Reading of Shakespeare's 'Antony and Cleopatra'* (1968), pp. 27–77.

6. Shakespeare found the point about false assumptions ready-made in the main source for *The Winter's Tale*, Robert Greene's prose romance *Pandosto* (1588). There it is the shepherd's shrewish wife who assumes that the baby is a bastard, 'as women are naturally given to believe the worst' (see J. H. P. Pafford, ed., New Arden *Winter's Tale* (1963), p. 200). In rehandling the story, Shakespeare eliminates the shepherd's wife. He would obviously have had little or no further use for her after III.iii, and the transfer of her bawdy to the shepherd has the advantage of helping to keep at a distance the horror of Antigonus's death. With the Shepherd's surmises about the baby's origins, plus the Clown's amusingly confused account of the shipwreck, Shakespeare seems to be guarding against any risk of having our sympathy diverted from Perdita to Antigonus and the drowned sailors.

7. The importance of Autolycus's role in the play is well argued by R. A. Foakes, *Shakespeare: The Dark Comedies to the Last Plays* (1971), pp. 137–41.

8. Anne Righter, ed., *The Tempest* (New Penguin edn, 1968), p. 14.

9

Among His Private Friends

As the soule of *Euphorbus* was thought to live in *Pythagoras*: so the
sweete wittie soule of *Ovid* lives in mellifluous & hony-tongued
Shakespeare, witnes his *Venus* and *Adonis*, his *Lucrece*, his sugred Sonnets
among his private friends, &c.

Francis Meres, *Palladis Tamia*

To talk of dramatic uses of bawdy in non-dramatic poems sounds
paradoxical, but with Shakespeare the paradox is apparent rather than
real. Just as a stage character's ribald speech or behaviour will make itself
felt as a breach of social decorum, so too in a narrative poem or a sonnet
particular lines, particular attitudes, can strike through the conventional
framework to startle, amuse or enlighten the reader. In Shakespeare's
first verse narrative, *Venus and Adonis*, and again in the sonnets, his
preoccuption with the relationship between love and lust makes this
kind of device not merely useful to him but a part of his basic method.

Like Marlowe's *Hero and Leander*, the quasi-Ovidian *Venus and Adonis*
(1593) is never out of cooing distance from the sexually indecent. Shakespear's translation of the great hunter Adonis into a shrinking adolescent,
and of the goddess of love into a pushing young matron, straight away
gives their encounter a hot sweaty feel: 'She red and hot as coals of
glowing fire, / He red for shame, but frosty in desire.' The sun shines
warmly down on them as they wrestle, as much in heat as the goddess
herself. The more Venus tries to strike a tone of light and companionable
flirtatiousness, the more lubricious she becomes, and the more disdain
she inspires in Adonis:

> 'Fondling,' she saith, 'since I have hemmed thee here
> Within the circuit of this ivory pale,
> I'll be a park, and thou shalt be my deer:
> Feed where thou wilt, on mountain or in dale;
>   Graze on my lips; and if those hills be dry,
>   Stray lower, where the pleasant fountains lie.

> 'Within this limit is relief enough,
> Sweet bottom-grass, and high delightful plain,
> Round rising hillocks, brakes obscure and rough,
> To shelter thee from tempest and from rain.
>   Then be my deer, since I am such a park.
>   No dog shall rouse thee, though a thousand bark.'   229

Here we have a situation that is paralleled many times in the plays: a bawdy conceit, put into the mouth of a character who hopes it to be seductive, proves counter-productive, eliciting only scorn from the person to whom it has been addressed. Shakespeare's contemporaries seem to have enjoyed Venus's topographical extravaganza for its own sake—it was still being quoted as late as 1607, in Tom Heywood's *Fair Maid of the Exchange*—but its ingenuity gains extra point from its dramatic placing in the poem, with Adonis an unwilling prisoner of his captor's locked arms. There follows the episode in which Adonis's horse breaks its tether to chase a jennet. Venus then tries again, in more straightforward vein.

> 'Who sees his true-love in her naked bed,
> Teaching the sheets a whiter hue than white,
> But, when his glutton eye so full hath fed,
> His other agents aim at like delight? . . .'   397

This is rather more winning—or would be, to anyone less of a hearty than Shakespeare's Adonis. ' "I know not love," quoth he, "nor will not know it, / Unless it be a boar, and then I chase it. . . ." ' With this unguarded remark from the hero, bawdy in *Venus and Adonis* enters on a new function. It has played its due part in characterising Venus and the limitedly sensual nature of the love she is offering; now its job is to underline the fact that Adonis too is living less fully than he might. The motif of his having a coital relationship with the hunted boar returns near the end of the poem, when Venus is bewailing his death:

> ' 'Tis true, 'tis true! thus was Adonis slain:
> He ran upon the boar with his sharp spear,
> Who did not whet his teeth at him again,
> But by a kiss thought to persuade him there;
>   And nuzzling in his flank, the loving swine
>   Sheathed unaware the tusk in his soft groin. . . .'   1111

Even in a poem as mannerist as *Venus and Adonis*, this is an exceptionally fanciful notion, and not any the less so for having a long pre-Shakespearean pedigree.[1] But its value here is twofold. It re-stresses the point that the shortcomings have not all been on the side of bawdily sensual Venus. In

addition, it communicates to the reader Venus's sense of loss, and does so
in terms that are all the more convincing for being consistent with her
earlier lustfulness. In these closing pages of the poem, Shakespeare is not
going to gainsay the strictures that he has by implication already passed
on his ultra-Wagnerian Venus, but he does at least ask us to spare a sigh
for her frustration by the potentially virile Adonis. Had she been toothed
like the boar,

> '. . . I must confess,
> With kissing him I should have killed him first;
> But he is dead, and never did he bless
> My youth with his—the more am I accurst.'   1117

This makes possible the very Shakespearean sympathy of the poem's
ending, where Venus, once so hot and pressing but now 'weary of the
world', disappears dove-drawn into empty skies.

Shakespeare's next-published poem, *The Rape of Lucrece* (1594), is
again concerned with sexual assault, but this time the tone is too sombre
to admit lighthearted bawdy and the characterisation too sober to have
need of the bitterer kind. One short passage does, admittedly, strike a
quietly ribald note. As Tarquin approaches Lucrece's chamber, we are
told, his heart, corrupted,

> heartens up his servile powers,
> Who, flattered by their leader's jocund show,
> Stuff up his lust, as minutes fill up hours;
> And as their captain, so their pride doth grow,
> Paying more slavish tribute than they owe.
> By reprobate desire thus madly led,
> The Roman lord marcheth to Lucrece' bed.   295

Bearing in mind the common Elizabethan meaning of *pride* as a swelling
or tumescence, one can detect here a suggestion of Tarquin's being led
along by his own erect penis. Yet the hint never becomes anything more
than a hint, perhaps because too close a view of the rapist at such a
moment would involve more of the grotesque than the poem could
successfully accommodate. At the same time, though, the fleeting
suggestion of penial tumescence is useful in solidifying the physical threat
to Lucrece, and hence in heightening the suspense of this early part of
the poem.

Later, when he is blackmailing Lucrece into silent submission, Tarquin
is given some lines of less equivocal indecency. He will murder her *and*
one of her slaves, he says, and will place the slave's body in her dead
arms, 'Swearing I slew him, seeing thee embrace him':

> 'So thy surviving husband shall remain
> The scornful mark of every open eye;
> Thy kinsmen hang their heads at this disdain,
> Thy issue blurred with nameless bastardy;
> And thou, the author of their obloquy,
> Shalt have thy trespass cited up in rhymes
> And sung by children in succeeding times. . . .'   519

That vicious stroke of Tarquin's guile was ready to Shakespeare's hand both in Ovid's *Fasti* and in Livy's *History of Rome*,[2] but its clear and forceful wording in *Lucrece* is worth noting because of the importance that the poem gives to the idea of pregnancy as a part-cause of Lucrece's suicide. Shakespeare, even in this formal narrative poem, is too much the dramatist to content himself with a statuesque gesture of Roman self-sacrifice. Guarding against the possibility that the heroine's suicide might strike us as irrational or even wicked after her husband's acknowledgement of her innocence, the poet establishes firmly (and urges again in Lucrece's long lament at the centre of the poem) her fearful determination that a 'bastard graff shall never come to growth' (1062). The thought—as so often in this poem—is conventional, but the human anxieties associated with it are better handled than some of the poem's critics have allowed.

Advancing from the narrative poems to the sonnets, we immediately run into a long-standing complex of demarcation disputes. Thomas Thorpe's quarto of 1609, which does not read as though it was proof-read by Shakespeare, gives 154 sonnets in all, prefaced by the infamously arcane dedication to 'the onlie begetter of these insuing sonnets Mr W.H.' and followed by the eleven-page poem 'A Lover's Complaint'. The last two of the sonnets are variations on an antique conceit that had already been handled by a number of Renaissance poets, and need not concern us here. The other 152 fall into three broad groups: numbers 1–17 urge a handsome youth to marry and beget children; numbers 18–126 are mainly (perhaps entirely) addressed to a male friend who is, in one sense or another, the poet's lover; and numbers 127–152 are mostly concerned with the poet's mistress. Since this mistress comes under reproach for having a love-affair with the poet's friend, and since just such an entanglement has already been glanced at in sonnets 40–42, it seems reasonable to regard the story underlying 127–152 as being simultaneous with, or at least overlapping, that of 18–126. Beyond this, however, the sequential appearance of the poems allows many different interpretations. Is the friend always to be thought of as one and the same friend? the mistress always one and the same mistress? Should the sonnets be regarded as autobiographical?

This last question, having befuddled the critical appreciation of the sonnets for 150 years or more, has in recent times been handed over to the biographers whose proper concern it is. Encouraged by two seminal books of the mid-1950s, Patrick Cruttwell's *The Shakespearean Moment* (1954) and J. W. Lever's *The Elizabethan Love Sonnet* (1956), literary critics in the past few decades have been more intent on stimulating the enjoyment of the sonnets as poems, without fussing over which of their implied events might once have been fact rather than fiction. In any case, like other Elizabethan sonnet sequences, this one is much more lyrical in impulse than it is narrative, and it may well be that its sonnets addressed to a boy or man are calculated primarily to give Petrarchan and Sidneyan conventions a new twist—at least for English Renaissance readers, if not for their Italian contemporaries. The well-worn theme of jealousy also gains a new poignancy when the jealousy is said to have been inspired by a sexual liaison between the poet's male lover and female mistress.

Yet even after conjectural biography has been set aside in favour of sonneteer's fiction, the demarcation struggle begins anew. Precisely in what sense are sonnets 1–126 love poems? Endearments are there in plenty as the 'I' of the poems pours forth affection for his 'love . . . dear my love', while references to the lovely boy's masculinity are frequent enough to encourage the supposition that all of these first 126 sonnets are homosexually-orientated letters to one or more male lovers. John Benson, a dishonest publisher who put out a pirated edition of the Sonnets in 1639, was obviously alarmed by the recurrent suggestion of sodomy. Besides jumbling the 1609 order of the poems and thereby making their underlying narrative difficult to discern, he tried to change the sex of the poet's friend by tampering with the wording. Sonnet 19, in which the poet pleads with Time—

> O, carve not with thy hours my love's fair brow,
> Nor draw no lines there with thine antique pen;
> Him in thy course untainted do allow
> For beauty's pattern to succeeding men

—this sonnet is omitted entirely from Benson's edition, together with 56 ('Sweet love, renew thy force'), 75, 76 and 96 (for no obvious reason), and, of course, 126 ('O thou, my lovely boy'). In several other sonnets, though with nothing like consistency, Benson changed masculine pronouns to feminine and heterosexualised the nouns: *him* and *he* became *her* and *she* in 101 and 108, while 108's 'sweet boy' became 'sweet love', and 104's 'fair friend' became 'fair love'. Sonnet 20 he surprisingly left alone, save for the pointless, and perhaps merely accidental, change of *wert* to *went* in its ninth line. Since this skittishly conceited piece has more than once been claimed as crucial to the whole question of homosexual bawdy in the collection, it needs to be quoted in full:

> A woman's face, with Nature's own hand painted,
> Hast thou, the Master Mistress of my passion;
> A woman's gentle heart, but not acquainted
> With shifting change, as is false woman's fashion;
> An eye more bright than theirs, less false in rolling,
> Gilding the object whereupon it gazeth;
> A man in hue all hues in his controlling,
> Which steals men's eyes and women's souls amazeth.
> And for a woman wert thou first created;
> Till Nature, as she wrought thee, fell a-doting,
> And by addition me of thee defeated
> By adding one thing to my purpose nothing.
>   But since she pricked thee out for women's pleasure,
>   Mine be thy love, and thy love's use their treasure.

A glance at H. E. Rollins's Variorum edition of the Sonnets[3] shows that down the centuries number 20 was to strike alarm into some sensitive breasts.

> It is impossible to read this fulsome panegyrick, addressed to a male object, without an equal mixture of disgust and indignation.
>
> George Steevens, 1780
>
> One of the most painful and perplexing [poems] I ever read. . . . I could heartily wish that Shakespeare had never written it.
>
> D. L. Richardson, 1840

But there were other views too on the nature of sonnet 20, and the record, as seen by Rollins in 1944, had a happy ending. H. M. Young, in a psychosexual analysis of the poems (1937), had argued that no homosexual starts by persuading his lover to marry, and that sonnet 20 in particular

> simply could not have been written by a homosexual. . . . 'A woman's face' would add no charm in the eyes of a homosexual, and the one thing which nature so carelessly added would not have been to his purpose nothing. It would, so far from defeating him, have been the one thing absolutely essential.[4]

This, and the scholarly reviewers' general acceptance of it, seemed to Rollins to be the end of the question of homosexuality in the sonnets. But Young had only proved afresh what the sonnets themselves go on to contemplate—that it is an unusual and disturbing thing to languish over a lovely boy and at the same time adore a mistress. Sonnet 20 decides nothing, either way. Far from providing final identification of a non-homosexual relationship, it could well be a deliberate smoke-screen, a haze expressly contrived to obscure that homosexual feeling which the poet's keen interest in his friend's physical beauty repeatedly suggests. The smoke-screen is not even laid seriously. With bawdy quibbles setting its tone (*thing, nothing, pricked, use*), number 20 is like the cheekily absurd ending of such a comedy as *The Two Gentlemen of Verona*. Viewed simply as narrative, it looks clumsy, contradictory, incredible; but as a transparently fictional way out of a complex situation, an escape hatch supplied for those readers who feel the need of one, it fulfils a useful artistic function.

Nowadays, of course, we have to read the Sonnets historically to gauge the distress-potential of their homosexual element. In our English language culture the taboo around sodomy has largely dissolved. But at least we have the advantage that simplistic notions of what constitutes (or governs) 'a homosexual' have dissolved too. In the present far-from-unanimous state of scientific opinion on homosexuality, the best formulation we have on this aspect of the sonnets is probably Martin Seymour-Smith's. They provide, he has suggested, 'a poetic insight into what may be described, paradoxically, as a heterosexual's homosexual experience'.[5]

Among the poems themselves, the inner conflict set up by such experience is brought to the surface in 40–42, the first 'eternal triangle' sequence, and again, more bitterly, in the later sonnets concerning the mistress (127–152). The brooding 129, 'Th'expense of spirit in a waste of shame', heralds the latter mood, though in my view there is nothing at all bawdy in this poem itself. Its contemplation of lust is steadily serious, and the proposition that a *double entendre* links the first and last lines (*spirit* = spermal fluid, *waste* = waist, *hell* = vagina) is super-ingenious —a hangover from the 1950s, when fashion decreed that the truest poetry was the most ambivalent. Sonnet 129, on the contrary, is a plain and unequivocal warning. Out of it comes the doubting, questioning atmosphere in which Shakespeare will bring bawdy to bear on the poet-mistress relationship with all the glare of a moral searchlight. This happens in sonnets 135–138, when the background story has reached, for the second time, the seduction of the friend by the mistress. The absent poet bodies forth his sense of betrayal by playing wryly with the thought of coitus. This is suggested in 135, first by *will* in the sense of libido or sexual desire, then by the word's extension to mean also an actual sex-organ, male or female. All this is done without jettisoning the more ordinary senses of *Will*—volition, determination, wilfulness, plus the poet's name and perhaps also his friend's name (or the mistress's husband's, or somebody's). The *tour de force* of word-play comes to a well-delayed climax in the poem's last word, which would seem to carry every meaning for *Will* that has occurred earlier:[6]

> Whoever hath her wish, thou hast thy Will,
> And Will to boot, and Will in over-plus;
> More than enough am I that vex thee still,
> To thy sweet will making addition thus.
> Wilt thou, whose will is large and spacious,
> Not once vouchsafe to hide my will in thine?
> Shall will in others seem right gracious,
> And in my will no fair acceptance shine?
> The sea, all water, yet receives rain still,
> And in abundance addeth to his store;
> So thou, being rich in Will, add to thy Will
> One will of mine, to make thy large Will more.
>   Let no unkind, no fair beseechers kill;
>   Think all but one, and me in that one Will.

For J. W. Lever, this richly indecent sonnet lies at the masochistic nadir of a satiric spiral. 'Courtship,' he comments, 'has become a joyless mating of human animals in rut.'[7] If I were to differ from that estimate, it would only be to place this particular poem somewhere just ahead of the spiritual nadir of the sequence. The lady's 'will' is large and spacious, perhaps distended through ordinary tumescence, perhaps permanently enlarged by excessive use, yet to the poet it is also sweet; and the brilliant ingenuity of a dozen consecutive puns on *will* surely enacts playfulness rather than bitterness.

Sonnet 136, a weaker set of variations on 135's theme, continues the series of innuendos.

> If thy soul check thee that I come so near,
> Swear to thy blind soul that I was thy Will,
> And will, thy soul knows, is admitted there;
> Thus far, for love, my love-suit, sweet, fulfil.
> Will will fulfil the treasure of thy love,
> Ay, fill it full with wills, and my will one.

That there is a physical sense alongside the metaphorical in 'the treasure of thy love' is indisputable: the only question is whether we choose to interpret this physical sense as 'vagina' or, with more varied implications, 'womb'. Either way, the *fulfil/full-fill* pun is supported later in the poem by 'thy store's account' (line 10), which could be punning on *cunt*. And the 1609 printers' hyphenation of 'some-thing' in line 12—

> For nothing hold me, so it please thee hold,
> That nothing me, a some-thing sweet to thee

—supports the view of two modern editors[8] that the same line's 'nothing' should be interpreted as 'no-thing': 'rate me as a mere cipher if you like, provided that you hold that no-penis, me, close to you, as if I were a real penis, some actual thing'.

The next sonnet, 137, suddenly cuts through all the clever-cleverness. It makes use of only two bawdy innuendos, but together they strike a hostile chord that far outgoes the preceding poems in disillusion:

> Thou blind fool, Love, what dost thou to mine eyes
> That they behold, and see not what they see?
> They know what beauty is, see where it lies,
> Yet what the best is take the worst to be.
> If eyes, corrupt by over-partial looks,
> Be anchored in the bay where all men ride,
> Why of eyes' falsehood hast thou forged hooks,
> Whereto the judgement of my heart is tied?
> Why should my heart think that a several plot,
> Which my heart knows the wide world's common place?
> Or mine eyes, seeing this, say this is not,
> To put fair truth upon so foul a face?
>   In things right true my heart and eyes have erred,
>   And to this false plague are they now transferred.

Now that the men who would copulate with this deceptive woman are riders on a horse as well as ships at anchor, not to mention crowds taking their recreation on a common, we have indeed reached the nadir. A limited recovery begins in the poem (138) that Thorpe printed next, 'When my love swears that she is made of truth'. Wry humour now returns and creates a relatively gentle tonal setting for the single bawdy pun which comes wittily at the end:

> Therefore I lie with her, and she with me,
> And in our faults by lies we flattered be.

It is perhaps no accident that three of the leading concerns of the sonnets have converged here. The poet is subject to time, love is subject to falsehood, and falsehood itself is the only defence against both time and love. Having brought their poet to this sad but at least self-aware position, the sonnets never move beyond it. They circle round it, broodingly—though whether this is because Shakespeare worked them out that way, or just because of a random ordering of these later sonnets by Thorpe, we have no means of telling.

After 138, the sonnets continue to have their bawdy moments, most of them still related to the faithlessness of the dark woman, but only in 144 and 152 is the ribaldry either extensive or dramatic. Sonnet 144 revives the ferocity of 137. Its imagery of saint and fiend becomes disconcertingly erotic when the poet's 'better angel . . . a man right fair' is corrupted by his 'worser spirit', his 'female evil', wooing the young man's purity 'with her foul pride'. That this pride is the sexual excitement of an animal rather than either hauteur or finery is indicated partly by the force of the adjective *foul*, and partly by the erotic suggestions in the poem's last four lines:

> But being both from me, both to each friend,
> I guess one angel in another's hell.
> Yet this shall I ne'er know, but live in doubt,
> Till my bad angel fire my good one out.

The evil angel's hell could be, *inter alia*, her vagina: commentators have often invoked comparison with the yonic hell in Boccaccio's Rustico and Alibech story.[9] More certainly, the final couplet suggests venereal infection as well as the smoking-out of a hunted animal.

As against that return to bitterness, sonnet 151 swings back to the more lighthearted manner of 135. Its phallic conclusion shows a bold rehandling of the Petrarchan theme of the lady's courtly servant being at once humble and triumphant:

> flesh stays no farther reason,
> But, rising at thy name, doth point out thee
> As his triumphant prize. Proud of this pride,
> He is contented thy poor drudge to be,
> To stand in thy affairs, fall by thy side.
> No want of conscience hold it that I call
> Her 'love' for whose dear love I rise and fall.

The sense of a throwback to an earlier mood could be accounted a dramatic stroke on Shakespeare's part only if one were placing firm reliance on the sonnets as narrative and on Thorpe's ordering of them in a proper sequence. Since both of those are open to doubt, it is impossible to claim special significance for the return to cheerful indecency in what happens to be the last but one of the mistress-sonnets. Yet in one way, at least, sonnet 151 does typify an aspect of the collection as a whole. Here, just as in *Venus and Adonis*, we see Shakespeare taking up a fashionable literary kind and leaving it the stronger for some firmly placed injections of sexual realism.

NOTES

1. F. T. Prince, in his New Arden edition of *The Poems* (1960), p. 59, traces the conceit back to Theocritus, and mentions its use in several sixteenth-century poems before Shakespeare's.
2. See Bullough, i, 191, 195 and 198.

3. H. E. Rollins, ed., *The Sonnets* (2 vols, 1944), i, 55–6 and ii, 232–9. Steevens and Richardson are quoted in i, 55.

4. H. M. Young, *The Sonnets of Shakespeare: a psycho-sexual analysis* (1937), p. 11; quoted by Rollins, ii, 239.

5. Martin Seymour-Smith, ed., *Shakespeare's Sonnets* (1963), p. 34. For a recent medical view of homosexuality in general, see (for instance) John Loraine, 'Hormones and homosexuality', *New Scientist*, liii (1972), 270–1.

6. See W. G. Ingram and Theodore Redpath, eds, *Shakespeare's Sonnets* (1964), pp. 312–3.

7. J. W. Lever, *The Elizabethan Love Sonnet* (1956), p. 179.

8. Ingram and Redpath, *ed. cit.*, p. 315.

9. Boccaccio, *Decameron*, iii, 10.

10

Some Conclusions

Many, out of their owne obscene Apprehensions, refuse proper and fit
words; as *occupie*, *nature*, and the like: So the curious industry in some of
having all alike good, hath come neerer a vice, then a vertue.

Ben Jonson, *Discoveries*

Before attempting any panoramic review of the development of Shakespeare's bawdy, I first have to exorcise a shade—the spectral thought that
bawdy, being often just playful, is really less decisive an element in the
plays and poems than the foregoing chapters would suggest. Even if one
distrusts the theories of an E. E. Stoll or a T. W. Baldwin about Eliza-
than acting companies,[1] at least some of the ribald jokes in Shakespeare's
text must owe their place to suggestions—even interpolations?—from
resident clowns or fools of the King's Men, and perhaps for no very compelling artistic reason. This being so, there is always the risk that we may
be wasting critical effort, as Dr Johnson put it in a different connection,
upon unresisting imbecility. Conversely, a study of the kind I have been
attempting suffers inevitably from a pressure towards tidying up the
plays. If some particular line or phrase of bawdy refuses to fit into the
categories that the enquiry offers, it easily finds itself being ignored as of
no account. An example is *Hamlet* IV.vii.170–2, where Gertrude's
reference to liberal shepherds' grosser name for what she calls 'long
purples' strikes a weirdly dissonant note in her description of Ophelia's
death, but is difficult to relate critically to anything else in the play.

Over both these issues, the reader who has persevered as far as this last
chapter can only be asked to judge each case on its merits. As was acknowledged at the outset, not all the indecency in Shakespeare is dramatically
significant, or even provable *as* indecency. Rather than agonise repeti-
tiously over the peripheral or the merely arguable, I have concentrated
on those many other instances of ribaldry that do seem to throw positive

light either on Shakespeare's developing skill as a playwright or on the distinctive qualities of particular works. It is the perennial weakness of all aspective criticism that it is too narrow, but if it serves to open up fresh possibilities of interpretation and evaluation in other directions, its limited perspective may be justified.

Recognising such limitation, what tentative conclusions can be drawn from the study of Shakespeare's bawdy?

First, one can discern a growing diversity in Shakespeare's ways of using this kind of material. The earliest comedies are the only plays that appear to use indecency solely for laughter's sake, while *Titus Andronicus* and the early histories use it mainly to indicate nuances of character. In *Romeo and Juliet* and the more mature histories and comedies these functions still exist, but scurrility takes on a new importance as a mode of deflation or would-be deflation. As a source of comic realism it is at its most potent in *2 Henry IV*, *As You Like It* and *Measure for Measure*. The more fully it becomes engaged in commentary on non-licentious people or events, the less farcical it grows, so we need feel no surprise when the aggressive indecencies of Hamlet and Thersites separately inaugurate a quite new style of Shakespearean indecency, one that is bitter and un-funny. This grotesque but humourless exaggeration and distortion of sexual behaviour remains prevalent with Shakespeare throughout the early years of the seventeenth century, but it never becomes totally dominant. *Twelfth Night*, *All's Well That Ends Well* and *Measure for Measure* all work without it, as also do *Macbeth* and *Coriolanus*. And first in *Troilus and Cressida*, then in *Antony and Cleopatra*, the two modes—the comic and the darkly grotesque—combine in marking out spiritual limits for human love. *The Winter's Tale* again makes use of both bawdy-as-disgust and bawdy-as-delight, this time in a balance that gives the impression of including the whole of human sexual experience, fair and foul.

Another general feature of Shakespeare's indecency—not a trend but an unchanging characteristic—may be seen in his handling of source materials. Many of his sources are too straightforward in narrative style to have room for the kind of detail that can be identified as bawdy. It is understandable that in creating dramatic dialogue out of such materials Shakespeare devises ribaldry of his own when he needs it. Even in cases where the source does offer erotic material ready-made, however, he almost always passes it by. This is particularly noticeable with *The Taming of the Shrew*, *Henry V*, and *Twelfth Night*. A special instance is *King Lear*, where the indecencies of the source play are rejected in favour of fiercer ones from Harsnett's *Declaration of Egregious Popish Impostures*. Again, in

Antony and Cleopatra we find the dramatist inventing both the perky indecencies of Cleopatra's courtiers and the scathing reproaches that follow the Thidias incident, while he totally omits from Antony's role a quite lengthy speech of lighthearted bawdy reported by Plutarch:

> He that could finely cloak his shameful deeds with fine words said that the greatness and magnificence of the Empire of Rome appeared most, not where the Romans took, but where they gave much; and nobility was multiplied amongst men by the posterity of kings when they left of their seed in divers places; and that by this means his first ancestor was begotten of Hercules, who had not left the hope and continuance of his line and posterity in the womb of one only woman, fearing Solon's laws or regarding the ordinances of men touching the procreation of children; but that he gave it unto nature, and established the foundation of many noble races and families in divers places.[2]

This deliberateness in Shakespeare's selection of ribald material goes far towards stilling the doubts that I raised at the start of this chapter. When you compare his finished plays with as many of their sources as have been satisfactorily identified, all the evidence points one way—to a dramatist who quite deliberately selected or invented bawdy in the interests of each play as a whole, and otherwise tended to exclude it.

Finally, it seems appropriate to ask which of the dramas would seem to call for some reinterpretation in the light of this study. Not, I think, any of the early comedies, though Jan Kott has proved sufficiently influential to place the image of *A Midsummer Night's Dream* in need of repair. *Romeo and Juliet* demands a good deal of critical reorientation if, as I suggested in chapter 5, Franco Zeffirelli's slightly sardonic presentation of Mercutio is justified by the text. In Shakespeare's middle years, *The Merry Wives of Windsor* takes on a new balance when considered from the point of view of its use of ribaldry, with the role of Falstaff becoming less undignified than stage tradition has commonly allowed. Among the later plays, *Lear* and *Antony* would seem to me to be those in which new relations of part to part, and increased coherence as wholes, become apparent. Amidst so much that is poetically forceful, scurrilous lines are not always particularly striking in performance, but their cumulative effect is indispensable to the complex statement that each of these great tragedies makes. With the romances also, directors do the plays a disservice if they either jettison the bawdy lines or blur their effect in the immediate interest of a noisy hilarity. Just as Shakespeare's sonnets treat of sex as both a threat *to* happiness and a source *of* happiness, so also do the late plays—most finely of all when sex exerts its irrepressible force of renewal in *The Winter's Tale*.

NOTES

1. E. E. Stoll, *Art and Artifice in Shakespeare* (1933); T. W. Baldwin, *The Organization and Personnel of the Shakespearean Company* (1927).
2. T. J. B. Spencer, ed., *Shakespeare's Plutarch* (Penguin Books, 1964), p. 223.

Bibliography

Editions of Shakespeare

Mr. Wm Shakespeares Comedies, Histories, & Tragedies (London, 1623): The Norton
Facsimile, prepared by Charlton Hinman (New York, 1968)
The Works of Mr William Shakespear, ed. Sir Thomas Hanmer (6 vols, Oxford,
1743–44)
The Family Shakespeare, ed. Thomas Bowdler (10 vols, London, 1818; 7th end,
1 vol, 1839, repr. 1861)
A New Variorum Edition of Shakespeare, edd. H. H. Furness *et al.* (Philadelphia,
1871–)
The Complete Works of Shakespeare, ed. Peter Alexander (4 vols, Collins, 1958). This
reprints, with corrections, the same editor's one-volume *Tudor Shakespeare* (1951)
The New Shakespeare, edd. J. Dover Wilson *et al.* (38 vols, Cambridge University
Press, 1921–66)
The Arden Shakespeare, gen. eds Harold F. Brooks and Harold Jenkins (Methuen,
1951–)
New Penguin Shakespeare, gen. ed. T. J. B. Spencer (Penguin Books, 1967–)
Shake-speares Sonnets (London, 1609): Menston, Scolar Press Facsimile, 1968
Shakespeare's Sonnets, ed. Martin Seymour-Smith (Heinemann, 1963)
Shakespeare's Sonnets, edd. W. G. Ingram and Theodore Redpath (University of
London Press, 1964)

Reference Books

BARTLETT, JOHN. *A New Concordance . . . of Shakespeare*, 1894, repr. New York, St
Martin's Press, 1956
CARY, M. *et al. The Oxford Classical Dictionary*, Oxford University Press, 1949
COTGRAVE, RANDLE. *A Dictionary of the French and English Tongues*, London, 1611;
Menston, Scolar Press Facsimile, 1968
FARMER, JOHN S. and HENLEY, W. E. *A Dictionary of Slang and its Analogues*, 7 vols,
[New York], 1890–1903
FLORIO, JOHN. *Queen Anna's New World of Words*, London 1611; Menston, Scolar
Press Facsimile, 1968
MURRAY, JAMES A. H. *et al. A New English Dictionary*, 20 vols, Oxford University
Press, 1888–1928; *Supplement*, 1933
ONIONS, C. T. *A Shakespeare Glossary* (1911) 2nd edn, Oxford University Press, 1919,
corr. repr. 1949
SCHMIDT, ALEXANDER. *Shakespeare-Lexicon*, 2 vols, Berlin and London, 1874–75

SPEVACK, MARVIN. *A Complete and Systematic Concordance to the Works of Shakespeare*, 6 vols, Hildesheim, Georg Olms, 1968–70

SUGDEN, E. H. *A Topographical Dictionary to the Works of Shakespeare and his Fellow Dramatists*, Manchester University Press, 1925

TILLEY, M. P. *A Dictionary of the Proverbs in England in the Sixteenth and Seventeenth Centuries*, University of Michigan Press, 1950

WRIGHT, JOSEPH. *The English Dialect Dictionary*, 6 vols, London, 1898

Biography and Background

ALEXANDER, PETER. *Shakespeare's Life and Art*, Nisbet, 1939

BALDWIN, T. W. The Organization and Personnel of the Shakespearean Company, Princeton University Press, 1927

BENTLEY, GERALD EADES. *Shakespeare: A Biographical Handbook*, Yale University Press, 1961

BUCKNILL, J. C. *The Medical Knowledge of Shakespeare*, London, 1860

CHAMBERS, E. K. *William Shakespeare: A Study of Facts and Problems*, 2 vols, Oxford University Press, 1930

CLOWES, WILLIAM. *Treatise, touching the cure of the disease called Morbus Gallicus*, London, 1579; 1585

HARBAGE, ALFRED. *Shakespeare's Audience*, Columbia University Press, 1941

JUDGES, A. V., ed. *The Elizabethan Underworld*, Routledge, 1930

LEE, SIR SIDNEY, et al. *Shakespeare's England*, 2 vols, Oxford University Press, 1916

MADDEN, D. H. *The Diary of Master William Silence*, London, 1897; 2nd edn, 1907

The Mirror for Magistrates, London, 1559, etc.; ed. Lily B. Campbell, Cambridge University Press, 1938

MONTAIGNE, MICHEL DE. *The Essays*, trans. John Florio, London, 1603; Dent, Everyman's Library edn, 3 vols, 1910

SIMPSON, R. R. *Shakespeare and Medicine*, E. and S. Livingstone, 1959

STOW, JOHN. *A Survey of London*, London, edn of 1603, ed. C. L. Kingsford, 2 vols, Oxford University Press, 1908

STUBBES, PHILIP. *The Anatomy of Abuses*, London, 1583

Tarlton's Jests, London, edn of 1613

VICARY, THOMAS. *The Anatomy of the Body of Man*, London, 1548, reissued 1577; ed. F. J. and P. Furnivall, London, 1888

WELSFORD, ENID. *The Fool: his social and literary history*, Faber, 1935; repr. 1968

WILCOX, R. TURNER. *The Mode in Costume*, Scribner, 1948

WRIGHT, LOUIS B. *Middle-Class Culture in Elizabethan England*, Cornell University Press, 1935

ZALL, P. M., ed. *A Hundred Merry Tales and Other English Jestbooks of the Fifteenth and Sixteenth Centuries*, University of Nebraska Press, 1963

Shakespeare's Language, Imagery and Conventions

ARMSTRONG, E. A. *Shakespeare's Imagination*, London, 1946; 2nd edn, University of Nebraska Press, 1963

BABB, LAWRENCE. 'The physiological concept of love in the Elizabethan and early

Stuart drama', *Publications of the Modern Language Association of America*, lvi (1941) 1020–35

BAKER, ANTHONY. 'Mistress Quickly's Bawdy', *N&Q*, n.s. xiii (1966) 132

CLEMEN, WOLFGANG H. *The Development of Shakespeare's Imagery* (Bonn, 1936, as *Shakespeares Bilder*); rev. and trans, Methuen, 1951

HULME, HILDA M. *Explorations in Shakespeare's Language*, Longmans, 1962

JORGENSEN, PAUL A. *Redeeming Shakespeare's Words*, University of California Press, 1962

KÖKERITZ, HELGE. *Shakespeare's Names*, Yale University Press, 1959

KÖKERITZ, HELGE. *Shakespeare's Pronunciation*, Yale University Press, 1953

LEWIS, C. S. *Studies in Words*, Cambridge University Press, 1960; 2nd edn, 1967

PARTRIDGE, ERIC. *Shakespeare's Bawdy: a literary and psychological essay and a comprehensive glossary*, Routledge 1947; 3rd edn, 1969

PYLES, THOMAS. 'Ophelia's "Nothing" ', *Modern Language Notes*, lxiv (1949) 322–3

SISSON, C. J. *New Readings in Shakespeare*, 2 vols, Cambridge University Press, 1956; n.e. Dawsons, Pall Mall, 1966

SPURGEON, CAROLINE. *Shakespeare's Imagery*, Cambridge University Press, 1935

STOLL, E. E. *Art and Artifice in Shakespeare*, Cambridge University Press, 1933

WILLIAMS, G. I. 'Serious uses of sexual imagery in the Elizabethan drama', Ph.D. thesis, University of Wales, 1964

Sources and Influences

BULLOUGH, GEOFFREY, ed. *Narrative and Dramatic Sources of Shakespeare*, 7 vols, Routledge and Columbia University Press, 1957–72

MUIR, KENNETH. 'Pyramus and Thisbe: A Study in Shakespeare's Method', *SQ*, v (1954) 141–53

MUIR, KENNETH. *Shakespeare's Sources, I: Comedies and Tragedies*, Methuen, 1957

RADOFF, M. L. 'Influence of French farce in *Henry V* and the *Merry Wives*', *Modern Language Notes*, xlviii (1933), 427–35

SATIN, JOSEPH. *Shakespeare and his Sources*, Houghton Mifflin, 1966

SPENCER, T. J. B., ed. *Elizabethan Love Stories*, Penguin Books, 1968

SPENCER, T. J. B., ed. *Shakespeare's Plutarch*, Penguin Books, 1964

Criticism

BARBER, C. L. *Shakespeare's Festive Comedy*, Princeton University Press, 1959

BAYLEY, JOHN. *The Characters of Love*, Chatto & Windus, 1960

BETHELL, S. L. *Shakespeare and the Popular Dramatic Tradition*, Staples Press, 1944

BETHELL, S. L. *'The Winter's Tale': a study*, Staples Press [1947]

BONJOUR, ADRIEN. 'The road to Swinstead Abbey: a study of the sense and structure of *King John*', *ELH*, xviii (1951) 253–74

BONNARD, GEORGES A. 'Shakespeare's purpose in *Midsummer-Night's Dream*', *Shakespeare Jahrbuch*, xcii (1956) 268–79

BRADBROOK, M.C. *Shakespeare and Elizabethan Poetry*, Chatto & Windus, 1951

BRADBROOK, M. C. *Themes and Conventions of Elizabethan Tragedy*, Cambridge University Press, 1953

BROOKE, NICHOLAS. *Shakespeare's Early Tragedies*, Methuen, 1968

BROOKS, HAROLD F. 'Two clowns in a comedy (to say nothing of the dog): Speed, Launce (and Crab) in *The Two Gentlemen of Verona*', *Essays and Studies*, n.s. xvi (1963) 91–100

BROWN, JOHN RUSSELL, and HARRIS, BERNARD, eds. *Early Shakespeare*, E. Arnold, 1961

CALDERWOOD, JAMES L. '*Love's Labour's Lost:* a wantoning with words', *SEL 1500–1900*, v (1965) 317–32

COLERIDGE, S. T. *Coleridge on Shakespeare*, ed. T. Hawkes, Penguin Books, 1969 (New York, 1959, as *Coleridge's Writings on Shakespeare*)

COOK, DAVID. '*Timon of Athens*', *SS* 16 (1963) 83–94

CRAIG, HARDIN. *An Interpretation of Shakespeare*, New York, 1948; repr. Hardin, 1966

CRUTTWELL, PATRICK. *The Shakespearean Moment*, Chatto & Windus, 1954

EDWARDS, PHILIP. *Shakespeare and the Confines of Art*, Methuen, 1968

EMPSON, WILLIAM. 'Falstaff and Mr Dover Wilson', *The Kenyon Review*, xv (1953) 213–62

EMPSON, WILLIAM. *Some Versions of Pastoral*, London, 1935; Peregrine edn, Penguin Books, 1966

FOAKES, R. A. '*Troilus and Cressida* reconsidered', *University of Toronto Quarterly*, xxxii (1962–63) 142–54

FOAKES, R. A. *Shakespeare: The Dark Comedies to the Last Plays*, Routledge, 1971

FRENCH, A. L. 'Hamlet's Nunnery', *English Studies*, xlviii (1967) 141–5

FRYE, DEAN. 'The question of Shakespearean "parody" ', *EC*, xv (1965) 22–6

FRYE, NORTHROP. 'Characterization in Shakespearian comedy', *SQ*, iv (1953) 271–7

FRYE, NORTHROP. *Anatomy of Criticism*, Princeton University Press, 1957

FRYE, NORTHROP. *A Natural Perspective*, Columbia University Press, 1965

GODDARD, HAROLD C. *The Meaning of Shakespeare*, 2 vols, University of Chicago Press, 1951

GRANVILLE-BARKER, HARLEY. *Prefaces to Shakespeare*, ed. M. St Clare Byrne (1927–47), 4 vols, Batsford, 1958–63

GREEN, WILLIAM. *Shakespeare's 'Merry Wives of Windsor'*, Princeton University Press, 1962

GRIVELET, MICHEL. 'Shakespeare, Molière, and the comedy of ambiguity', *SS* 22 (1969), 15–26

HERFORD, C. H. *Shakespeare's Treatment of Love and Marriage*, London, 1921

HINMAN, CHARLTON. *The Printing and Proof-reading of the First Folio of Shakespeare*, 2 vols, Oxford University Press, 1963

HOTSON, J. L. *Shakespeare's Motley*, Hart-Davis, 1952

HOTSON, J. L. *The First Night of 'Twelfth Night'*, Hart-Davis, 1954

JENKINS, HAROLD. '*As You Like It*', *SS* 8 (1955) 40–51

JENKINS, HAROLD. 'Hamlet and Ophelia', *Proceedings of the British Academy*, xlix (1963) 135–51

JOHNSON, SAMUEL, *Dr Johnson on Shakespeare*, ed. W. K. Wimsatt, Penguin Books, 1969 (New York, 1960, as *Samuel Johnson on Shakespeare*)

JONES, ELDRED. *Othello's Countrymen*, Oxford University Press, 1965

JONES, ERNEST. *Hamlet and Oedipus*, Gollancz, 1949

KNIGHT, G. WILSON. *The Sovereign Flower*, Methuen, 1958

KNIGHTS, L. C. *Some Shakespearean Themes* and *An Approach to 'Hamlet'* Chatto & Windus, 1959, 1960; combined Peregrine edn, Penguin Books, 1966

KOTT, JAN. *Shakespeare Our Contemporary*, trans. Boleslaw Taborski, Methuen, 1965; 2nd edn, 1967

LAWRENCE, W. W. *Shakespeare's Problem Comedies*, New York, 1931; Penguin Books, 1969

LEECH, CLIFFORD. '*Twelfth Night*' *and Shakespearean Comedy*, Toronto University Press, 1965

LEVER, J. W. *The Elizabethan Love Sonnet*, Methuen, 1956

LEVIN, RICHARD. 'Elizabethan "clown" subplots', *EC*, xvi (1966) 84–91

LEWIS, C. S. *Hamlet, the Prince or the Poem?*, London, Humphrey Milford [for the British Academy] 1943

MAHOOD, M. M. *Shakespeare's Wordplay*, Methuen, 1957

MARSH, D. R. C. *The Recurring Miracle*, University of Natal Press, Pietermaritzburg, 1962

MARSH, D. R. C. 'Interpretation and misinterpretation: the problem of *Troilus and Cressida*', *Shakespeare Studies*, i (1965) 182–98

MCCOLLOM, W. G. 'The role of wit in *Much Ado About Nothing*', *SQ*, xix (1968) 165–74

MILES, ROSALIND M. 'A Study of *Measure for Measure*', Ph.D. thesis, University of Birmingham, 1968

MUIR, K., ed., *Shakespeare, The Comedies: a collection of critical essays*, Prentice-Hall, 1965

POWELL, A. W. 'The Language and Procedures of Shakespearean Criticism', Ph.D. thesis, University of Bristol, 1967

PRICE, H. T. 'Mirror-scenes in Shakespeare', in James G. McManaway *et al.*, *Joseph Quincy Adams Memorial Studies*, Folger Shakespeare Library, Washington, 1948, pp. 101–13

RABKIN, NORMAN. *Shakespeare and the Common Understanding*, Collier-Macmillan, 1967

RIEMER, A. P. *A Reading of Shakespeare's 'Antony and Cleopatra'*, Sydney University Press, 1968

ROSSITER, A. P. *Angel with Horns*, Longmans, 1961

SCHANZER, ERNEST. '*A Midsummer-Night's Dream*', in Muir, ed., *Shakespeare, The Comedies* (see above), pp. 26–31

SCHANZER, ERNEST. *The Problem Plays of Shakespeare*, Routledge, 1963

SENG, PETER J. *The Vocal Songs in the Plays of Shakespeare*, Harvard University Press, 1967

SISSON, C. J. *The Mythical Sorrows of Shakespeare*, Oxford University Press, 1935

SMITH, LOGAN PEARSALL. *On Reading Shakespeare*, Constable, 1933

STIRLING, BRENTS. *The Populace in Shakespeare*, Columbia University Press, 1949

VICKERS, BRIAN. *The Artistry of Shakespeare's Prose*, Methuen, 1968

WAITH, EUGENE M. 'The metamorphosis of violence in *Titus Andronicus*', *SS* 10 (1957) 39–49

WELLS, STANLEY. 'The failure of *The Two Gentlemen of Verona*', *Shakespeare Jahrbuch*, xcix (1963) 161–73

WILSON, JOHN DOVER. *What Happens in 'Hamlet'*, Cambridge University Press, 1935; 3rd edn, 1951

WILSON, JOHN DOVER. *The Fortunes of Falstaff*, Cambridge University Press, 1943

WILSON, JOHN DOVER. *Shakespeare's Happy Comedies*, Faber, 1962

Related Material

BAKER, S. J. 'Shakespeare and sex', *The International Journal of Sexology*, iv (1950) 35–9

BERGSON, HENRI. *Laughter*, trans. Brereton and Rothwell, Macmillan, 1911

BRADLEY, S. A. J. and DUARTE, JOHN W., eds. *Sixty Ribald Songs from 'Pills to Purge Melancholy'*, Deutsch, 1968

BRISSENDEN, A. T. 'Sexual themes in Jacobean drama', Ph.D. thesis, University of London, 1962

DAVIDSON, SIR STANLEY, ed. *The Principles and Practice of Medicine*, 1952; Churchill Livingstone, 10th edn, 1971

DOUGLAS, MARY. *Purity and Danger*, Routledge, 1966; Penguin Books, 1970

FERGUSON, GEORGE. *Signs and Symbols in Christian Art*, 1954; 2nd edn, New York, Hesperides, 1959

FRAZER, SIR JAMES GEORGE. *The Golden Bough*, abridged edn, 2 parts, London, 1922

FREUD, SIGMUND. *Jokes and their Relation to the Unconscious*, trans. and ed. James Strachey, Routledge, 1960

HALE, J. R. *Renaissance Europe 1480–1520*, Fontana, 1971

RABELAIS, FRANCOIS. *Gargantua and Pantagruel*, trans. J. M. Cohen, Penguin Books, 1955

REEVES, JAMES. *The Idiom of the People*, Heinemann, 1958

ROBERTSON, D. W. *A Preface to Chaucer*, Princeton University Press, 1962

SPENCE, LEWIS. *The Minor Traditions of British Mythology*, London, Rider, 1948

WILSON, JOHN. *Logic and Sexual Morality*, Penguin Books, 1965

YOUNG, H. M. *The Sonnets of Shakespeare: a psycho-sexual analysis*, Columbia University Press, 1937

Glossary

Bawdy does not readily lend itself to lexicographical treatment: it is too volatile and too intimately related to particular contexts. It has seemed useful, nevertheless, in listing words and phrases which Shakespeare uses with indecent connotation, to add brief notes on those meanings which could be obscure to the modern reader.

Italic figures immediately following a word or phrase are page numbers showing where it has already been quoted or discussed in this book. Cross-references within the glossary are shown by the use of small capitals.

List of Abbreviations

SHAKESPEARE'S WORKS

AC	Antony and Cleopatra	Mac	Macbeth
Ado	Much Ado About Nothing	MM	Measure for Measure
AW	All's Well That Ends Well	MND	A Midsummer Night's Dream
AYL	As You Like It	MV	The Merchant of Venice
CE	The Comedy of Errors	MWW	The Merry Wives of Windsor
Cor	Coriolanus	Oth	Othello
Cym	Cymbeline	Per	Pericles
Ham	Hamlet	R2	Richard II
1H4	Henry IV, Part 1	R3	Richard III
2H4	Henry IV, Part 2	RJ	Romeo and Juliet
H5	Henry V	Son	Sonnets
1H6	Henry VI, Part 1	TA	Titus Andronicus
2H6	Henry VI, Part 2	Tem	The Tempest
3H6	Henry VI, Part 3	TGV	The Two Gentlemen of Verona
H8	Henry VIII	Tim	Timon of Athens
JC	Julius Caesar	TN	Twelfth Night
KJ	King John	TrC	Troilus and Cressida
KL	King Lear	TSh	The Taming of the Shrew
LC	A Lover's Complaint	VA	Venus and Adonis
LLL	Love's Labour's Lost	WT	The Winter's Tale
Luc	The Rape of Lucrece		

F1   The First Folio (1623);   Q, Q1, Q2   Quarto editions.

WORKS BY SHAKESPEARE'S CONTEMPORARIES

Chapman, *Widow's Tears*
> George Chapman, *The Widow's Tears*, in *The Plays and Poems*, ed. T. M. Parrott (London, 1910–14), ii, 363–434.

Cotgrave
> Randle Cotgrave, *A Dictionary of the French and English Tongues* (London, 1611; Menston, Scolar Press Facsimile, 1968).

Dekker, *1 Hon. Whore*
> Thomas Dekker and Thomas Middleton, *The Honest Whore, Part I*, in *The Dramatic Works of Thomas Dekker*, ed. Fredson Bowers (Cambridge University Press, 1953–61), ii, 1–130.

Dekker, *2 Hon. Whore*
> Thomas Dekker, *The Honest Whore, Part II*, in Bowers, *ed. cit.*, ii, 131–227.

Dekker, *Northward Ho*
> Thomas Dekker and John Webster, *Northward Ho*, in Bowers, *ed. cit.*, i, 405–90.

Dekker, *Sel. Writings*
> Thomas Dekker, *The Wonderful Year, The Gull's Horn Book, Penny-Wise Pound-Foolish, English Villainies Discovered by Lantern and Candlelight and Selected Writings*, ed. E. D. Pendry (E. Arnold, 1967).

Dekker, *Shoemaker's Hol.*
> Thomas Dekker, *The Shoemaker's Holiday*, in Bowers, *ed. cit.*, i, 7–104.

Florio
> John Florio, *Queen Anna's New World of Words* (London, 1611; Menston, Scolar Press Facsimile, 1968).

Ford, *'Tis Pity*
> John Ford, *'Tis Pity She's a Whore*, ed. N. W. Bawcutt (E. Arnold, 1966).

Heywood, *WKK*
> Thomas Heywood, *A Woman Killed with Kindness*, ed. R. W. Van Fossen (Methuen, 1961).

Jonson, *Alch.*
> Ben Jonson, *The Alchemist*, ed. F. H. Mares (Methuen, 1967).

Jonson, *Bart. Fair*
> Ben Jonson, *Bartholomew Fair*, ed. E. M. Waith (Yale University Press, 1963).

Jonson, *Discoveries*
> Ben Jonson, *Discoveries*, in *Works*, edd. C. H. Herford and Percy Simpson (Oxford University Press, 1925–52), viii, 555–649.

Jonson, *EMI*
> Ben Jonson, *Every Man in His Humour*, ed. Gabriele Bernhard Jackson (Yale University Press, 1969).

Jonson, *Epicoene*
> Ben Jonson, *Epicoene*, ed. Edward Partridge (Yale University Press, 1971).

Jonson, *Volpone*
> Ben Jonson, *Volpone*, ed. Alvin B. Kernan (Yale University Press, 1962).

Marlowe, *Faustus*
> Christopher Marlowe, *Doctor Faustus*, ed. J. D. Jump (Methuen, 1962).

Marston, *A &M*
> John Marston, *Antonio and Mellida*, ed. G. K. Hunter (E. Arnold, 1965).

Marston, *Dutch Court.*
John Marston, *The Dutch Courtesan*, ed. M. L. Wine (E. Arnold, 1965).
Marston, *Malcontent*
John Marston, *The Malcontent*, ed. M. L. Wine (E. Arnold, 1965).
Massinger, *City Madam*
Philip Massinger, *The City Madam*, ed. Cyrus Hoy (E. Arnold, 1964).
Middleton, *Changeling*
Thomas Middleton and William Rowley, *The Changeling*, ed. N. W. Bawcutt (Methuen, 1958).
Middleton, *CMC*
Thomas Middleton, *A Chaste Maid in Cheapside*, ed. R. B. Parker (Methuen, 1969).
Middleton, *Mich. Term*
Thomas Middleton, *Michaelmas Term*, ed. Richard Levin (E. Arnold, 1967).
Middleton, *Roaring Girl*
Thomas Middleton and Thomas Dekker, *The Roaring Girl*, in Bowers, *ed. cit.*, iii, 1–112.
Middleton, *TCOO*
Thomas Middleton, *A Trick to Catch the Old One*, ed. G. J. Watson (Benn, 1968).
Middleton, *WBW*
Thomas Middleton, *Women Beware Women*, ed. Roma Gill (Benn, 1968).
Stow
John Stow, *A Survey of London*, ed. C. L. Kingsford (Oxford University Press, 1908).
Tourneur, *Atheist's Trag.*
Cyril Tourneur, *The Atheist's Tragedy*, ed. Irving Ribner (Methuen, 1964).
Tourneur, *Rev. Trag.*
Cyril Tourneur (attrib.), *The Revenger's Tragedy*, ed. R. A. Foakes (Methuen, 1966).
Webster, *Wh. Devil*
John Webster, *The White Devil*, ed. John Russell Brown (Methuen, 1960).

OTHER BOOKS

Publication details of books listed in the Bibliography (p. 173) are not repeated here.

Alexander
Peter Alexander, ed., *The Complete Works of Shakespeare*.
Ard.
The Arden Shakespeare.
Armstrong
E. A. Armstrong, *Shakespeare's Imagination*.
Aubrey
John Aubrey, *Brief Lives*, ed. Oliver Lawson Dick (5th edn, Penguin Books, 1962).
F &H
John S. Farmer and W. E. Henley, *A Dictionary of Slang and its Analogues*.
Hulme
Hilda M. Hulme, *Explorations in Shakespeare's Language*.

Kökeritz
> Helge Kökeritz, *Shakespeare's Pronunciation.*

NPS
> *New Penguin Shakespeare.*

OED
> *New English Dictionary* (Oxford, corr. repr. 1933).

Onions
> C. T. Onions, *A Shakespeare Glossary* (1949).

Partridge
> Eric Partridge, *Shakespeare's Bawdy* (3rd edn, 1969).

Rabelais
> François Rabelais, *Gargantua and Pantagruel*, trans. J. M. Cohen.

Sugden
> E. H. Sugden, *A Topographical Dictionary to the Works of Shakespeare and his Fellow Dramatists.*

Tilley
> M. P. Tilley, *A Dictionary of the Proverbs in England in the Sixteenth and Seventeenth Centuries.*

ABHORSON. *MM* dram. pers. Cf. WHORESON.

ABILITY. *TrC* III.ii.82. Virility, sexual potency. Cf. Tourneur, *Atheist's Trag.* I.iv.140, 'Poor wench, for thy sake may his ability die in his appetite'.

ABLE. *H8* II.ii.139. Virile.

ABRAHAM CUPID, *11. RJ* II.i.13. Dekker, *Sel. Writings*, p. 289, 'going Abr'am (that is to say, "naked")'.

ACCOST, *85. TN* I.iii.52–6. Sir Andrew (alone) takes this in a copular sense.

ACCOUNT, *165. Son* 136. With possible pun on *cunt*. Cf. *H5* III.iv.47–52 and COUNT.

ACHE, ACHING. See BONES.

ACHILLES' BRACH. *TrC* II.i.111. Brach = hunting-hound, and more especially the bitch. Hence, homosexually, Patroclus.

ACT (n), *118. TrC* III.ii.80, *MM* II.iii.26. Coitus.

—— OF DARKNESS, *129. KL* III.iv.84.

—— OF LUST. *Luc* 1636.

—— OF SHAME. *Oth* V.ii.210.

—— OF SPORT. *Oth* II.i.221.

ACTAEON. *TA* II.iii.63, *MWW* II.i.106 and III.ii.36. In myth, Actaeon was changed into a stag by Artemis and killed by his own hounds; hence, here, a type-figure of cuckoldry. Cf. BUCK, HORN, STAG.

ACTION, *139. 2H4* II.i.1–4, *Per* IV.ii.9. Sexual activity. Cf. ENTER.

ACTIVITY, *134. H5* III.vii.96 (by quibble), *TrC* III.ii.55, *Tim* IV.iii.164. Sexual busy-ness.

ACTURE. *LC* 185. Copulation.

ADULTERY. *H5* II.i.35. A Quicklyism for *battery*.

AFFAIRS, *167. Son* 151. Quibble, (a) everyday business, household affairs, (b) female sex-organs. Cf. THING, WOMEN'S MATTERS.

AJAX. *LLL* V.ii.573. Punning on 'a jakes'. Cf. Sir John Harington, *The Metamorphosis of Ajax* (1596): Harington's invention was to improve a jakes by making it into a water-closet.

ANOTHER THING. *TGV* III.i.341. Here = female pudendum. Cf. ETCETERAS.

APPETITE, *9*, *59*. *TN* II.iv.96, *R3* III.v.80, *Oth* I.iii.259, *Son* 110. Sexual appetite.

APRONS MOUNTANT. *Tim* IV.iii.136. These are courtesans' aprons, regularly raised for fornication, though now only to receive Timon's gift of gold. Cf. LAP.

APT. *Tim* I.i.136. Sexually willing or inclined.

AQUA VITAE, *71*. *RJ* III.ii.88. Brandy or other spirits: a restorative for Juliet's Nurse—as also for bawds, according to Marston, *Malcontent* V.i.19.

AUNT, *9*, *152*. *Ham* II.ii.372 (with quibble), *WT* IV.iii.11. A procuress or trollop. Middleton, *TCOO* II.i.11, 'I need not say bawd, for everyone knows what "aunt" stands for in the last translation'.

 MAID'S —— OF BRAINFORD, *84*. *MWW* IV.ii.150. A description of MOTHER PRAT not calculated to reassure the jealous Ford. A maid's aunt has to live somewhere, and Brainford, = Brentford, is within fourteen miles of Windsor; but *aunt* can also mean *bawd*, and Brainford, with some other country villages within easy reach of London, was known as a place for furtive sexual adventure— like the Brighton of a later generation. Cf. Massinger, *City Madam* II.i.106, 'pleasures stoln being sweetest, apprehend / The raptures of being hurried in a coach / To Brainford, Staines, or Barnet.' (See also H. J. Oliver, Ard. *MWW*, p. lxii, on Q's 'Gillian of Brainford'.)

BACHELORSHIP. See FRUIT.

BACK, -S (n). With coital implication.

 BACK-TRICK. *TN* I.iii.116. Quibble, (a) *riccacciata*, a backward leap, (b) copulation.

 BEAST WITH TWO BACKS. *Oth* I.i.117. Man and woman in coital attitude.

 HOT ——, *79*. *MWW* V.v.9.

 SHOOK YOUR ——. *H5* III.vii.47.

 UPON MY ——, *TrC* I.ii.252.

BAG (n). *Oth* III.i.19. Where musicians' pipes are to be put up 'in your bag', one sense of *bag* is probably baggage, a loose girl. Cf. PIPES.

BALD, *133*. *Tim* IV.iii.161. Loss of hair through venereal disease could be a direct result of syphilis but may have been brought on by the fumigation and sweating with which the veneral infections were treated. Cf. POWDERING TUB, HOT-HOUSE.

BALLS. *H5* I.ii.283. Probable quibble, (a) tennis balls, (b) the Dauphin's testicles. Cf. EMBALLING; and Middleton, *WBW* III.iii.85, '*Ward*. Why, can you catch a ball well? *Isabella*. I have catched two in my lap at one game.'

BARBARY HORSE, *122*. *Oth* I.i.112. A breeding stallion from the North African coast.

BARNES. *Ado* III.iv.43. Pun *barns/bairns* (children).

BARRICADO FOR A BELLY. *WT* I.ii.204.

 BARRICADO [VIRGINITY] AGAINST HIM, *89*. *AW* I.i.112.

BASIMECU, *54*, *66*. *2H6* IV.vii.25. Nickname for the Dauphin: *baisez-ma-queue*, kiss my arse. Cf. QUEUBUS.

BASTARD, -S, -Y, *52*, *94*, *96*, *120*, *132*, *152*. *1H6* V.iv.70, etc. (by no means always bawdy in Shakespeare).

BASTARDLY. *2H4* II.i.47. Quicklyism for *dastardly*.

BASTARDIZING. *KL* I.ii.132. The begetting of a bastard.

BATHS. *Tim* IV.iii.87. Hot baths as a treatment for venereal disease. Cf. HOT-HOUSE.

BAUBLE. *RJ* II.iv.90. *AW* IV.v.28. Quibble, (a) fool's sceptre, (b) phallus. Cf. Ford, '*Tis Pity* I.ii.123, 'They say a fool's bauble is a lady's playfellow'.

BAWD, *99*, *129*. *VA* 792, *RJ* II.iv.127, etc. A procurer or brothel-keeper, male or female.

BAWD'S HOUSE. *MM* II.i.173. A brothel.

BAWDY-HOUSE, -S. *1H4* III.iii.16, 98 and 156, *2H4* II.iv.136, *H5* II.i.33, *Per* IV.v.6. A brothel.

PARCEL-BAWD. *MM* II.i.61. A part-time pimp.

BE OUT. *AYL* IV.i.74–80. Quibble, (a) be at a loss for words, (b) have penis out of loved-one's vagina. See also at HAND.

BEAR (vb), *38*. *TSh* II.i.200, *RJ* II.i.76, *2H4* II.i.32 and II.iv.57, *H5* III.vii.43, *AC* I.v.21 and III.vii.8. To support a man's weight during coitus: with various quibbles.

BEAST, -LY, *78*, *146*. *MWW* V.v.5–8, *Ham* I.v.42, *Oth* IV.i.62, *MM* III.ii.22. Man or god reduced to beastliness by carnality or by being cuckolded. Cf. HORNS, MONSTER.

—— WITH TWO BACKS. *Oth* I.i.117. Man and woman in coital attitude.

BESTIAL APPETITE, *59*. *R3* III.v.80.

BEAT LOVE DOWN. *RJ* I.iv.28. Probable quibble, (a) discourage love, (b) induce orgasm and detumescence. Cf. Modern American, 'beat my meat'.

BED, -S (n), *3*, *77*, *116*, *124*, *132*, *154*. *MV* V.i.228, etc.

BEDFELLOW, *77*. *MV* V.i.223.

BED-MATE. *TrC* IV.i.6.

BEDS OF LUST. *Tim* IV.iii.258.

BEDS' REVENUES. *Son* 142. Legitimate sexual enjoyment.

BED-SWERVER. *WT* II.i.93. An adulteress.

BLAMEFUL ——. *2H6* III.ii.212.

DAY-BED. *TN* II.v.47.

DOWN ——. *H8* I.iv.18.

DULL, STALE, TIRED ——, *127*. *KL* I.ii.13.

ENSEAMED ——. *Ham* III.iv.92.

FEATHER-BED, *75*. *MV* II.ii.153. As place of physical peril.

GO TO ——. *AW* V.iii.262, possibly *WT* IV.iv.105; *Per* IV.ii.102. (1) For sexual intercourse; (2) in *Per*, a euphemism for premature male orgasm.

HIGHWAY TO MY ——. *RJ* III.ii.134.

LOVE-BED. *R3* III.vii.71.

UNPROPER BEDS. *Oth* IV.i.68. Shared with wives' lovers.

BEHIND-DOOR-WORK, *152*. *WT* III.iii.72. Illicit sex. Cf. STAIR-WORK, TRUNK-WORK.

BELGIA, THE NETHERLANDS. *CE* III.ii.136. The low countries of the female body.

BELL-WETHER. *MWW* III.v.96. A noisy ram, and hence Falstaff's term for an aggressive cuckold.

BELLY, -IES, *108*, *132*, *VA* 594, etc. Used with various coital implications.

CHILD BRAGS IN HER ——. *LLL* V.ii.665.

BEWHORE. *Oth* IV.ii.114. To call a woman a whore.

BIG. *WT* II.i.61. Pregnant.

BLAINS, *133*. *Tim* IV.i.28. Boils or blisters, regarded as venereal symptoms.

BLOW (n), *57*, *119*. *3H6* III.ii.23, *TrC* I.ii.261. A coital thrust.

BLOW UP, *89*. *AW* I.i.118–23. Conflates (a) war/sex imagery (cf. BREACH, CHARGE, CITY, PIKES, SIEGE, UNDERMINE) and (b) the idea of swelling in pregnancy.

BOAR, *136*. *Cym* II.v.16. Type of bestial lust.

   BOAR'S HEAD. Sign of several London taverns. That of *H4* and *H5* was in Eastcheap. Another, in Southwark High Street, was once the property of Sir John Fastolfe (Sugden, p. 66). Cf. CARDINAL'S HAT.

BOILED STUFF, *135*. *Cym* I.vi.124. Prostitutes who have been overworked, and/or sweated in tubs to treat their venereal diseases. Cf. BATHS, POWDERED BAWD, SODDEN, STUFF.

BOILS (n). *TrC* II.i.2–5. Probably as a venereal symptom.

BOLSTER (vb). *Oth* III.iii.396. Share a bolster.

BONA-ROBA, *103*. *2H4* III.ii.23 and 200. Prostitute. Florio: 'good stuff, that is, a good wholesome plumcheeked wench.'

BONES. *Cor* III.i.178. As supposed to be harmed by venereal disease. Untreated or wrongly treated gonorrhoea can produce, amongst other effects, chronic arthritis. The general malaise associated with syphilis in its secondary stage could also cause the sensation still popularly described as 'aching bones'. Cf. HAMS, SCIATICA.

   ACHE IN MY ——, *118*. *TrC* V.iii.104.

   ACHING ——. *TrC* V.x.35 and 49.

   DRYNESS OF HIS ——. *AC* I.iv.27.

   HOLLOW ——, *133* *MM* I.ii.55, *Tim* IV.iii.154.

   INCURABLE BONE-ACHE, *7*. *TrC* V.i.21. Cf. Jonson, *Alch*. III.ii.38.

BOSOM (vb). *KL* V.i.13. To clinch, amorously.

BOTTOM-GRASS. *VA* 236. Although *bottom* as = human posterior is not recorded in *OED* before 1794, it is hard to resist Partridge's gloss 'the hair growing in and about the crutch'. Bottoms, in Venus's primary sense, are meadows, where 'sweet' lush grass grows. But see also *OED*, *bottom*, 16; and Boswell's *Life of Johnson* (ed. Hill, rev. Powell), iv, 99.

BOULT, *139–40*. *Per* dram. pers. Hulme (p. 54) suggests that *bolt* can mean pimp or pander, perhaps by association with door-holding. The name Boult for this particular fastener of doors is apparently of the dramatist's own choice, as the corresponding character in the prose source is not named. Cf. BUM, OVERDONE, TEARSHEET, VEROLES.

BOUT. *1H6* III.ii.56–8. Talbot means 'a fight', but La Pucelle ('Are ye so hot, sir?') quibbles on the idea of a sexual encounter. Cf. Middleton, *CMC* II.i.76–78.

BOW (n), *36*. *LLL* IV.i.103, *TrC* III.i.109. Both contexts raise the suspicion that *bow* could, in suggestive contexts, carry the sense *vulva*. See also Middleton, *Mich. Term* II.i.97.

   BOW-HAND. *LLL* IV.i.126. Cf. HAND IS OUT.

BOW (vb) IN THE HAMS, *69*. *RJ* II.iv.52. Through sexual excess, and perhaps venereal BONE-ACHE.

BRAKES. *VA* 237. Quibble, (a) thickets, (b) pubic hair.

BRAN AND WATER. *LLL* I.i.280. Low diet to 'cure' lechery. See also WATER AND BRAN.

BRAWN-BUTTOCK. *AW* II.ii.17. Fleshy buttock. Cf. *brawns* in *Cym* IV.ii.312.

BREACH (n), *89*, *102*. *2H4* II.iv.49, *AW* I.i.124. Female pudendum.

BROACH (vb). *AC* I.ii.167. Quibble, (a) begin, (b) stick into.

BROKER. *KJ* II.i.568, *Ham* I.iii.127, *LC* 173. A go-between.
  BROKER-LACKEY. *TrC* V.x.33.
  BROKERS-BETWEEN. *TrC* III.ii.199.

BROTHEL, -S, *132*. *Ham* II.i.61, *Tim* IV.i.13, *KL* I.iv.241 and II.iv.93.
  BROTHEL-HOUSE. *Ado* I.i.233.

BROW, -S. *LLL* IV.i.110, *Ham* IV.v.116, *WT* I.ii.119 and 146. In a man, this is the forehead horned by cuckolding, or potentially so. In an adulterous woman, *whore* or *harlot* is fancied written on the forehead. Cf. *Oth* IV.ii.70–1.

BUCK, *84*. *MWW* III.iii.138-9. Quibble, (a) lye for bleaching dirty clothes, (b) stag, (c) horned cuckold.

—— AND DOE. *TrC* III.i.110. Male and female, shot by Cupid's arrows.

BUCKLERS. *Ado* V.ii.18. Quibble, (a) small shields, (b) female pudenda—the inserted swords being phallic.

BULL, *30*, *43*, *44*, *102*. *MND* II.i.180, *2H4* II.ii.151, *MWW* V.v.4, *Ado* I.i.242-3, V.i.174, V.iv.43-51. A regular and powerful copulator, sometimes deceptively passive: cf. EUROPA.
  BULL ... DOG. *TrC* V.vii.9–11. As = 'The cuckold and the cuckold-maker', embattled. Cf. HORNS.
  THE ——. *TrC* V.i.51. Menelaus, as cuckold, HORNED.

BULLETS. *2H4* II.iv.107-15. *Two* bullets, as = testicles.

BULLY STALE, *83*. *MWW* II.iii.27. *Bully* is a more-or-less affectionate form of address; *stale* = urine, forms one of the Host's cheerful nicknames for Dr Caius because Elizabethan quacks were often willing to prescribe for patients whom they had not seen, but whose urine they had inspected. Simpson, *Shakespeare and Medicine*, p. 22, quotes a statute of the College of Physicians denouncing such water-casting (*c.* 1601). Cf. CASTALION-KING-URINAL, MOUNSEUR MOCK-WATER, and *2H4* I.ii.1–4.

BUM, -S (n). *MND* II.i.53, *MM* II.i.206-7, *Tim* I.ii.236. Buttocks, and Pompey's surname.

BURDEN (n). *RJ* II.v.76, *H8* II.iii.43. Man's weight, in coitus.

BURDEN (vb). *TSh* II.i.202, *RJ* I.iv.23. To apply weight, and perhaps pressure, during coitus. Cf. HEAVIER, WEIGHT.

BURIED ... FACE UPWARDS. *Ado* III.ii.63. By quibble based on DIE, the fate of female during sexual intercourse.

BURN (vb), *26*, *32*, *130*, *133*. *CE* IV.iii.51, *TGV* II.v.45, *2H4* III.iv.326, possibly *TrC* V.ii.193, *KL* III.ii.84 and glancingly IV.vi.129, *Tim* IV.iii.142. To infect with gonorrhoea or any other urethral disorder with a burning sensation among its symptoms.

BUTT (n), *39–40*. *TSh* V.ii.40. An obscure cuckoldry joke.

BUTTOCK, -S. *CE* III.ii.116, *AW* II.ii.16–18, *Cor* II.i.48.

CAKE. *CE* III.i.71, *TSh* I.i.15. As = woman.

CALF. *Ado* V.iv.50, *WT* I.ii.127. Son of a BULL.

CALLET, -AT, *55*. *2H6* I.iii.81, *3H6* II.ii.145, *Oth* IV.ii.120, *WT* II.iii.90. Contemptuous term for a woman: a drab.

CALM (n). *2H4* II.iv.36–40. Quicklyism for *qualm*, taken up by Falstaff as = abstinence from sexual intercourse.

CAMP (n). *AW* V.iii.194, *Oth* III.iii.342. As place of business for soldiers' whores.

CAP (b), *42*. *Ado* I.i.185. Worn uneasily over HORNS.

CAPABLE. *LLL* IV.ii.76, glancingly *AW* I.i.206. Sexually.

CARDINALLY. *MM* II.i.77. Malapropism for *carnally*.

CARDINAL'S HAT. *1H6* I.iii.36 and 49. In Southwark, some brothels ordered to be 'put downe' in 1546 included one at the sign of the Boar's Head, another at the Cardinal's Hat (Stow, ii, 55). Sh. may be glancing at that. Cf. WINCHESTER GOOSE.

CARET, *82*. *MWW* IV.i.48–9. Quicklyism, (a) Latin for 'is missing', (b) carrot, (c) phallus, 'a good root'.

CARPET-MONGERS. *Ado* V.ii.32. Men 'whose achievements belong to the lady's boudoir' (Onions).

CARRIAGE. *RJ* I.iv.94. 'Good carriage' here quibbles on (a) ability to bear the weight of a man, (b) ability to bear children, (c) good demeanour, (d) good moral conduct.

CARRION. *RJ* III.v.156, *MV* III.i.32, *MWW* III.iii.170, *Ham* II.ii.181. Corrupted flesh; hence a term of abuse, sometimes with sexual implications. Cf. *OED*, 3b.

CARRY. *AW* III.vii.19. To carry a woman by storm (or by attrition).

CART (n and vb), *9, 41, 109*. *TSh* I.i.55, *AYL* III.ii.7. Prostitutes were sometimes whipped while exposed on, or at the tail of, a cart.

CARVE. *LLL* V.ii.323, *MWW* I.iii.41. To make advances by signalling with the fingers—'a sort of digitary ogle' (F. L. Lucas, *Works of Webster*, i, 209).

CASE (n), *4, 69, 71, 82, 90, 149*. *KJ* I.i.147, *RJ* II.iv.50–1, III.iii.85–91, IV.v.97, *1H4* II.iv.243 (bow-case). *2H4* II.i.28, *MWW* IV.i.52–70, *AW* I.iii.21–3, *AC* I.ii.160, *Cym* II.iii.75. Cotgrave, glossing Fr. *cas*: 'also, the privities (of man, or woman)'.

CASTALION-KING-URINAL, *83*. *MWW* II.iii.30. Nickname for Dr Caius, alluding to urine-inspection as a form of quackery. See also BULLY STALE and MOUNSEUR MOCKWATER. 'Castalion' suggests Castilian pride, foreignness and aggressiveness; with a glance too, perhaps, at the spring of Castalia, near Delphi. Being sacred to Apollo and the Muses, the spring was a source of inspiration to those who drank of it.

CATASTROPHE. *2H4* II.i.58. As = bottom, posterior.

CATCH (vb), *102*. *2H4* II.iv.45. Catch venereal diseases.

—— A BLOW, *57*. *3H6* III.ii.23. Sexually.

CENTAURS, *130*. *KL* IV.vi.124. As type of bestial lechery. Cf. NESSUS.

CHAMBER, *118*. *TrC* III.ii.207. Private room for fornication.

CHAMBER-LYE. *1H4* II.i.22. Urine.

CHANGING PIECE. *TA* I.i.309. Woman as small-change coin, passed from hand to hand.

CHARGE (vb). *2H4* II.iv.114–19. To assail, sexually.

CHARGED CHAMBERS, *102*. *2H4* II.iv.51. Quibble, (a) small cannon, loaded; (b) ovaries; perhaps also (c) female cavities where gonorrhoeal infection is encountered.

CIRCLE (n), *13, 18, 105*. *RJ* II.i.24, *H5* V.ii.289. Vulva.

CISTERN OF MY LUST. *Mac* IV.iii.63. As unfilled container.

CITY, *89*. *AW* I.i.125, *LC* 176. Citadel of chastity.

CLACK-DISH. *MM* III.ii.120. Possibly a quibble, (a) beggar's wooden bowl with noisy lid, (b) female pudendum.

CLASPS, -INGS. *Oth* I.i.127, *Per* I.i.128.

CLEAVING THE PIN. *LLL* IV.i.129. Quibble, (a) splitting the pin in centre of archery target, (b) masturbation of male by female.

CLEF. *TSh* III.i.75. Possible quibble, (a) sign on musical stave, (b) Hortensio's penis. But the cryptic message may simply allude to his double identity when disguised.

CLIFF. *TrC* V.ii.11. Quibble, (a) clef, key in music; (b) cleft, vulva. Cf. Marlowe, *Faustus* (Appendix I) A-version iv.56, 'all she-devils has clefts and cloven feet.' See also SING.

CLIFFS. *CE* III.ii.125. In the geography of Nell = breasts.

CLOSE (vb). *TrC* III.ii.48. To embrace, to engage sexually.

CLOSE-STOOL. *LLL* V.i.572, *AW* V.ii.17. Chamber-pot enclosed in a box or stool.

CLYSTER-PIPES. *Oth* II.i.173. Syringes, with a vague indecent implication here.

COCK, *39*. *TSh* II.i.224–5, *H5* II.i.49. Penis (with quibbles).

COD, -S, *107*. *AYL* II.iv.47. Strictly, *cod* = scrotum. More loosely, in plural, testicles.

CODDING SPIRIT. *TA* V.i.99.

MASTER PEASCOD, *27*. *MND* III.i.182.

QUOD ... QUODS. *MWW* IV.i.70–1. Punning on COD and CODS (Kökeritz, p. 119).

COD-PIECE, *36, 128, 146*. *TGV* II.vii.53–5, *LLL* III.i.174, *Ado* III.iii.133, *MM* III.ii.109, *KL* III.ii.27, *WT* IV.iv.607. Flap on breeches or hose, enclosing male genitalia. By extension, the organs themselves.

COIN HEAVEN'S IMAGE. *MM* II.iv.45–6. Beget children, illicitly. Cf. STAMP.

COINER WITH HIS TOOLS. *Cym* II.v.5. Quibble, (a) illicit coin-maker with his stamping tools, (b) illicit lover (begetting a bastard) with his sexual organs.

COLT (vb), *136*. *Cym* II.iv.133. To copulate with. Cf. MOUNT.

COLT'S TOOTH ... NOT CAST YET. *H8* I.iii.48. Proverbial expression for youthful promiscuity. See Tilley, C525.

COME, *12–13*. No orgasmic denotation in Shakespeare.

—— HALTING OFF, *102*. *2H4* II.iv.49. Limping away after (a) battle, (b) coitus.

—— OFF THE BREACH, *102*. *2H4* II.iv.49. The same quibble repeated.

—— OVER. *Ado* V.ii.9. Either 'to overcome sexually' or simply 'to top (someone) sexually'.

—— TO [SOMEONE'S] BED, *116*. *TN* III.iv.29, *Ham* IV.v.64. Malvolio is quoting from a song whose words are in *Tarlton's Jests*, 1601 (Mahood, NPS *TN*, p. 169).

COMING-IN, *74*. *MV* II.ii.151. Quibble, (a) income, (b) coitus.

COMMIT (vb, trans.), *121*. *Oth* IV.ii.71–9, *KL* III.iv.78. Commit adultery.

COMMON, -EST (adj.). *R2* V.iii.17, *2H4* II.ii.161, *Ado* IV.i.63, *AW* V.iii.188 and 284, *Oth* III.iii.299, *Cym* I.vi.104. Available as prostitute.

—— HOUSES. *MM* II.i.43.Brothels.

COMMONER (n), *121*. *AW* V.iii.194. *Oth* IV.ii.72. Prostitute.

COMMONWEALTH, *44*. *LLL* IV.ii.73, possibly *1H4* II.i.81, *Ado* III.iii.162, *MM* I.ii.105. With pun on COMMON.

CONCEIVE, *126*. *TSh* V.ii.22–5, *KL* I.i.11–12. Quibble, (a) understand, (b) become pregnant.

CONCUPY (n). *TrC* V.ii.175. Either 'concupiscence' or 'concubine'. See *OED*, *concupy* and *concuby*.

CONFESSOR. *H8* I.iv.15. A confessor whose intent is lecherous. Cf. SHRIVE.

CONFLICT (n). *TA* II.iii.21. Amatory engagement.

CONGER, *102*. *2H4* II.iv.52. Large eel—the term being applied to Falstaff abusively and with penial connotation.

CONJURE UP, *105*. *H5* V.ii.284. Raise (with coital suggestions). In *conjure*, as also in *consign*, *consort* and *constable*, there may be a jingle on Fr. *con*, Lat. *cunnus*, Eng. *cunt*.

—— DOWN. *RJ* II.i.26. Induce male orgasm, and hence detumescence.

CONSUMPTION. *KL* IV.vi.129. With allusion to gonorrhoea. Cf. BURN.

CONTEND. *TGV* I.ii.129. Struggle together, sexually.

CONVERSATION. *R3* III.v.31. Guilty intercourse.

CONVINCE. *Oth* IV.i.28, *Cym* I.iv.91. Make a sexual conquest of.

COOL (vb), *147*. *KL* III.ii.79, *AC* I.i.10. To lessen sexual heat.

COPE (vb). *Oth* IV.i.86, *WT* IV.iv.421. To copulate with. Partridge cfs Scots *coup* (to throw) and comments, 'yet another of those sadistic verbs of copulation: cf. *hit*, *strike*, *thump*, and *fuck* itself'.

COPESMATE. *Luc* 925. Sexual partner.

COPULATION. *AYL* III.ii.76, *KL* IV.vi.114.

COPULATIVES. *AYL* V.iv.54.

CORINTH. *Tim* II.ii.74. City notorious for luxury and profligacy. Perhaps also the name of a brothel.

CORINTHIAN. *1H4* II.iv.11. Easygoing, friendly and brazen roisterer.

CORNER, -S. *MV* III.v.27, *MM* IV.iv.156. As place for furtive sexual dealings.

—— IN THE THING I LOVE. *Oth* III.iii.269. Cf. THING, USES.

CORNUTO. *MWW* III.v. 63. Cuckold, a horned man.

COUCH (vb), *125*. *MV* V.i.305, *Oth* IV.iii.55.

COUNSEL-KEEPER. *2H4* II.iv.256. Bawd, hold-door. Cf. *Oth* IV.ii.21–9, 90–3.

COUNT (n), *4, 19, 105*. *H5* III.iv.48–52, probably *H8* II.iii.41. Pun, *gown/count/cunt*. Cf. Webster, *Wh. Devil* I.ii.57.

COUNTRY. With pun on *cunt*—

—— COPULATIVES. *AYL* V.iv.54. The pun may be present, or it may not.

—— MATTERS, *16*. The pun surely is present.

—— MISTRESSES. *Cym* I.iv.53. The pun could be present.

COURTESAN, *24*. *CE* dram. pers., *1H6* III.ii.45, *R3* III.vii.73, *KL* III.ii.79. Prostitute.

COVER (vb), *17, 122*. *Oth* I.i.112, glancingly *WT* I.ii.294. To mount, coitally.

COW (n), *44, 45*. *Ado* II.i.21 and V.iv.49. As = woman or wife.

CRACK (vb)-

—— THE GLASS OF HER VIRGINITY, *140*. *Per* IV.vi.141.

—— THE LAWYER'S VOICE, *133*. *Tim* IV.iii.152. The reference is to syphilitic ulcerations of the larynx.

BOND OF CHASTITY QUITE CRACKED. *Cym* V.v.207.

CRESSID, -A, *104, 117, 120*. *H5* II.i.73. *TN* III.i.51, *AW* II.i.97, *TrC passim* but especially III.ii.180–202. As type of highly sexed, inconstant woman.

CROP (n). *AW* I.iii.45. Crop of illegitimate children.

CROP (vb). *AC* II.ii.232. To bear (illegitimate) children. Cf. EAR, GROUND, PLOUGH.

CROWN, -S (n). See FRENCH CROWN, SCATTER HIS CROWNS.

CRY 'HEM'. *AYL* I.iii.19, *Oth* IV.ii.28. Give the brothel-keeper's call of warning if somebody approaches during copulation. Cf. HOLD-DOOR TRADE.

CUCKOLD, -RY, *9*, *90*, *120*, *151*. *LLL* V.i.59, etc. Husband of an adulterous wife. As a type-figure, he was usually thought of as growing horns.

  CUCKOLD-MAD. *CE* II.i.58. Driven mad by supposition of being a cuckold.

  CUCKOLD-MAKER. *TrC* V.vii.9, *H8* V.iv.27. Adulterer.

CUCKOLD (vb). *MWW* III.v.122, *Oth* I.iii.363, IV.i.199. To make someone a cuckold.

  CUCKOLDY, -LY (adj). *MWW* II.ii.240 and 244, V.v.108, *AYL* III.ii.79.

CUCKOO, *28*. *LLL* V.ii.885-98, *MND* III.i.124-8. *MWW* II.i.111, *AW* I.iii.62. Symbolic bird of cuckoldry, since it lays its eggs in the nests of other birds.

CUPID, *36*. *LLL* III.i.169-76, IV.iii.54. Eros, god of love.

  CUPID'S CARRIERS, *81*. *MWW* II.ii.122. Go-betweens.

  SIGN OF BLIND —. *Ado* I.i.233. Brothel-house sign.

CUSTOMER, *26*. *CE* IV.iv.57, *AW* V.iii.284, *MM* IV.iii.4, *Oth* IV.i.120, *Per* IV.vi.18. A prostitute plying for custom (*AW*, *Oth*); a prostitute's 'client' (*CE*, *MM*, *Per*).

CUSTOM-SHRUNK. *MM* I.ii.83. Having fewer customers at the brothel.

CUT (n), *85*, *149*. *TN* II.v.87-9, *AC* I.ii.160. Vulva (by quibbles). Cf. *OED*, sb, 20; German *Kutt*; and Middleton, *CMC* II.i.135, 'Can any woman have a greater cut?'

CUT A MORSEL OFF THE SPIT. *Per* IV.ii.132. To have sexual intercourse with a woman who is already not a virgin. Cf. STEAL A SHIVE; WATER . . . BY THE MILL.

DALE. *VA* 232. Partridge: 'the valley between her breasts; the vulva-valley; and perhaps the rearward ravine'.

DARK (n). *LLL* V.ii.24, *TrC* III.ii.48, *Oth* IV.iii.64. As cover for sexual activity.

  ACT OF DARKNESS. *KL* III.iv.84.

  DEED OF DARKNESS. *Per* IV.vi.28.

DAUGHTERS OF THE GAME. *TrC* IV.v.63. Harlots.

DAY-BED. *TN* II.v.47. With copulation implied.

DEAD MEN'S FINGERS, *169*. *Ham* IV.vii.172. Polite name for 'long purples', flowers of phallic appearance. The euphemism reappears in Middleton, *CMC* II.i.59.

DEAL (vb), *139*. *Per* IV.vi.25 and 137. To have sexual business.

DEED, -S, *13*. *LLL* III.i.188, *MV* I.iii.82, *TrC* III.i.126 and III.ii.54, *AC* I.v.14-16, *Per* IV.vi.28. Coitus. Cf. Middleton, *CMC* II.i.146.

  DARK DEEDS. *MM* III.ii.167.

DEER, *36*. *LLL* IV.i.107, *MWW* V.v.15, *Cym* II.iii.70. With pun on *dear*, sexual quarry to be hunted.

DEFLOWER. *TA* II.iii.191, II.iv.26 and V.iii.38, *Luc* 348, *RJ* IV.v.37, *MM* IV.iv.19.

  DEFLOWERED MY DEAR, *28*. *MND* V.i.284. Bottom's slip for *devoured*.

DEMESNES. *RJ* II.i.20. Rosaline's pelvic region.

DIAN, -A. *TA* II.iii.57, *AW* I.iii.110, *Per* IV.ii.150, *Cym* II.v.7 and V.v.180. As goddess of chastity: sometimes used sarcastically. (Not usually bawdy in Sh.)

  DIAN'S RANGERS. *Cym* II.iii.69. Virgins who escort Diana.

DIE (vb). Possibly *2H6* II.iii.46; more clearly *Ado* V.ii.92, *TrC* III.i.114–19, *KL* IV.vi.198. Quibble, (a) loss of life, (b) detumescence following orgasm, in male or female.

DIET (n). *Tim* IV.iii.88. Prescribed for venereal patients. Cf. TUB-FAST.

DILDOS, *153*. *WT* IV.iv.196. Although this masquerades here as the kind of nonsense-word common in ballads, the nearness of 'jump her and thump her' suggests also the more concrete sense of *dildo*, an artificial phallus. Cf. Florio, '*Puga*, a pricke, a pillicocke, a dildoe'; and Middleton, *CMC* I.ii.56–8, where *dildo* appears in both its roles.

DINE (vb). *Cym* III.v.143. Of lust—to be satiated.

DIS, *154*. *Tem* IV.i.89. As rapist of Persephone.

DISCHARGE (vb). *2H4* II.iv.106–13 and probably III.ii.254. Quibble, (a) fire a pistol or other weapon, (b) ejaculate semen.

DISEASE, -S (n), *102*. *2H4* I.ii.234 and II.iv.42–5, *TrC* V.x.55, *MM* I.ii.45, *Per* IV.ii.109 and IV.vi.97. Specifically, venereal disease.

  DISEASED PERFUMES. *Tim* IV.iii.208. Infected and perfumed concubines.

  DISEASED VENTURES, *135*. *Cym* I.vi.122. Infected prostitutes.

  HAVE THE —. *WT* I.ii.207. To be cuckolded.

DISEDGE (vb). *Cym* III.iv.92. To satisfy a man's sexual appetite.

DISH (n). *AC* II.vi.122 and V.ii.271. As = woman.

DISHONEST. *H5* I.iii.49, *TN* IV.ii.31 and possibly I.v.37. Unchaste or indecent.

DISTAIN (vb). *R3* V.iii.323, *Luc* 786. To defile sexually.

DO, *62*, *95*, *121*, *129*, *139*. *TA* IV.ii.73, etc. Quibble, (a) be active, (b) copulate, or copulate with. Cotgrave: '*Besongner*. To worke, labour . . . Also, to doe, or leacher with.'

  —— FOR CLIENTS HER FITMENT. *Per* IV.vi.5. Copulate with customers, as a prostitute should.

  —— MY OFFICE. *Oth* I.iii.382. To copulate (as *de facto* husband).

  —— NAUGHT WITH, *17*, *58*. *R3* I.i.99. To copulate with.

  —— THE DEED, *13*. *LLL* III.i.188, *MV* I.iii.82, *Per* IV.vi.28.

  GREAT DOERS IN OUR TRADE. *MM* IV.iii.17. Frequent users of prostitutes.

  MISTRESS OVERDONE, *145–6*. *MM* dram. pers. and II.i.190–2. See OVERDONE.

DOE. *TA* II.i.93 and 117, II.iii.26, *Luc* 581, *MWW* V.v.16, *TrC* III.i.110. As = woman.

DOLL TEARSHEET, *104*. *2H4* dram. pers., *H5* II.i.74 and (probably through an error) V.i.77. 'Doll' was to become a favourite name for prostitutes in Jacobean drama: cf. *Alch.*, *2 Hon. Whore*, *Northward Ho*. 'Tearsheet' is unique and splendid.

DOOR KEEPER. *Per* IV.vi.117. Boult, employed in the brothel.

DOUBLE-DEALER. *Ado* V.iv.112. Unfaithful husband.

DOVE. *MWW* I.iii.94, *Ham* IV.v.164. As = loved one.

  DOVES. *TrC* III.i.121. Eaten, with supposed aphrodisiac effect. Cf. QUAILS.

DOWN WITH THEM, *36*. *LLL* IV.iii.364. For sexual intercourse.

  DOWNRIGHT WAY OF CREATION. *MM* III.ii.100. Coitus.

  BROUGHT THEM —. *Per* IV.ii.16.

  LAY —— LADIES, *155*. *H8* I.iii.40.

DOXY, *143*. *WT* IV.iii.2. Vagabond's *de facto* wife.

DRAB, -S (n), *152*. *1H6* V.iv.32, etc. Cheap and beggarly whore.

  DRABBING. *Ham* II.i.26. Using prostitutes.

DRAW (vb). *RJ* I.i.30 and II.iv.156. By quibble, to uncover (a) sword, (b) penis.

DUCK (n). *TrC* III.ii.51. As = paramour. Cf. the 'wild ducks' of Webster (*Wh. Devil* II.i.89) and waterfowl generally. Elsewhere in Sh., 'my duck' or 'my dainty duck' is a simple term of endearment.

EAR (vb), *90. AW* I.iii.44. To plough, with quibble on copulation.

EAT, *132.* Probably *2H4* II.iv.332, certainly *Oth* III.iv.101, *Tim* I.i.206–8. Quibble, (a) to consume food, (b) to use up, coitally. Cf. DISH, FLESH, FRAGMENT, MORSEL, MUTTON, STEWED PRUNE.

—— MUTTON ON FRIDAYS. *MM* III.ii.171. Transgress, especially in a sexual way, since MUTTON can = prostitute.

EDGE (n), *114. Son 56, Ham* III.ii.244, *MM* I.iv.60, *Tem* IV.i.29. Sexual appetite in a man. Cf. WHETSTONE.

EELS, *128. KL* II.iv.117–19, *Per* IV.ii.144. Stirring eels likened to rising penises. Cf. CONGER.

EGGS, *78. MWW* III.v.25–6. As aphrodisiac, which Falstaff denies needing. The custom of serving liquor with raw egg in it lives on: Dylan Thomas, *Under Milk Wood* (1954), has Mr Waldo cancelling the order for an egg in his pint of stout when the postman delivers his latest paternity summons.

EMBALLING, *156. H8* II.iii.47. Quibble, (a) investiture with royal orb, (b) involvement in coitus. Cf. BALLS.

EMPLOY (vb), *95. KJ* I.i.98. Sexually.

ENCOUNTER, -S (n). *MWW* III.v.66, *Ado* IV.i.91, *AW* III.vii.32, *TrC* III.ii.204, *MM* III.i.252, *Cym* II.v.19. Assignation, sexual accosting.

ENCOUNTER (vb). *1H6* II.ii.46. To engage with, sexually.

ENCOUNTERERS. *TrC* IV.v.58. Brash women.

ENFORCE. *TA* V.iii.38, *MND* III.i.195, *Cym* IV.i.14. To rape.

ENFORCEMENT. *R3* III.vii.8, *Luc* 1623.

ENJOY, *52. 1H6* V.iv.73, etc. Sexually.

ENTER, *106. 2H4* II.i.9, *H5* V.ii.317. By quibble, to enter (or cause to enter) coitally.

ENTERTAINMENT, *78. MWW* I.iii.40, *MM* I.ii.153, *Per* IV.ii.54. Sexual amusement or hospitality.

ERECTION, *78, 134. MWW* III.v.36, *Tim* IV.iii.165. Phallic erection, and a Quicklyism for *direction*.

ERINGOES, *79. MWW* V.v.19. Sugared roots of sea-holly, eaten as a sweetmeat and thought to be aphrodisiac.

ESTATE. *Per* IV.ii.31. Literally, property: here = girls to stock a brothel.

ETCETERAS, *17. 2H4* II.iv.174. Vulvas. Cf. Cotgrave, translating Fr. *con*, 'A womans &c.'

EUNUCH, *61, 137, 148. 2H6* IV.iv.161, *TA* II.iii.128, *AC* I.v.10, *Cym* II.iii.30. A castrated male.

EUROPA, *44, 78. TSh* I.i.165, *MWW* V.v.3, *Ado* V.iv.45–8. Princess deceived, then carried off, by Jupiter in the form of a snow-white BULL.

EVILS, *146. MM* II.ii.172, *H8* II.i.67. Meaning uncertain. Apparently scruffy buildings of some kind—perhaps privies.

EWE, *122. Oth* I.i.90. As type of innocent female. Cf. MUTTON.

EXCHANGE FLESH. *WT* IV.iv.278. To copulate.

EXCREMENT. *LLL* V.i.89. Don Armado exclaims quickly that by this he only means his moustache, but Holofernes might well smell false Latin, here as elsewhere. Shakespeare underlines the *double entendre*: 'sweet heart, let that pass'.

EXPENSE OF SPIRIT, *164. Son* 129. Pouring-forth of (primarily) vital energy, but with a suggestion of seminal fluid also. Cf. 'vitall spirits' in quotation from Reginald Scot's *Discovery of Witchcraft* on p. 29.

FADINGS, *153. WT* IV.iv.196. 'Fading' was the name of an Elizabethan dance, but 'With a fading, fading, fading' occurs as the refrain of a ribald song. Partridge points out that the pairing of *fading* with *dildo* is suggestive, especially in conjunction with 'jump her and thump her'. His proposal that *fading* = fading-away, an orgasmic 'death', is reasonable.

FALL (n). *AYL* I.iii.25. Quibble, (a) in wrestling, (b) from sexual grace. Cf. THROW.

FALL (vb), *57, 71. 3H6* III.ii.24, *RJ* III.iii.11, *Oth* IV.iii.86. Of a woman: to fall from virtue. Cf. prostitution in Dekker, *1 Hon. Whore* II.i.30, 'that, of down and arise, or the falling trade'.

—— BACKWARD. *RJ* I.iii.43. For copulation.

—— BY THY SIDE. *Son* 151. Of a man's 'flesh': to detumesce after coitus.

FALLING IN. *TrC* III.i.96. Making up, amorously, after a quarrel.

FARTUOUS. *MWW* II.ii.87. A Quicklyism for *virtuous*.

FEATHER-BED, *75. MV* II.ii.153. A suggestive source of physical peril.

FEE (n). *TA* II.iii.179, *VA* 609. Quibble, (a) gamekeeper's reward, (b) rapist's or seductress's gratification. Cf. Tourneur, *Rev. Trag.* II.ii.79, and Richard Lovelace, 'La Bella Bona-Roba'.

FEED (vb). *CE* II.i.101, *VA* 232, *Cym* II.iv.138. Quibble, (a) deer grazing, (b) man wandering amorously.

FEEL (vb), *56. RJ* I.i.26–7. Coitally.

FEELINGLY. *MM* I.ii.33–5. Quibble, (a) to the point, (b) probingly, painfully (because of venereal disease).

FICO (n). *MWW* I.iii.27. See at FIG.

FIDDLE (vb), *155. H8* I.iii.42. Part of a vaguely sexual imprecation. Cf. *fiddle* and *fiddlestick* as = penis.

FIG (n), *54. 2H6* II.iii.65, *H5* II.vi.58, *Oth* I.iii.316. Contemptuous expletive with sexual implications; often accompanied by the insulting gesture of biting the thumb. Cf. ——

FIG ME. *2H4* V.iii.117. An amalgam, presumably, of (a) fuck me, and (b) ——

A FICO FOR. *MWW* I.iii.27. *Fico* is Italian for *fig*, and an anecdote in Rabelais, p. 544, throws some light on its lewd implications. The story is that after putting down a revolt in Milan, the Emperor Frederick Barbarossa (*c.* 1123–90) forced all his prisoners to choose between being hanged and undertaking to extract and replace, by means of their teeth, a fig specially inserted for the purpose in the vulva of a mule. Half-way through this feat, each candidate had to announce *Ecco lo fico*, 'Behold the fig.'

FIGO (n). *H5* III.vi.56 and IV.i.60. Spanish for FICO and FIG. The thumb-biting gesture may have been thought to be Spanish in origin rather than Italian. The reputation of Spaniards as braggarts and lechers would give extra virulence to the insult.

FILLING A BOTTLE WITH A TUN-DISH. *MM* III.ii.162. Copulating. See TUN-DISH.

FINGERING, *137. Per* I.i.82, *Cym* II.iii.13. Quibble, (a) playing a musical instrument,

(b) toying with female sexual organs. Cf. Marston, *Malcontent* V.v.38: 'busy-fingered lords . . . put the beauties to squeak most hideously'.

FIRE (n), *133*. *VA* 94, 334, 348, *AW* V.iii.7, *Tim* IV.iii.143, *Tem* IV.i.53. Fierce sexual heat; probably also, in *Tim* IV.iii.143, venereal infection.

FIRK (vb). *H5* IV.iv.29. Literally, to beat; but a pun on *fuck* is also likely. Cf. Marston *A&M* III.ii.13, and Dekker, *Shoemaker's Hol.* I.i.129–30.

FISH (n), *100*. *RJ* I.i.29, *1H4* III.iii.125, *WT* IV.iv.277. As counterpart of male flesh, fish can be (a) salted and rigid, like dried hake, (b) female, (c) cold-blooded. Cf. LING.

    FISHMONGER. *Ham* II.ii.173. Possible quibble, (a) seller of fish, (b) seller of women.

    FLESH . . . FISHIFIED. *RJ* II.iv.37.

FISH (vb), *151*. *WT* I.ii.195. To copulate with, illicitly, as a poacher.

FIT (adj). *Cym* IV.i.4. Of suitable measure or size, vaginally.

    FITMENT. *Per* IV.vi.5. What is fitting (for a prostitute).

    FITNESS. *Cym* IV.i.5. Readiness for sexual activity.

FITCHEW, *130*. *Oth* IV.i.146, *KL* IV.vi.122. The polecat, as type of lechery. This relative of the weasel emits a fetid smell.

FLAMES. *Luc* 6, *MWW* V.v.95. Of sexual ardour.

    FLAMING. *Ham* III.iv.84.

FLESH (n), *100*, *133*, *135*. *RJ* I.i.28, etc. With emphasis on carnality. Cf. EAT, MUTTON.

    FLESHMONGER. *MM* V.i.331. A user of whores.

    EXCHANGE ——. *WT* IV.iv.278. Fornicate.

FLESHES HIS WILL. *AW* IV.iii.15. Achieves coitus. Partridge cfs 'flesh one's sword'. See also HONOUR and WILL.

FLIRT-GILLS. *RJ* II.iv.150. Wantons, strumpets. *Gill* is short for Gillian, and *flirt* is stronger than in modern usage. Cf. Cotgrave: '*Gaultière*. A whore, punke, drab, queane, gill, flirt, strumpet, cockatrice, mad wench, common hackney, good one.'

FOCATIVE (adj), *4*, *82*. *MWW* IV.i.45–8. *Vocative* mispronounced, yielding jingle on *fuck* (Kökeritz, p. 74).

FOH! *H5* III.iv.52, *Oth* V.i.123. Exclamation of disgust, specifically in a sexual context. Cf. Marston, *Dutch Court.* dram pers., Mistress Mary Faugh, a bawd.

FOIN (vb), *4*. *2H4* II.i.16 and II.iv.222. To thrust, (a) in fencing, (b) priapically.

FOOT (n), *19*, *105*. Possibly *LLL* V.ii.658, possibly *TSh* IV.i.24, certainly *H5* III.iv.48. Pun on indecent Fr. *foutre* = to fuck. Cf. YARD.

FOREHEAD, *43*, *123*. *MWW* IV.ii.21, *Ado* I.i.244, *AYL* III.iii.54, *Oth* II.iii.281. Where the cuckold's horns would appear.

FORFENDED PLACE. *KL* V.i.11. Vagina of another man's wife.

FORGET TO DRINK AFTER THEE. *MM* I.ii.38. Avoid sharing your cup, for fear of venereal infection.

FORKED (adj). With horns.

    —— ONE, *151*. *TrC* I.ii.158–60, *WT* I.ii.186. A cuckold.

    —— PLAGUE. *Oth* III.iii.273. Cuckoldry.

FORKS (n). *KL* IV.vi.119. The crutch.

FORT. *Luc* 482. Lucrece's chastity.

FORTUNE, *115*. *KJ* III.i.60–1, etc. Goddess Fortune as hussy or whore: an Elizabethan commonplace.

FOUNTAINS, *158*. *VA* 234. Breasts.

FOUTRA (n). *2H4* V.iii.97 and 114. Pistol's expletive adapts Fr. verb *foutre*, = to fuck.

FRAGMENT (n). *AC* III.xiii.117. Discarded mistress as = leftover scrap of food. Cf. DINE.

FRANCE. See MALADY OF FRANCE.

FREE (adj). *1H6* V.iv.82, *2H6* IV.vii.117, *AC* I.v.11. Sexually unrestrained.

FRENCH CROWN, *27, 89*. Probably *LLL* III.i.133, certainly *MND* I.ii.90, *H5* IV.i.218–22, *AW* II.ii.21, *MM* I.ii.51. Quibble, (a) the Fr. coin called *écu*, (b) bald head, with the baldness attributed to venereal disease. See also SCATTER HIS CROWNS.

—— VELVET. *MM* I.ii.34. Quibble, (a) costly and soft velvet, the opposite of a rough 'English kersey'; (b) patch of velvet used in treating syphilis, to cover lanced chancres. See also PILED.

FRIEND, *3*. *RJ* III.v.43 and 77, *Oth* IV.i.3, *MM* I.iv.29, *AC* III.xii.22, *Cym* I.iv.65. Lover, mistress or paramour.

FRUIT. *2H6* III.ii.214. Illicit progeny.

—— WITHIN MY WOMB. *1H6* V.iv.63.

FRUITION OF HER LOVE. *1H6* V.v.9. Coitus.

FRUITS OF LOVE. *3H6* III.ii.58. Copulation.

FIRST —— OF MY BACHELORSHIP. *1H6* V.iv.13.

FRY (vb). *TrC* V.ii.56. Thersites tells lechery to go on frying in its own heat.

FRY OF FORNICATION. *H8* V.iv.35. (a) Offspring resulting from fornication, (b) a shoal of fornicators, or (c) both of these.

FUBBED OFF. *2H4* II.i.33. Mistress Quickly's twice-repeated phrase sounds like a portmanteau one—(a) fobbed off, (b) copulated with. (Kökeritz, p. 75.)

FULL-ACORNED BOAR, *136*. *Cym* II.v.16. The boar as type of lustfulness—all the more eager, here, for being well fed.

FULL POINTS, *17*. *2H4* II.iv.174. Quibble, (a) full stops (as in a play-script, leading to silences); (b) erect penises. Cf. ETCETERAS, another 'literal' equivoque.

FUT! *KL* I.ii.130. Edmund's expletive may be influenced by FOUTRA. Cf. FOOT.

GALLOWAY NAGS. *2H4* II.iv.180. As = prostitutes. 'Doll is like a Galloway nag, because anyone may ride her' (Sugden).

GAME (n), *57, 122*. *3H6* III.ii.14, *Oth* II.iii.19. (a) Sexual quarry being hunted, (b) sexual play.

—— OF TICK-TACK. See TICK-TACK.

DAUGHTERS OF THE ——. *TrC* IV.v.63. Randy women.

GAMESTER. *AW* V.iii.188, *Per* IV.vi.73. Prostitute.

GANYMEDE, *108*. *AYL* I.iii.123, etc. As girl-boy, Rosalind goes by the name of Jove's page, with pederastic associations. (Sh. is following Thomas Lodge, *Rosalind*, 1590.)

GATES. *WT* I.ii.197. Quibble, (a) sluice-gates, (b) vulvas.

GEAR, *118*. *TrC* I.i.6 and III.ii.207. Probable quibble, (a) business, affairs, stuff; (b) the sexual organs, male and female (F&H). Cf. Florio, glossing Italian *mozza*, 'a wench, a guirle, a lasse. Also used for a womans geare or quaint.'

GELD, *151*. *2H6* IV.iv.160, *MV* V.i.144, *MM* II.i.219, *WT* II.i.147 and IV.iv.607, *Per* IV.vi.124. To castrate.

GENDER (vb). *Oth* IV.ii.61. To breed.

GERMENS. *KL* III.ii.8, *Mac* IV.i.58. Spermatozoa.

GET, -TING, *91, 95*. *KJ* I.i.237, etc. To beget. (Not always bawdy in Sh.)

—— THE SUN OF THEM. *LLL* IV.iii.365. Quibble, (a) gain advantage by attacking from sunny direction, (b) beget their sons.

—— WITH CHILD, *151*. *AW* V.iii.299, *MM* I.ii.72, *WT* III.iii.60.

GETTER. *Cor* IV.v.231. Begetter.

GETTING UP OF THE NEGRO'S BELLY, *75*. *MV* III.v.34. Both (a) entering her vagina, and (b) making her swell in pregnancy.

GIGLOT, -S. *1H6* IV.vii.41, *MM* V.i.344, *Cym* III.i.31. Harlot.

GILLYVORS, *152*. *WT* IV.iv.82. Gillyflowers, clove-scented pinks: 'Nature's bastards' perhaps because streaked. Cf. also, *OED*, *gillyflowers*, 2b.

GIVE UP (trans or intrans). *MM* II.iv.54, *Cym* II.ii.46. Surrender to sexual advances.

GIVE THYSELF. *AW* IV.ii.35.

GLIB (vb). *WT* II.i.149. To castrate.

GO (vb). *R3* III.v.85, *LLL* V.ii.661, *AC* I.ii.59, *H8* IV.i.77. Usually refers to pregnancy, but in *AC* could = any, or all, of (a) copulate, (b) achieve orgasm, (c) conceive.

—— BACK. *Cym* I.iv.101. To lose ground, (a) in fencing, (b) in sexual self-defence. Cf. YIELD.

—— BETWEEN. *AW* V.iii.257. As pimp.

—— THE WAY OF WOMENKIND. *Per* IV.vi.148. To accept men coitally.

—— TO BED. *AW* V.iii.262, possibly *WT* IV.iv.105; *Per* IV.ii.102. (1) For sexual intercourse; (2) in *Per*, a euphemism for premature male orgasm.

—— TO'T, *130*. *KL* IV.vi.112 and 122, *Per* IV.vi.73. To copulate. Cf. Jonson, *Bart. Fair* II.v.117; also TO'T and SET ME TO'T.

GOAT, -S, *10, 30, 123*. *H5* IV.iv.20, *Oth* III.iii.400 and IV.i.265, *Cym* IV.iv.37. As type of lechery.

GOATISH, *128*. *KL* I.ii.127.

GO-BETWEEN. *MWW* II.ii.234.

GOERS-BETWEEN. *TrC* III.ii.196. Panders.

GOOSE (n). Can mean 'girl' or 'female simpleton', but not bawdy in Sh. except as WINCHESTER GOOSE or

—— OF WINCHESTER. *TrC* V.x.53. Prostitute.

GOSSIPS, *32*. *TGV* III.i.268. Female friends attending a lying-in or christening.

GOTH, -S, *10*. *TA* II.iii.110, *AYL* III.iii.5–7. Possible pun on GOAT.

GREASILY. *LLL* IV.i.130. Bawdily, indecently, foully.

GREASY. *1H4* II.iv.224, *MWW* II.i.95.

GREAT-BELLIED. *MM* II.i.95. With child.

GREAT BELLIES, *132*. *Tim* I.i.208. Of pregnant women.

GREENSLEEVES, *79*. *MWW* II.i.55 and V.v.17. The tune so named; reputedly erotic, it would seem. Certainly some of the ballads that used it were love-songs.

GRINDSTONE. *RJ* I.v.9. Susan's equivocal surname. STONES can be testicles, but two metaphors could also apply. (a) As the sexual EDGE or APPETITE is sharpened, the grinding-stone is gradually worn away. Cf. *Son* 110. (b) F &H quote Florio: '*Macinio*, greest or grinding-corne, taken also for carnall copulation.'

GROAN, -S (n). *TrC* V.x.48, *Per* IV.ii.108. Caused by syphilitic pains or gonorrhoeal arthritis. Cf. BONES, VEROLES.

GROAN OUT. *TrC* III.i.119. Apparently in wordless erotic ecstasy.

GROANING (n), *114*. *Ham* III.ii.244. Probably an orgasmic exclamation, whether of pleasure or pain. Cf. Tourneur, *Atheist's Trag.* II.iii.29, "Sh' had rather you would wake and make her groan."

THE GROANING JULIET. *MM* II.ii.15. Groaning because she is in labour. Cf. Mistress Allwit 'upon the point of grunting'—Middleton, *CMC* I.ii.30.

GROPING FOR TROUTS. *MM* I.ii.89. Copulating.

GROUND (n), *140*. See PIECE OF GROUND.

GROW. *RJ* I.iii.96. In pregnancy.

GUINEA-HEN. *Oth* I.iii.312. A courtesan. Cf. Jonson, *Alch.* IV.i.38 (to Doll), 'Well said, my guinea-bird.'

HACK (vb), *82*. *MWW* II.i.44 and IV.i.60. Of uncertain meaning, but very probably sexual. Cf. *OED* vb¹ 1, 5a, 8; and HACKNEY.

HACKNEY (n). *LLL* III.i.29. Woman as = horse for everyday riding. See also at FLIRT-GILLS.

HAIR. *RJ* II.iii.93. Quibble, (a) grain, as in 'against the grain', (b) pubic hair. The pun TALE/TAIL is also involved. Cf. Tourneur, *Rev. Trag.* I.iii.131, 'the wagging of her hair . . . shall put you in, my lord.'

LOSE HIS ——. *CE* II.ii.82–93. Through venereal disease or its treatment. See BALD and cf. THIN ROOFS.

NO —— AT ALL. *MND* I.ii.90. As above. Cf. FRENCH CROWN.

HALF-WORKERS. *Cym* II.v.2. Women as sharers in procreation.

HALF-BLOODED (adj). *KL* V.iii.81. Onions: 'of superior blood by one parent only.'

HALT (vb). *2H4* I.ii.232 and II.iv.49. To limp, because of venereal disease.

HAMS, *69*, *139*. *RJ* II.iv.52, *Per* IV.ii.104. The upper part of the legs, weakened by sexual excess and (in *Per*) by venereal disease.

HAND (n) ——

—— IS OUT, . . . IS IN, *36*. *LLL* IV.i.128. Boyet accuses Maria of masturbating.

—— OF THE DIAL. *RJ* II.iv.109. Mercutio calls the clock's hand bawdy because it touches the PRICK ((a) mark, (b) penis) of noon.

DRY ——. *Ado* II.i.105, *TN* I.iii.70–2. A sign of old age, but commonly also, among the Elizabethans, a sign of impotence. Sir Andrew, missing the point, replies that he has wit enough to keep his hand dry—when urinating, presumably.

HANDLE [WOMEN] (vb), *104*, *106*. *H5* II.iii.34 and V.ii.305, *MM* V.i.272–5. To fondle.

HANG (vb) ——

THEREBY HANGS A TALE, *110*. *AYL* II.vii.28. Probable quibble, (a) 'there is a story concerning that', (b) 'a penis dangles because of that'. For the *double entendres*, see TALE, HOUR, ROTTEN.

HARD. *Ado* V.ii.38, *H5* V.ii.294. Probable quibble, (a) difficult, (b) related to phallic erection.

HARE, *82–3*, *92*. *RJ* II.iv.129–36. The hare, like the rabbit, has long been associated with lust and fecundity, but the much-repeated claim that Mercutio means *prostitute* is unsubstantiated. For other occurrences of *hare* as a very general type-animal of lechery, see *MWW* IV.i.55 and Ford, *'Tis Pity* V.iv.31.

HARLOT, -S, *59*, *65*. *CE* V.i.205, etc. A person (male or female) of loose sexual morals.

HARLOTRY (n). *RJ* IV.ii.14, *1H4* III.i.193,*Oth* IV.ii.232. Means *courtesan* in *Oth*, but only *hussy* in *RJ* and *1H4*.

HARLOTRY (adj). *1H4* II.iv.388. Pejorative word, but not specifically bawdy. Modern equivalent might be *hippie* or *gipsy*.

HATCH (n), *95*. *KJ* I.i.171. The lower half of a divided door. To vault over it instead of opening it is to arrive irregularly: hence proverbial for illegitimate birth (Tilley W456). Cf. IN AT THE WINDOW.

  KEEP OUR DOOR HATCHED. *Per* IV.ii.31. Operate a brothel. It was usual for Elizabethan brothels to have a half door surmounted by a row of spikes, and for this to be kept shut and guarded.

HAVE, *100*. *1H4* III.iii.126, *MWW* V.v.183, *AYL* I.iii.19. Coitally.

—— IT, *54*. *2H6* IV.vii.116.

HEAD, -S (n). *RJ* I.i.22–5, probably *MM* IV.ii.5. As = maidenhead or prepuce.

HEAT (n). *Luc* 706 and 1473, *Ado* IV.i.39, *Oth* I.iii.260. Sexual enthusiasm.

HEAVIER. *Ado* III.iv.24–31, *TrC* IV.i.68. By the weight of a lover, in coitus. Cf. BURDEN, WEIGHT.

HEELS (n). Probably *Ado* III.iv.41. As raised by female in coitus.

HEIFER, -S, *102*. *2H4* II.ii.151, *WT* I.ii.124. Sexual partner of steer or BULL.

HEIR. *CE* III.ii.123, *Oth* II.i.135. (1) Pun on *hair*, with probable allusion to venereal baldness: cf. FOREHEAD. (2) Heir as = child, fruit of a woman's folly.

HELL, *167*. *2H4* II.iv.326, possibly *Son* 144. As place of fiery punishment, hell is where a diseased harlot 'burns poor souls'. In *Son* 144, *vagina* may also be implied.

HEM! See CRY 'HEM'.

HERB-WOMAN. *Per* IV.vi.83. Euphemism for bawd.

HICK (vb), *82*. *MWW* IV.i.60. Meaning uncertain, and not necessarily bawdy.

HIGHWAY. *RJ* III.ii.134. To Juliet's bed.

HILLOCKS. *VA* 237. Buttocks.

HILL OF BASAN, *149*. *AC* III.xiii.127. Thinking of himself as horned, Antony would outroar the compassing bulls of Psalm 22.

HIREN. *2H4* II.iv.151 and 165. Allusively, a prostitute. The name, a corruption of Irene, comes from Peele's play *The Turkish Mahamet and Hyrin the Fair Greek* (*c.* 1594). F&H quote two other occurrences of the allusion.

HIT (vb), *61*, *69*, *119*. *TA* II.i.97, *LLL* IV.i.111–21, possibly *TSh* V.ii.185, *RJ* II.i.33, *TrC* I.ii.260. Via various quibbles, notably from archery, this = 'achieve coitus with a woman'.

HOAR (adj), *83*. *RJ* II.iv.130–4, *Tim* IV.iii.36. Meaning *white*, but also punning on *whore*. See also at HARE.

HOAR (vb), *133*. *RJ* II.iv.136, *Tim* IV.iii.157. Meaning 'turn white' or 'make white-haired', but punning on WHORE (vb).

HOBBY-HORSE, *124*. *LLL* III.i.27, *Oth* IV.i.154, emended *WT* I.ii.276 (F1 Holy-Horse). By extension from the antics of a morris-dance character, this came to = 'a loose-living person'—female in Sh., though not necessarily a prostitute; male in Jonson, *Epicoene* IV.iii.49.

HOLD-DOOR TRADE. *TrC* V.x.50. Brothel-keeping.

HOLE (n), *28*. *MND* V.i.197–8, probably *RJ* II.iv.90, and possibly *TGV* II.iii.17. Vulva.

HOLLOW BONES, *133*. *MM* I.ii.55, *Tim* IV.iii.154. Supposedly made so by venereal disease.

HONEST. *MWW* II.i.211, etc. Chaste.

HONESTY, *17. TA* II.iii.135, etc. In *WT* I.ii.288 Sh.'s usage is quasi-physical, suggesting *hymen*. Cf. HONOUR.

HONEY, *61, 118. TA* II.iii.131, *Luc* 493, *TrC* V.x.42–4. As = sexual satisfaction.

HONEYING, *114. Ham* III.iv.93.

—— SECRETS. *VA* 16.

HONOUR (n), *77, 89. MV* V.i.232. Quibble, (a) chastity, (b) hymen. Cf. *OED* 3b, and *3H6* III.ii.124, 'Ay, Edward will use women honourably.'

HORN, -S (n), *6, 36, 40, 43, 90, 95. TA* II.iii.62–71, etc. Generally, symbolic of cuckoldry; but sometimes only suggestive of any erect penis: cf. *MWW* V.v.3 and *Ado* V.ii.38.

HORNED, *124, 149. Oth* IV.i.62, *AC* III.xiii.128.

HORNER, *54, 66. 2H6* dram. pers. and II.iii.60–103. As = cuckoldmaker? Cf. Wycherley, *The Country Wife*, dram. pers. and epilogue; and see STOCK-FISH, THUMP, VEROLES.

HORNING, *63. TA* II.iii.67. Cuckold-making.

HORN-MAD. *CE* II.i.57–8, *MWW* I.iv.44 and III.v.133, *Ado* I.i.249. (a) Stark mad, (b) mad with rage at being made a cuckold.

HORN-MAKER. *AYL* IV.i.56. Cuckold-maker.

HORSE (n). *H5* III.vii.43–65. With allusions to bestiality. Cf. MOUNT, RIDE.

BARBARY ——, *122. Oth* I.i.112. A breeding stallion from the North African coast.

SOILED ——, *130. KL* IV.vi.122. A horse stall-fed with fresh-cut green fodder, and hence mettlesome and sexually eager. But see also SOIL, on which there may also be a quibble here.

HORSE-PISS. *Tem* IV.i.199. Cf. STALE (n²).

HOT, *79, 99, 123, 149, 154. TGV* II.v.44, etc. Sexually ardent, eager, lascivious; or (of blood or foodstuffs) deemed conducive to those feelings.

HOT-HOUSE. *MM* II.i.64. Ostensibly a bath-house; actually a brothel. Cf. Jonson's epigram 'On the New Hot-House', and *MM* I.ii.101–8.

HOTLY. *VA* 178, *KL* IV.vi.163.

HOUR, *110. AYL* II.vii.26–7. Probably with pun on *whore* (Kökeritz, p. 117). Cf. HANG, ROTTEN, TALE.

HOUSE, -S (n). *MM* I.ii.95–102, II.i.62 and 154–5, *Per* IV.vi.118 and 189. Used as brothel.

—— OF PROFESSION. *MM* IV.iii.2.

—— OF RESORT. *MM* I.ii.101.

—— OF SALE. *Ham* II.i.60.

BAWD'S ——. *MM* II.i.73.

BAWDY-HOUSE, -S. *1H4* III.iii.16, 98 and 156, *2H4* II.iv.136, *H5* II.i.33, *Per* IV.v.6.

BROTHEL-HOUSE. *Ado* I.i.233.

COMMON HOUSES. *MM* II.i.43.

HOT-HOUSE. *MM* II.i.64. Ostensibly a bath-house.

LEAPING-HOUSES. *1H4* I.ii.9.

NAUGHTY HOUSE. *MM* II.i.74.

HOUSEWIFE, -VES, *105, 122*. F1 spelling usually = Huswife. *H5* V.i.76, *Oth* II.i.111 and IV.i.94, *AC* IV.xv.44. Hussy; light woman.

OVERSCUTCHED HUSWIFES. *2H4* III.ii.308. Prostitutes who have been whipped so often as to be either hardened to their trade or deadbeat.

HUSBANDRY. *Son* 3, possibly *2H4* III.ii.113, *MM* I.iv.44. Quibble, (a) conscientious farming, (b) role of husband. See also TILLAGE, and cf. PLOUGH.

HUSWIFE. See HOUSEWIFE.

HYMEN. Not bawdy in Sh.

ILLEGITIMATE CONSTRUCTION. *Ado* III.iv.44. Quibble, (a) improper construing, (b) illegal building, (c) imputation of bastardy.

IN AT THE WINDOW, *95*. *KJ* I.i.171. Born illegitimately. Tilley W456, 'To come in at the window'. Cf. HATCH.

INCESTUOUS . . . ADULTERATE BEAST. *Ham* I.v.42.

INCONTINENT (adj and adv), *108*, *132*. *AYL* V.ii.37, *Tim* IV.i.3. Quibble, (a) immediately, (b) unable to contain one's sexual urge.

INDULGENCES TO SIN. See WINCHESTER GOOSE.

IO. *TSh* Ind.ii.53–4. Nymph seen, pursued and raped by Zeus.

IRELAND. *CE* III.ii.115–16. In the geography of Nell, the buttocks—'I found it out by the bogs'.

ITALY. A byword for its courtesans. Hence—
GIRLS OF ——. *AW* II.i.19.
JAY OF ——. *Cym* III.iv.47. A light, flashy woman.

ITCH, -ES (n). *Tim* IV.i.28, *AC* III.xiii.7. Sexual urge. Cf. Ford, *'Tis Pity* IV.iii.8, 'your hot itch and pleurisy of lust'. In *Tim*, probably a symptom of venereal disease too. Cf. Webster, *Wh. Devil* I.ii.136–9.

ITCH (vb). *Tem* II.ii.52. See at TAILOR.

JADE, -S (n), *38*. *TGV* III.i.274, *TSh* II.i.201, *H5* III.vii.57, *AW* II.iii.282. A tired, out-of-condition horse. *TGV* and *H5* quibble on (a) worn-out horse, (b) perverse and over-worn trollop. Cf. NAG.

JAKES, *19*. *KL* II.ii.64. A privy. See also AJAX and WHAT-YE-CALL'T.

JAQUES, *19*, *109*. *AYL* dram. pers. See AJAX, JAKES and WHAT-YE-CALL'T.

JAY, -S. *MWW* III.iii.35, *Cym* III.iv.47. A flashy, unfaithful woman.

JEWEL. *Luc* 1191, *Per* IV.vi.153. As = married chastity in *Luc*, virginity in *Per*. (Not bawdy elsewhere in Sh.)

JORDAN. *1H4* II.i.21, *2H4* II.iv.33. Chamber-pot.

JOVE, JUPITER, *44*, *78–9*, *122*. *MWW* V.v.2–13, *Ado* V.iv.48, *Oth* II.iii.17. As arch-lover. Cf. BULL, EUROPA.

JOY (vb). *TA* II.iii.83. To enjoy someone sexually.

JUGGLE (vb), *52*. *1H6* V.iv.68. To perform dexterously, and also sexually.
JUGGLING (n and adj). *TrC* II.iii.68 and V.ii.24. Cf. TRICK.
STALE JUGGLER, *102*. *2H4* II.iv.124. (a) An insulting allusion to Pistol's histrionic gifts; or (b) = tired fornicator; or (c) both.

JUMP (vb, trans.), *153*. *WT* IV.iv.196. Partridge: 'To coit athletically and vigorously with'. Cf. DILDOS, LEAP, VAULTING VARIABLE RAMPS.

KATE KEEPDOWN. *MM* III.ii.190. Name of the prostitute who bore a child to Lucio. Cf. GRINDSTONE, NIGHTWORK and OVERDONE.

KITCHEN-VESTAL, *25*, *33*. *CE* IV.iv.72. Ironic reference to the kitchen-maid's virginity.

KNOG [HIS] URINALS. *MWW* III.i.12 and 80. To knock Dr Caius's (medical) urine-flasks. Cf. CASTALION-KING-URINAL.

KNOT (vb). *Oth* IV.ii.61. To intertwine coitally.

LANGUAGE, *120*. *TrC* IV.v.55. Sexual invitation, excitement.

LANTHORN, *2H4* I.ii.44. Quibble, (a) lantern, lit up by a wife's LIGHTNESS; (b) cuckold's HORN. Cf. *MND* V.i.233–4.

LAP, -S (n), *64, 101, 147. 2H6* III.ii.390, *3H6* III.ii.148, *TA* IV.iii.64, *Ham* III.ii.108–12, probably *Oth* IV.iii.87, *AC* II.i.37. Both (a) skirt from waist to knees, and (b) the vulva or vagina. Cf. *OED* 2b, 4; Hulme, pp. 119 and 124; Jonson, *Alch.* IV.i.126, 'And it shall rain into thy lap, no shower, / But floods of gold, whole cataracts, a deluge, / To get a nation on thee!'

LAY (vb) ——

—— DOWN LADIES, *155. H8* I.iii.40. For sexual intercourse.

—— DOWN THE TREASURES OF YOUR BODY. *MM* II.iv.196.

—— HIS SWORD TO BED. *AC* II.ii.231. Quibble, (a) retire from war, (b) fornicate.

—— IT. *RJ* II.i.26. Quibble, (a) exorcise a spirit, (b) induce detumescence in penis.

LAZAR KITE, *104. H5* II.i.73. A venereally diseased and rapacious person. Cf. CRESSID, LEPROSY. In *The Testament of Cresseid* (pr. 1532) Robert Henryson describes her as 'ane lazarous'.

LEAK (vb), *100. 1H4* II.i.21. To urinate.

LEAKY. See UNSTANCHED WENCH.

LEAP (vb), *44. Ado* V.iv.49. To mount, coitally. Cf. MOUNT, JUMP.

LECHER, -S (n). *Luc* 1637, *MWW* III.v.127, *TrC* IV.i.65, *KL* III.iv.108.

LECHERY. *Ado* III.iii.162, *TN* I.v.120, etc. As malapropism for *treachery* in *Ado*; mishearing of *lethargy* in *TN*.

LECHER (vb), *129. KL* IV.vi.113. To copulate.

LEDA, *79. MWW* V.v.6. Seduced by Zeus, who approached her in form of swan.

LEMAN. *2H4* V.iii.47, *MWW* IV.ii.145, more innocently *TN* II.iii.24. Illicit lover.

LEPROSY, *133, 148. Tim* IV.i.30 and IV.iii.36, *AC* III.x.11. Thought-of as a venereal infection. Cf. Ford, *'Tis Pity* I.i.74 and IV.iii.61, 'leprosy of lust . . . Thy lust-be-leper'd body'. See also LAZAR KITE.

LIBERAL. *1H6* V.iv.82, etc. Unrestrained, licentious.

LIBERTINE, -S. *Ado* II.i.125, *AYL* II.vii.65, *Ham* I.iii.49, *AC* II.i.23.

LIBERTY. *Ham* II.i.24, *Oth* III.iv.40, *MM* I.ii.124, *Tim* IV.i.25. As = (specifically) sexual licence.

LIE (n). *Mac* II.iii.33. Punning on *lye* (urine).

LIE (vb) ——

—— BETWEEN MAIDS' LEGS, *16. Ham.* III.ii.114.

—— BY. *TN* III.i.8, *H8* IV.i.70. Implying *copulate with*.

—— LONG. *TrC* IV.i.4–6. Staying late in bed, with a lover.

—— ON HER. *Oth* IV.i.34–5. In coitus.

—— ON THEIR BACKS. *RJ* I.iv.92.

—— UNDER. *MWW* II.i.69. As woman lies beneath man in coitus.

—— UPON MY BACK. *TrC* I.ii.251.

—— WITH, *166. 3H6* III.ii.69, etc. To copulate with.

LYING DOWN, *101. 1H4* III.i.221. As if for sexual intercourse.

—— LIKE DOGS. *Tem* III.ii.18. Quibble, (a) to lie still, like sleeping dogs; (b) to urinate as readily as dogs.

LIGHT (adj), *9, 26, 36, 149. CE* IV.iii.51, etc. Wanton, sexually easy.

LIGHTNESS. *2H4* I.ii.43, *MM* II.ii.170.

LINED. *AYL* III.ii.101. Lined or padded on the inside: hence, = fucked. Cf. CASE.

LING, *90*. *AW* III.ii.12–13. As = woman, venally considered. *Old ling* is salted fish: cf. SALT and FISH.

LOAF (n). See STEAL A SHIVE.

LONG PURPLES. See DEAD MEN'S FINGERS.

LOOSE-WIVED. *AC* I.ii.66. Having an unfaithful wife.

LOVE'S QUICK PANTS. *Oth* II.i.80. Rapid breathing.

LOVER, -S. *VA 573*, *LLL* II.i.125, etc., *MM* I.iv.40, *Per* IV.ii.121. As = illicit lover. (Elsewhere in Sh., the word is much less loaded.)
   BE SO LOVERED. *LC* 320. Have such a lover.

LOW COUNTRIES. *2H4* II.ii.22. Pubic (perhaps also anal) region of Poins's body. Cf. *CE* III.ii.136–7.

LOWER PART, *19*. *AW* II.iii.250. Euphemism for YARD = penis.

LUNGS. *TrC* V.i.18. As affected (supposedly) by venereal disease. Cf. TISICK.

LUST, -S (n). *1H6* V.iv.43, etc.

   LUST-DIETED. *KL* IV.i.66. (a) Accustomed to indulging lust; or (b) overfed; or (c) both.

   LUSTFUL PARAMOURS, *50*. *1H6* III.ii.53.

   LUST-STAINED. *Oth* V.i.36. Othello pictures Desdemona's bed physically as well as figuratively stained.

   LUSTY. *TSh* IV.ii.50, *RJ* I.ii.26, *Oth* II.i.286, *KL* I.ii.11. With strong overtones of *lustful*.

LUST (vb), *130*. *KL* IV.vi.163.

LUXURIOUS, *62*. *TA* V.i.88, *Ado* IV.i.39, *TrC* V.iv.7, *Mac* IV.iii.58. Lascivious, lustful.

   LUXURIOUSLY, *149*. *AC* III.xiii.120.

LUXURY, *59*, *130*. *LC* 314, etc. Lasciviousness, lavish sexual indulgence.

LYING DOWN, *101*. *1H4* III.i.221. For sexual intercourse.

MADAM MITIGATION. *MM* I.ii.44. Nickname for Mistress Overdone, who as a brothel-keeper sells the means of mitigating lust.

MAID, -EN, *32*, *68*, *81*, *97*, *116*, *128*. *1H6* V.iv.65, etc. Virgin.

   —— MARIAN, *100*. *1H4* III.iii.113. A character from the morris dance and Robin Hood plays: a type-figure of promiscuity.

   MAIDENHEAD, *54*, *143*. *2H6* IV.vii.115, etc. Hymenal membrane; virginity itself.

   MAIDENHOOD, -S. *RJ* III.ii.13, *AW* III.v.22. Virginity.

MAKE (vb). *Cym* IV.i.3. With suggestion of 'make love to' or 'achieve sexually'.

   —— IT SHORT. *RJ* II.iv.95. *Double entendre*, (a) to keep the story short, (b) to make the penis short (by orgasm and detumescence). See TALE.

   —— LOVE. *Ham* III.iv.93.

   —— MY PLAY. *H8* I.iv.46. Quibble: win what I play for, (a) generally, (b) sexually.

   —— WATER, *31*. *TGV* IV.iv.36, *TN* I.iii.123, *MM* III.ii.104. To urinate.

   —— YOURSELF A SON. *AW* II.iii.96. To beget a son.

   HIS MAKING. *KL* I.i.22. His conception.

MALADY OF FRANCE, *105*. *H5* V.i.78. Syphilis.

MALE VARLET, *7*. *TrC* V.i.14. Patroclus, as Achilles' 'masculine whore'.

MANDRAKE, *103*. *2H4* I.ii.14 and II.ii.304: not bawdy elsewhere in Sh. The Mandragora, a poisonous plant of the potato family, used from early times in fertility potions. Its branching roots were popularly thought to resemble a skinny and naked man or woman. Cf. POTATO.

MANLY MARROW. *AW* II.iii.279. Quibble, (a) mettle, essence, (b) semen. Cf. STUFF.

MANNER. *LLL* I.i.199. The thing stolen—in this case Jaquenetta. Costard has been 'taken with the manner', caught in the act.

MARK (n), *36*. *LLL* IV.i.124-30, *RJ* II.i.33. Vulva, as point of aim for a man. Cf. DEER, HIT, PRICK.

MARKET-PRICE. *AW* V.iii.219. Of a prostitute. Cf. RATE.

MARROW. See MY MANLARROW.

MARS, *154*. *AC* I.v.18, *Tem* IV.i.98. As adulterous lover of Venus, wife of Vulcan.

MART (vb). *Cym* I.vi.150. To shop around, sexually.

MASCULINE WHORE, *7*. *TrC* V.i.14.

MASTER PEASCOD. See PEASCOD.

MASTER WHAT-YE-CALL'T, *19*. *AYL* III.iii.67. See WHAT-YE-CALL'T.

MATCH (n). *RJ* III.ii.212, *MM* V.i.209. Love-game, assignation.

MATTER (n), *108*. *AYL* IV.i.69. Quibble, (a) small-talk, (b) semen.

MATTERS. See WOMEN'S MATTERS.

MEAT, *102*. Possibly *RJ* II.iv. 133, certainly *2H4* II.iv.118, *Per* II.iii.32. As lust-fodder. Cf. the 'meat twice sod' of Jonson, *EMI*, IV.x.37.

ROAST —— FOR WORMS, *26*. *Per* IV.ii.23. Corpse of a syphilitic. Cf. BURN, HOT, POOP.

MEDDLE, *30, 53, 62, 86*. *RJ* I.i.39, probably *MND* II.i.181, *JC* I.i.22, *TN* II.iv.245, *Cor* IV.v.48-50. To masturbate and/or copulate. Cf. MEDLAR; and Dekker, *1 Hon. Whore* IV.i.95, 'If it be a woman, mary-bones and Potato pies keepe me for medling with her'.

MEDDLERS, *69*. *Tim* IV.iii.311. Intriguers, with suggestion of sexual intrigue. Cf. MEDLAR.

MEDLAR, -S, *69, 109*. *RJ* II.i.34-6, *AYL* III.ii.116, *MM* IV.iii.170. (a) A type of fruit eaten when it has grown soft and pulpy. It has been thought to resemble in shape the female genitals. Hence, (b) slang for *prostitute*; and (c) a doubly sexual pun on MEDDLER. Cf. Tourneur, *Atheist's Trag.* IV.i.19-43.

MELL WITH. *AW* IV.iii.223. To mix with, sexually.

MEMBERS, *149*. *AC* I.ii.159. Possible quibble, (a) people, (b) male sexual organs.

MENELAUS, *55*. *3H6* II.ii.147; also, allusively, *TrC* V.i.50-3. The husband of Helen of Troy, as archetypal cuckold.

MILK (vb). *TGV* III.i.293-4. Possible quibble, (a) to milk cows, (b) to cause male ejaculation. Hulme, p. 140, cfs Jonson, *Alch.* III.iii.22, 'she must milk his epididimis'.

MILLER. See WATER . . . BY THE MILL.

MINGLE BLOODS. *WT* I.ii.109. To engage in coitus.

MINION, -S, *26, 61, 154*. *CE* II.i.87, etc. Pejorative word for a lover or paramour, but not always bawdy.

MISTAKE, MIS-TAKE (vb, trans), *7, 114*. *H5* III.ii.129-30, *Ham* III.ii.246. Probably = to have anal intercourse. (By quibble in *H5*.)

MISTRESS OVERDONE. See OVERDONE.

MISTRESS SQUASH. See SQUASH.

MOCKWATER. See MOUNSEUR MOCKWATER.

MOIST (adj). *Oth* III.iv.36–43. A moist hand was taken to signify fruitfulness and LIBERTY.

MONKEY, -S (n), *30, 103, 123. MND* II.i.181, *2H4* III.ii.303, *Oth* III.iii.400 and IV.i.265. As type of lechery. Cf. BOAR, GOAT, SPARROWS.

MONSIEUR VEROLES. See VEROLES.

MONSTER (n),*124. KJ* II.i.293. *Oth* IV.i.62–4. Man turned to horned beast by being cuckolded.

MOON (n), *35. LLL* V.ii.215. As = woman, with man in her.

MORSEL, *149. MM* III.ii.51, *AC* I.v.31 and III.xiii.116. As = woman. Cf. DISH.

  CUT A —— OFF THE SPIT. *Per* IV.ii.132. To fornicate with an already-deflowered girl. Cf. MEAT, MUTTON.

MOTHER PRAT. *MWW* IV.ii.160. Name for the 'maid's aunt of Brainford', who is fat Falstaff in disguise. Prat = the buttocks.

MOTION, -S, *83. MWW* III.i.94. Bowel-movements.

  —— GENERATIVE. *MM* III.ii.105. A puppet, and therefore without feelings, yet capable of breeding.

MOUNSEUR MOCKWATER, *83. MWW* II.iii.51-6. Nickname for Dr Caius: cf. BULLY STALE, CASTALION-KING-URINAL. Puns on *sewer* and *makewater* are probably combined here with a glance at Elizabethan quack-doctors who would give advice after inspecting urine yet without seeing the patient.

MOUNSIEUR BASIMECU, *54, 66. 2H6* IV.vii.25. Nickname for the Dauphin: *baisez-ma-queue*, kiss-my-arse. Cf. QUEUBUS.

MOUNT (vb), *136. Cym* II.v.17. For copulation. Cf. TUP.

MOUNTAIN. *VA* 232. In the topography of Venus, various raised and rounded parts: lips, breasts, buttocks and probably the *mons Veneris*.

MOUNTANTO. *Ado* I.i.28. Nickname for Benedick. The *montant* or *montanto* is an upward thrust in fencing, and Benedick goes in for verbal duelling. But *mountant* (adj, in heraldry) = mounting or rising, and I.i.36-9 confirms the phallic suggestion. Cf. FOIN, THRUST.

MOUSE-HUNT. *RJ* IV.iv.11. Girl-chaser.

MUDDY. *2H4* II.iv.38 and 52. Bawdy, foul-minded.

MUTTON, *10. TGV* I.i.97, glancingly *TN* I.iii.115 and *MM* III.ii.171. As food for lust; hence, loose woman. (The slang sense, *prostitute*, is never plainly present in Sh.) Cf. EWE.

MYSTERY, *49. Oth* IV.ii.29, *MM* IV.ii.31-5. Trade or profession—specifically that of brothel-keeping.

NAG (n). *AC* III.x.10. Woman as = small horse for everyday riding. Cf. HACKNEY, JADE, and Dekker, *2 Hon. Whore* IV.i.171, 'all your sex are but foot-cloth Nags: the Master no sooner lights, but the man leapes into the saddle'.

  GALLOWAY NAGS. *2H4* II.iv.180. As = prostitutes—sturdy, hardwearing beasts.

NAKED, *3, 18, 86, 105, 123, 150.*

NAPLES. *Oth* III.i.4. As supposed source of syphilis. See NEAPOLITAN BONE-ACHE.

NAUGHT (n), *17, 58. R3* I.i.97-9, *MND* IV.ii.14. Sexual sin. 'To do naught with' = 'to fornicate with' (*OED, nought,* sb 2b and 8c).

NAUGHTILY. *TrC* IV.ii.37. Improperly.

NAUGHTY. *TrC* IV.ii.25 and 32, *MM* II.i.74. Indecent, bawdy.

NEAPOLITAN BONE-ACHE. *TrC* II.iii.17. Syphilis. 'Syphilis, when it first struck Europe in 1494 (almost certainly brought in a virulent form from the new world) brought with it the terror of novelty. Its passage through Europe was frighteningly swift: from Naples it reached Bologna early in 1495 and crossed the Alps later that year as troops disbanded after the Italian campaign took it in all directions to their homes' (Hale, *Renaissance Europe 1480–1520*, p. 24).

NESSUS. *AW* IV.iii.245. Centaur who tried to rape Deianira, wife of Hercules. Cf. CENTAURS.

NEST OF SPICERY. *R3* IV.iv.424. The female genitals.

NETHERLANDS. *CE* III.ii.136. In the geography of Nell, the low countries. Cf. BELGIA, LOW COUNTRIES.

NICK (n). *H5* III.iv.30–3. Kökeritz, pp. 72, 131, 133, proposes that this = slit = vulva, and cfs BREACH, CASE, CUT, HOLE, O. The *H5* pun-sequence (III.iv.30–55) —with *chin/sin* adjoining [*neck*]/*nick*, and with horrified exclamations at FOOT and COUNT—supports Kökeritz's conjecture.

NIGHT, -S. *KJ* I.i.172, etc. As affording secrecy for sexual activity. Cf. DARK, -NESS.

NIGHT-CAP, *121*. *Oth* II.i.298. As = wife.

NIGHT-WALKING HERALDS. *R3* I.i.72. Go-betweens.

JANE NIGHTWORK, *102–3*. *2H4* III.ii.192. Name of an elderly ex-prostitute.. Cf GRINDSTONE, KATE KEEPDOWN, OVERDONE.

NOB. See SIR NOB.

NOSE (n), *20*. *AC* I.ii.57; probably also *TrC* III.i.120. A jocular avoidance of *yard* (penis).

COPPER ——. *TrC* I.ii.101. Syphilitic deterioration of the nose could be so complete as to cause rich patients to wear false noses made of various metals. Sir William Davenant 'gott a terrible clap of a Black handsome wench that lay in Axe-yard, Westminster, . . . which cost him his Nose' (Aubrey, p. 178), and there is a portrait of him wearing a metal one.

DOWN WITH THE ——, *133*. *Tim* IV.iii.158. Through syphilis.

SPEAK I'TH'NOSE. *Oth* III.i.4. Allusion to syphilis. Cf. NAPLES, NEAPOLITAN BONE-ACHE.

NOT. *KJ* I.i.275. Possible pun, (a) not so, (b) nought, naught.

NOTE (vb), *16*. *TA* II.iii.86, *TrC* V.ii.11 (with musical quibble). To brand with disgrace, on sexual grounds. Cf. Marston, *Dutch Court*. II.ii.8–9; Ford, '*Tis Pity* IV.iii.4, 'notable harlot'.

NOTE-BOOK. *2H4* II.iv.256. Woman as man's counsel-keeper, bawd.

NOTHING, -S, *15–18, 71*. *2H4* II.iv.174, *Ham* III.ii.114–16, *Oth* IV.i.9, glancingly *Son* 20. Possibly = vulva, rounded during coitus (but see discussions, pp. 15–18 and 163–4).

NOUGHT, *17, 71*. *MND* IV.ii.14. F1 spelling of *naught*. Elizabethan spelling did not consistently distinguish between the two. Cf., also, NOTHING and letter o.

O, *16, 71, 82, 136*. *RJ* III.iii.91, possibly *MWW* IV.i.47 (after FOCATIVE), probably *TrC* III.i.109, *Cym* II.5.17. (a) Echo of an orgasmic sigh or grunt, as in *Cym*; (b) euphemism for vagina, as is probable in *RJ*. Cf. NAUGHT, NOUGHT, NOTHING; and Kökeritz, pp. 74–5.

OBSCENE, -LY, *27, 169. LLL* I.i.232 and IV.i.136, *MND* I.ii.100, *1H4* II.iv.224. Abominable, abominably. (Misused by Costard and Bottom, both perhaps to be imagined aiming at *seemly*.)

OCCUPY, *169. RJ* II.iv.97, *2H4* II.iv.139. For a time, this was used as slang, = to fuck. Florio so applies it in the 1598 edn. of *A World of Words*: '*Scuotere il pellicione*, to ginicomtwig or occupie a woman'. Like Sh., Ben Jonson (*Discoveries*, ll. 1545-8) defends the word's respectability.

　　MEMBERS OF MY OCCUPATION. *MM* IV.ii.34. Probable quibble, (a) sharers in my trade, (b) people I have copulated with.

ŒILLADES. *MWW* I.iii.58, *KL* IV.v.25. Sexually appraising (and inviting) glances.

O'ER THE HATCH. See HATCH.

ON HER WAY. *LLL* V.ii.662. Pregnant. Cf. GO.

OPEN. *TrC* V.ii.24. Sexually available.

　　OPEN-ARSE, *69. RJ* II.i.38 editorially amended. Slang name for the MEDLAR.

OUCHES (n). *2H4* II.iv.48. Probable quibble, (a) brooches, bracelets, or other settings for gems; (b) carbuncles, sores. A. R. Humphreys, Ard. *2H4*, p. 66, quotes Chapman, *Widow's Tears* I.ii.118-20, where a diseased lord has 'ouches in's skin'.

OUT-PARAMOUR THE TURK, *129. KL* III.iv.88. To have even more concubines than the Sultan of Turkey, famous for his harem. See also TURK.

OVERDONE, *145-6. MM* dram. pers. and II.i.190-2. Bawd who has had nine husbands, not to mention the customers. 'Overdone by the last' quibbles on (a) 'her last husband gave her the name Mistress Overdone'; (b) 'worn out with copulating with him'. Cf. DO, GRINDSTONE, KATE KEEPDOWN, NIGHTWORK.

OVID. *TSh* I.i.33. As love-poet, more or less erotic.

OX. *LLL* V.ii.250, glancingly *MWW* V.v.117. Horned beast: hence, = cuckold. Cf. BULL, HORNS, MONSTER.

　　OX-HEAD, *97. KJ* II.i.292. As symbol of cuckoldry.

P'S, *85 TN* II.v. 88. Quibble, (a) letter P, handwritten, (b) pee, piss, urine. (Kökeritz, p. 133.

PAGAN (n). *2H4* II.ii.147. Sinner, trollop. Cf. Massinger, *City Madam* II.i.110.

PAIN, *134. Tim* IV.iii.163. Pain of venereal disease.

　　PAINS, *133. Tim* IV.iii.144. Almost certainly = menstrual pain, but the line is obscure.

PAINTED CLOTHS. *TrC* V.x.45. 'Canvas hangings painted with pictures and moral sentences were a cheap substitute for figured tapestries' (Alexander, III, 557). On the bareness and meanness of Elizabethan brothels, see Dekker, *2 Hon. Whore* IV.i.47, 'every roome with bare walls, and a halfe-headed bed to vault upon, (as all your bawdy-houses are.)'.

PANDAR, -US, *117-18. MWW* I.iii.72. *TN* III.i.50, *TrC* dram. pers., allusively *AW* II.i.97. As eponym of all pimps or procurers. Hence ——

　　PANDER (n), *118. MWW* V.v.161, etc.

PANDER (vb, trans). *Ham* III.iv.83. To act as procurer of.

PANEL. *AYL* III.iii.79. Hulme, pp. 105-6, argues for a pun here, *panel/panel*: the first being a piece of planed timber, the second a harlot (*OED pernel*). This linguistic case looks strong, but the stage situation works against it: Jaques is addressing only the male, Touchstone, and doubts the fidelity of bridegroom as well as bride.

PARAMOUR, -S. *1H6* III.ii.53, etc. Illicit lover.

PARCEL-BAWD. *MM* II.i.61. A part-time procurer. See also *MM* II.i.209–10.

PARITORS, *36. LLL* III.il.176. An apparitor was the summoning-officer of a bishop's court, frequently concerned with the sin of fornication.

PASTIMES. *TA* II.iii.26. Sexual play.

PEASCOD, *27, 107. MND* III.i.182, *AYL* II.iv.47. A pea-pod, symbolic of fecundity, and perhaps also quibbling on *cod* = testicle.

PEESEL. *2H4* II.iv.152. By so pronouncing the name Pistol, the Hostess unwittingly puns on *pizzle*, = the penis of an animal (Kökeritz, p. 135). Cf. BULL'S-PIZZLE.

PEN (n), *77. MV* V.i.237. As = penis.

PENANCE. *H8* I.iv.17. See CONFESSOR, and cf. SHRIVE.

PENETRATE, *137. Cym* II.iii.13. Quibble, (a) to touch someone's heart, (b) to enter the vagina. Cf. FINGERING.

PEOPLE (vb, trans), *154. Tem* I.ii.350. To populate (the island) by breeding.

PERFORMANCE. *2H4* II.iv.251, *TrC* III.ii.81, *Mac* II.iii.28. Virility.

PERFUMES. *Tim* IV.iii.208. Perfumed concubines.

PERVERT (vb). *LC* 329. To seduce.

PHILOMEL, *137. Cym* II.ii.46. In Greek myth, raped and mutilated by her sister's husband, TEREUS.

PHILOSOPHER [WITH TWO STONES]. *2H4* III.ii.316, *Tim* II.ii.113–14. Quibbling on (a) the philosopher's stone, an imaginary substance by which alchemists hoped to transmute base metals to gold; (b) a man's testicles, his STONES.

PHRYNIA, *133. Tim* IV.iii.48. One of Alcibiades's two concubines. She takes her name from Phryne, a famous Greek courtesan of the fourth century B.C.

PICK THE LOCK. *Cym* II.ii.41. Metaphor for act of adultery.

PICKT-HATCH. *MWW* II.ii.16. 'An infamous resort of thieves and prostitutes in Elizabethan London.' The name 'properly means a half-door, surmounted by a row of spikes, such as was often used in brothels'. (Sugden.) Cf. HATCH.

PIECE (n). *TrC* IV.ii.64, possibly *Per* IV.ii.42. Applied pejoratively to a woman. (But elsewhere a term of praise, = *example* or even *masterpiece*.)

—— OF GROUND. *Per* IV.vi.143. As = girl. Cf. PLOUGH.

CHANGING ——. *TA* I.i.309. Woman as small-change coin, passed from hand to hand.

PIKE, -S, *3, 102. 2H4* II.iv.50, *Ado* V.ii.21. Quibble, (a) the weapon of war, (b) penis.

PILED. *MM* I.ii.32–4. Quibble, (a) having a pile, or nap, like velvet; (b) having haemorrhoids, regarded by Elizabethans as a result of venereal disease (cf. Jonson, *Bart. Fair* II.v.121). A 'three-piled' piece of velvet had a nap of triple thickness, and hence was the most costly kind. For further extensions of the joke, see FRENCH VELVET.

PILLICOCK. *KL* III.iv.73. Name from a nursery-rhyme, probably here = penis. Cf. Florio, '*Puga*, a pricke, a pillicocke, a dildoe'.

PILLICOCK-HILL. *KL* III.iv.73. Possibly, as Partridge avers, = the female genitals. But Sugden (and others) may have been right in leaving Poor Tom's nonsense as nonsense: 'A hill in the land of Nursery Rhymes. . . . The full version of the rhyme runs: "Pillycock, Pillycock, sat on a hill, If he's not gone he sits there still." '

PIN (n). *LLL* IV.i.129. Quibble, (a) pin in centre of archery-target, (b) erect phallus. Cf. CLEAVING THE PIN, UPSHOOT.

PIPES (n). *Oth* III.i.19. Possibly a quibble, (a) musical instruments, (b) penises.

PISS (n). See HORSE-PISS, P'S.

PISSING CONDUIT. *2H6* IV.vi.3. A fountain in London—probably the Little Conduit at the west end of Cheapside. The name seems to have been suggested by the slenderness of the stream of water. (Sugden.)

A PISSING WHILE. *TGV* IV.iv.18. A short time, the time it would take Crab to empty his bladder.

PISS MY TALLOW, *79. MWW* V.v.13. Of a buck deer: to have his fat melt in the heat of RUT-TIME.

PISTOL-PROOF. *2H4* II.iv.111. Quibble, (a) bullet-proof, (b) impervious to penises. For ensuing complications, see FORGET TO DRINK, BULLETS.

PISTOL'S COCK IS UP. *H5* II.i.49. Quibble, (a) Ancient Pistol is angry, (b) the hand-gun is cocked, (c) the Ancient's penis is erect.

PIZZLE. See BULL'S-PIZZLE, PEESEL, PUZZEL.

PLACKET, -S, *36, 117, 129. LLL* III.i.174, *TrC* II.iii.18, *KL* III.iv.93, *WT* IV.iv.243 and 606. The opening in a petticoat or skirt, at the crotch. By extension, the female pudendum itself; by further extension, the whole woman.

PLAIN (n). *VA* 236. In the topography of Venus, either her belly or her back.

PLAIN DEALING, *36. LLL* IV.iii.366. Possible quibble, (a) honest talk, (b) practical love-making. Cf. DEAL.

PLAINER DEALER. *CE* II.ii.83. Quibble, (a) more honest man, (b) more un-skilled lover of women.

PLANTS IN OTHERS' ORCHARDS. *LC* 171. Illegitimate children.

PLAY (n). See MAKE MY PLAY.

PLAY (vb), *135, 151. TGV* IV.ii.69, etc. Sexually (sometimes with a quibble on non-sexual meanings).

—— [A HUSBAND] FAIR. *MM* III.i.144. By not being adulterous.

PLAY-FELLOW. *Per* I.Chor.34. In 'marriage-pleasures'.

PLEASE THEMSELVES UPON HER. *Per* IV.i.102. Euphemism for *rape*. Cf. ENJOY.

PLOUGH (vb, trans), *140. AC* II.ii.232, *Per* IV.vi.144. To copulate with a woman. Cf. CROP, PIECE OF GROUND, HUSBANDRY.

POINTS (n). *1H4* II.iv.210-1. Quibble, (a) sword-points, (b) laces holding up hose (breeches) by tying them to the doublet. But see also FULL POINTS.

POLECAT, -S, *81-2, 84. MWW* IV.i.25 and IV.ii.163. Slang for *prostitute*. Cf. *OED polecat*, 2; and FITCHEW.

POND, -S, *135, 151. Cym* I.iv.85, *WT* I.ii.95. As metaphor for invaded woman or her vagina. Cf. FISH, SLUICE; and the fishpond of Dekker, *2 Hon. Whore* III.i.35.

POOP (vb, trans). *Per* IV.ii.23. To kill by infecting with syphilis. Hulme, p. 114, suggests that Sh.'s nonce-verb adapts the noun *poop* as used by John Davies of Hereford in some such sense as *vagina* or *tail*. Alexander, IV, 551, prefers a straightforwardly nautical derivation—'to cause to founder'. Either way, in *Per* the little baggage that lay with the poor Transylvanian *ended* him.

POPPERING PEAR, *69. RJ* II.i.38. A type of pear (from Poperinghe, Belgium) thought to resemble the penis and scrotum. Cf. Tourneur, *Atheist's Trag.* IV.i.19-43.

POSTERIOR, -S. *LLL* V.i.76-8. Buttocks of the day: the afternoon.

POTATO, -ES, *79. MWW* V.v.16, *TrC* V.ii.55. The Spanish or sweet potato, *Ipomoea Batatas*, thought by Elizabethans to have aphrodisiac properties. Cf. the potato pies of Dekker, *1 Hon. Whore* IV.i.95.

POWDERED BAWD. *MM* III.ii.56. A procuress, 'salted' by having undergone fumigation and sweating treatment in a tub for her venereal diseases: thus the opposite of the 'fresh whore' she once was.

POWDERING TUB, *104*. *H5* II.i.72. A tub originally used for 'powdering' (that is, salting) beef, but now used for the treatment of venereal patients, by sweating and fumigation over roasted mercuric sulphide. Cf. *MM* III.ii.51–7, *Tim* IV.iii.86–8.

POX (n), *8, 9, 99*. *TGV* III.i.368, *1H4* I.ii.47, *2H4* I.ii.218, 231 and II.iv.39, *Per* IV.iv.14–5. Syphilis, which in its tertiary stage produces lesions on external and internal organs. (Elsewhere, expletive phrases 'A pox of/on/upon . . .' tend not to be bawdy. They usually lack metaphoric life, and they do not distinguish between venereal and other poxes. Cf. 'a plague on . . .'.)

PRACTICE. *Per* IV.ii.125. Sexual practice, action.

PRANKS. *Oth* II.i.140 and III.iii.200. Of a sexual kind. Cf. TRICK.

PRAT, *84*. *MWW* IV.ii.160–1. Slang for *buttocks*. Hence the name Mother Prat for 'the maid's aunt of Brainford', who is fat Falstaff in disguise. Frank Ford then picks up *prat* as a nonce-verb, = to beat. Cf. Dekker, *Sel. Writings*, pp. 299 and 362, where cant 'glimmer in the prat' = venereal disease in a female.

PRAY. See PREY (vb).

PREGNANT. *WT* V.ii.30. Quibble, (a) clear, obvious, (b) with child.

PREPOSTEROUS, *7*. *LLL* I.i.232, *TSh* III.i.9, *TrC* V.i.22. Ostensibly this = 'absurd, unnatural, inverting the normal order of things'; but it also = 'posterior-foremost'—as for buggery in *TrC*. Cf. Marston, *Dutch Court*. I.i.29: 'thrusts his wench forth of the window, and himself most preposterously, with his heels forward, follows.'

PRESS (n). See PUT INTO THE PRESS.

PRESS (vb). *RJ* I.iv.93, *Cym* II.iv.135. To weigh down, coitally. (In *RJ* the sense 'urge on, urge forward' is also present.)

—— TO DEATH. *TrC* III.ii.204, *MM* V.i.519. Quibble, (a) to torture to death by applying crushing weights, (b) to wear out (bed or man) through relentless coital pressures. Cf. LIE UNDER.

PREVAIL. *1H6* V.iv.78. Euphemism for *to seduce*.

PREY (n), *59*. *R3* III.v.83. Victim of lecher's hunting.

PREY (vb). *1H4* II.i.81. In addition to the obvious pun on *pray*, there may be a quibble on (a) be parasitic, (b) make a sexual victim. Cf. *Ham* I.v.57. See also RIDE.

PRIAPUS. *Per* IV.vi.3. God of fertility, often depicted with erect phallus.

PRICK, -S (n), *3, 19, 109*. *LLL* IV.i.125–32, *RJ* II.iv.110, *AYL* III.ii.108, *H5* II.i.32. With various quibbles on *prick* as slang for penis. Cf. Tourneur, *Atheist's Trag.* IV.i.52.

PRICK (vb). *RJ* I.iv.28, *2H4* III.ii.111, 152 and 158. With phallic play on other senses of *prick*, including (a) puncture, (b) turn sour, (c) vex, (d) mark (a name) on a list, (e) insert needle. Clearly, Romeo and Mouldy intend no bawdy: Mercutio and Falstaff intend much. Cf. Marston, *A &M* IV.i.269 and V.ii.257–60; Dekker, *1 Hon. Whore* V.ii.267–70; and HUSBANDRY.

—— OUT, *163–4*. Son 20. Quibble, (a) dress up, (b) equip with a penis.

PRIDE, *123*. *Luc* 438, *LLL* II.i.236, *Oth* III.iii.401, *Son* 144 and 151. Sexual desire; phallic turgidity. Cf. Marston, *Malcontent* II.v.114, 'They say there's one dead here, pricked for the pride of the flesh.' See also WOLVES.

PRIME (adj), *123*. *Oth* III.iii.400. Sexually excited. See also GOAT.

PRINCIPAL (n). *AW* I.i.146. Via the idea of virginity, Parolles conflates *womb* and *vagina* in a metaphor of usury: the original sum will increase, yet will not be much the worse for USE.

PRIVATES, *115*. *Ham* II.ii.232–5. Quibble, (a) unimportant people, (b) intimates (i.e., customers) of a strumpet, (c) genitals.

PROCREANTS. *Oth* IV.ii.27. Breeders, fornicators.

PROCURE. *MM* III.ii.51. To obtain girls for prostitution.

PROFESSION. *MM* IV.iii.2, *Per* IV.vi.71 and 134. The trade of whoring. Cf. GAMESTER, HOUSE, MYSTERY.

PROFIT (n). *Oth* II.iii.10. Sexual pleasure, reward.

PROSTITUTE (vb, trans). *Per* IV.vi.188. To hire out as a prostitute.

PROVOCATION. *MWW* V.v.19, *Oth* II.iii.22. Sexual incitement.

PROVOKE . . . UNPROVOKE. *Mac* II.iii.27. To stimulate, then dampen, lechery.
    PROVOKER. *Mac* II.iii.23. Of urine, *inter alia*.

PRUNE, –S. See STEWED PRUNE.

PUBLIC COMMONER, *121*. *Oth* IV.ii.72. Prostitute.

PUCELLE, *49–53*. *1H6* dram. pers. and I.iv.107, etc. Virgin, Maid. Cf. PUZZEL.

PULLET-SPERM, *78*. *MWW* III.v.28. Falstaff means eggs, which were thought of as aphrodisiac. See EGGS.

PUNK, *81, 89*. *MWW* II.ii.122, *AW* II.ii.21, *MM* V.i.179 and 519. Harlot.

PUR. *AW* V.ii.19. Animal dung. Cf. *OED pure*, sb, 5; and *F&H*, sb, 2.

PUT (vb) ——
    —— A MAN IN YOUR BELLY, *108*. *AYL* III.ii.197. Coitally.
    —— DOWN. *TSh* V.ii.35–6, *Ado* II.i.259–62. Quibble, (a) to defeat in argument, (b) to lay a woman down for sexual intercourse.
    —— INTO THE PRESS. *MWW* II.i.68. Quibble, (a) to set up [the two wives'] names in a printing press, (b) to lie on [the two wives] coitally.
    —— IT TO THEM. *LLL* IV.ii.76. Quibble, (a) put instruction to them (the parishioners' daughters), (b) to fornicate with them.
    —— STUFF TO SOME SHE-BEGGAR. *Tim* IV.iii.273–4. Put semen into some drab.
    —— TO. *WT* I.ii.277. To fornicate. Cf. GO TO'T, TO'T.
    —— UP, *73*. *RJ* IV.v.97, possibly *Oth* III.i.19. Quibble, (a) to put away musical instruments in their cases, (b) to insert penises. Cf. Marston, *Malcontent* I.vi.6, where Maquerelle, 'an old pand'ress', accepts jewels, saying 'As for my part, 'tis well known I can put up anything . . ., can bear patiently with any man'.

PUZZEL, *49*. *1H6* I.iv.107 (F1 sp. = Puzel). Drab, slut. See *OED pucelle*, 2. Cairncross, Ard. *1H6*, p. 30, further suggests that Sh. may be punning on PIZZLE.

PYGMALION'S IMAGES, NEWLY MADE WOMAN. *MM* III.ii.43. As = young, fresh girls available as prostitutes. Aphrodite brought a statue to life when Pygmalion, its sculptor, fell in love with it.

QUAILS (n). *TrC* V.i.49. Probable quibble, (a) the game-birds, quite rightly considered a delicacy; (b) loose women (because quails were thought to be especially amorous). Cf. DOVES, DUCK, MUTTON.

QUATCH-BUTTOCK. *AW* II.ii.17. The expression is not recorded elsewhere, and its meaning is uncertain. Apparently = squat, or perhaps pimple-like buttock. A quat (*Oth* V.i.11) is a pimple, and cf., in form, *Scot/Scotch*.

QUEAN, *84. MWW* IV.ii.151, *AW* II.ii.24. Hussy.

QUEUBUS. *TN* II.iii.23. Name quoted from Feste's mock-learning. A conjectural etymology would suggest Fr. *queue* + Eng. buss = tail-kiss, arse-kiss. Cf. BASIMECU.

QUICK (adj). *LLL* V.ii.665. Pregnant.

QUIVERING THIGH. *RJ* II.i.19.

QUOD ... QUODS. See COD, -S.

R. *RJ* II.iv.204. The Nurse's hesitations over the letter R have never been satisfactorily explained. Partridge suggests a suppressed allusion to *Roger*, = *roger*, = *penis*. Another possibility is *growl*; yet another is *arse*.

RAISE (vb). *RJ* II.i.24–9. Quibble, (a) call up a spirit, (b) cause a male erection.

RAM (n), *122. TA* IV.iii.72, *Oth* I.i.89. As owner of horns (*TA*), and as type of potent lechery. Cf. BARBARY HORSE, BOAR, BULL, GOAT.

RAMP, -S (n), *51. Cym* I.vi.133. Loose woman.

RANK (adj). *LC* 307, *MV* I.iii.77, *Cym* II.v.24. In heat, lascivious.

RAPE, -S (n). *TA* II.i.116, etc.

RAPINE. *TA* V.ii.103.

RATE (n). *AW* V.iii.217. Price of hire for a courtesan.

RAVISH. *TA* II.iv.2, etc.

RAVISHMENT, -S. *Luc* 430, *AW* IV.iii.245.

REBEL (vb), *76. MV* III.i.31–2, *2H4* II.iv.338, *Oth* III.iv.43. Alluding to rebellion of the flesh, a favoured topic in Elizabethan homilies.

REBELLION OF A COD-PIECE. *MM* III.ii.109. Cf. COD-PIECE.

RELIEF. *VA* 235. Quibble, (a) goemorphic variety, (b) release for pent-up desires.

RENTS (n). *Son* 142. Sexual dues. Cf. BEDS' REVENUES, USE.

RESORTERS, *139. Per* IV.vi.22. Customers (of the brothel).

RESPECT (vb). *MM* II.i.154–69. Elbow's word for *to suspect* (of fornication).

REVEL IN LAVINIA'S TREASURY. *TA* II.i.131. Rape her. Cf. JEWEL.

REVENUES. See BEDS' REVENUES.

REVOLTED WIVES. *WT* I.ii.199. Unfaithful wives. Cf. TURN (vb).

RHEUM IN MINE EYES, *118. TrC* V.iii.103. As symptom of venereal disease. (Both gonorrhoea and syphilis can affect the eyes.) The same idea is probably present in *MM* III.i.31, and could be in *Oth* III.iv.51. Cf. the 'raw eyes' of *TrC* V.i.18.

RHODOPE, *50. 1H6* I.vi.22. Greek courtesan, married to a pharaoh, and sometimes said to have had the third pyramid built for her.

RIBAUDRED NAG, *148. AC* III.x.10. Approximately = 'clapped-out bitch'. Cf. NAG. *Ribaudred* has not been found elsewhere, but strongly suggests *ribald*. The next line wishes LEPROSY upon Cleopatra.

RIDE (vb). *H5* III.vii.51–6; and perhaps glancingly *1H4* II.i.82. Quibble, defined by Cotgrave, '*Chevaucher*. To ride, or bestride a horse; ... also, to swive a woman.' (*F &H* provide ten columns of quotations and analogues.)

RIGGISH, *AC* II.ii.244. Sexually playful. Cf. GAME, GAMESTER.

RING (n), *77, 92. MV* V.i.307. Quibble, (a) wedding-ring, (b) vulva. Cf. *AW* IV.ii.45 and HONOUR. See also the Hans Carvel anecdote in Rabelais, p. 368.

RISE (vb), *71. RJ* III.iii.90, *Son* 151. With quibble on phallic erection. Cf. Donne, 'The Canonization', where the tumescence is female as well as male.

RIVER. *MM* I.ii.89. As = vagina. Cf. POND, GROPING FOR TROUTS.

ROAD, *102. 2H4* II.ii.160–2. As = trollop. Cf. Tilley C109 and H457 ('as common as the highway'); and COMMON.

ROAST MEAT FOR WORMS, *26. Per* IV.ii.23. Corpse of a syphilitic. Cf. BURN, HOT, POOP.

ROE. See WITHOUT HIS ROE.

ROOT (n), *82. MWW* IV.i.49, possibly *Per* IV.vi.83. Quibble, (a) root vegetable, (b) penis. Cf. Tourneur, *Atheist's Trag.* IV.i.40; and F &H.

ROSALIND, *109. AYL* III.ii.108. Probable pun—Rosa LINED.

ROSE, -S. *AYL* III.ii.107, *AW* IV.ii.18. The metaphor of a virgin or her virginity as a rose to be plucked, to wither, etc., is so commonplace as to be nearly beyond the reach of bawdy, but Touchstone and Diana both render the image unusually 'concrete', as = the female pudendum. Cf. PRICK, ROSALIND, SERVE.

ROTTEN,*109, 139*. Possibly *AYL* III.ii.115 and *Cor* III.i.178, probably *MM* IV.iii.170, certainly *Per* IV.ii.9. Putrefied with venereal disease. For quibble on *over-ripe* (*AYL, MM, Cor*), see MEDLAR.

—— ORANGE. *Ado* IV.i.30. Metaphor for debauched bride, a worthless gift.

ROTTENNESS, *135. Cym* I.vi.124.

ROUGH PASH AND SHOOTS. *WT* I.ii.128. Shaggy head and horns of a cuckold. Cf. BULL, CALF, MONSTER.

ROUND (vb, intrans). *WT* II.i.16. To grow round, in pregnancy.

ROUND-WOMBED. *KL* I.i.13.

RUB ON (vb). *TrC* III.ii.48. Quibble, (a) in bowls, to go on touching obstacles, (b) in love-making, to go on fondling someone. Pandarus extends the conceit with 'and kiss the mistress'.

RUBBING. *LLL* IV.i.132. Similar to RUB ON, but with more wry emphasis on opposition or friction.

RUFF. *2H4* II.iv.126 and 136. It seems that Elizabethan prostitutes wore particularly large ruffs. A. R. Humphreys, Ard. *2H4*, p. 71, quotes references in Dekker and Middleton (*The Roaring Girl*), Jonson (*Bart. Fair*) and Nathan Field (*A Woman's a Weathercock*). Cf., as later items of uniform for whores, *fin-de-siècle* feathers or the long umbrellas of the late 1940s.

RUMP. *TrC* V.ii.55. Posterior.

RUN AWAY, *91. RJ* I.i.9, *AW* III.ii.39–43. A possible quibble, (a) to escape, (b) to ejaculate prematurely, or perhaps in *coitus interruptus*. Cf. STAND, STIR, GET, WOMAN'S TAILOR.

RUNNING BANQUET (n). *H8* I.iv.12 and V.iv.64. Literally, a snack; but with quibbles on (1) sexual intercourse, (2) whipping through the streets.

RUT-TIME, *79. MWW* V.v.13. Rutting-time, when deer are on heat.

RUTTING, *140. Per* IV.v.9. Copulating.

RUTTISH. *AW* IV.iii.210. Lecherous, lustful.

SALLETS (n), *10. Ham* II.ii.435. Tasty bits—here = bawdy touches in a play.

SALT (adj), *123. Oth* II.i.233 and III.iii.401, *MM* V.i.398, *Tim* IV.iii.86, *AC* II.i.21. Lewd, lecherous.

SATE (vb). *Ham* I.v.56, *Oth* I.iii.346. To satiate, sexually.

SATIATE ... DESIRE. *Cym* I.vi.47.

SATISFY. *TA* II.iii.180, etc. Sexually—usually with a quibble on a non-sexual sense.

SAUCY. *TA* II.iii.60, *RJ* II.iv.142, *2H4* II.iv.123, *AW* IV.iv.23, *MM* II.iv.45, *KL* II.ii.95, *Cym* I.vi.150. Insolent in a bawdy or lascivious way.

SAUCINESS. *TA* II.iii.82.

SCALDING, *130*. *KL* IV.vi.129. The idea of infecting with venereal disease is probably present. Cf. BURN, HOT, CONSUMPTION.

SCALE THY . . . FORT. *Luc* 481–2. Euphemism for rape.

HIS HAND DID SCALE. *Luc* 440. Feeling its way up Lucretia's 'bare breast'.

SCAPE, -S (n), *151*. *Luc* 747, *MV* II.ii.153, *WT* III.iii.70–1. Wrongdoings, especially of a sexual kind.

SCATTER HIS CROWNS. *Per* IV.ii.113. Quibble concerning the French brothel-customer, Monsieur Veroles: (a) to pay out money in the form of *écus*, French crown-pieces; (b) to spread syphilitic baldness. See also FRENCH CROWN, HAIR, VEROLES.

SCIATICA, -S, *141*. *TrC* V.i.19, *MM* I.ii.58, probably *Tim* IV.i.23. As symptom of syphilis. Lever, Ard. *MM*, p. 12, notes that sciatica was associated with bawds in Latin comedy. Cf. BONES, HAMS.

SCRATCH HER WHERE'ER SHE DID ITCH. *Tem* II.ii.52. See at TAILOR.

SCUT. *MWW* V.v.16. A doe's short tail.

SECRET AS MAIDENHEAD. *TN* I.v.208.

SECRET-FALSE. *CE* III.ii.15. Discreetly adulterous.

—— PARTS OF FORTUNE. *Ham* II.ii.234. Strumpet Fortune's genitalia.

SECRETLY OPEN. *TrC* V.ii.24. Sexually available in private.

SECRETS. *TGV* III.i.372, *VA* 16. With vague sexual implication. Cf. HONEY.

SEDUCE. *KJ* I.i.254, etc.

SEDUCER. *AW* V.iii.145.

SEE THE PICTURE. *MWW* II.ii.78. Heavy-handed euphemism for a sexual assignation. Cf. Bianca's off-stage tour of Livia's rooms and pictures in Middleton, *WBW* II.ii.271–445.

SELLING HER DESIRES. *Oth* IV.i.94. Metonymic description of Bianca's trading as a courtesan.

SEMIRAMIS. *TA* II.i.22 and II.iii.118, *TSh* Ind.ii.38. Legendary Assyrian queen, reputedly voluptuous.

SERPIGO. *TrC* II.iii.70, *MM* III.i.31. Any spreading skin-disease: symptoms were often confused with those of syphilis. Cf. RHEUM IN MINE EYES.

SERVE (vb), *32*, *102*. Probably *TGV* III.i.269, certainly *2H4* II.iv.48, perhaps *H5* III.ii.30, *AW* IV.ii.18. This quibbles on the idea of copular service or mounting.

SERVE . . . LUST, *129*. *TA* IV.ii.42, *KL* III.iv.83.

—— . . . TURNS, *61*. *TA* II.i.96. See TURN.

SERVICE, -S. Probably *2H4* III.ii.244, certainly *AW* IV.v.22–9, *MM* I.ii.102 and III.ii.113, probably *Cor* IV.v.50. As with SERVE. Also, *MM's* Pompey and Lucio choose to regard prostitution as a form of national service.

SET ME TO'T. *MM* IV.iii.153. Awaken my sexual urge.

SHARPEN. *TrC* V.ii.74. To work someone up, sexually. Cf. EDGE, WHETSTONE.

SHEETS, *122*. *Ham* I.ii.157, etc. With various coital associations.

SHOOTS (n). *WT* I.ii.128. Cuckold's horns. See ROUGH PASH AND SHOOTS.

SHORT. See MAKE IT SHORT.

SHRIVE, *57*. *1H6* I.ii.119. Quibbling on religious and sexual confessions. Cf. CONFESSOR, PENANCE.

SIEGE. *RJ* I.i.212, *MWW* II.ii.211, *AW* III.vii.18. As = sustained attack on a woman's chastity.

—— OF THIS MOONCALF. *Tem* II.ii.104. Excrement of this abortion.

SIGNOR MOUNTANTO. See MOUNTANTO.

SING (vb, trans). *TrC* V.ii.10–11. To take on or tackle someone (sexually), just as readily as if they were a page of easy music. Cf. CLIFF, NOTE.

SINK (n). *Cor* I.i.120. Cesspool.

SINK IN IT (vb). *RJ* I.iv.23. To achieve coitus, to penetrate a woman.

SIR NOB, *95*. *KJ* I.i.147. Diminutive for Sir Robert (Faulconbridge), but possibly also with a play on *knob* as = penis. The immediate context includes STIR, FOOT, CASE.

SLACK THEIR DUTIES. *Oth* IV.iii.86. Of husbands, sexually and otherwise. Cf. HUSBAND, HUSBANDRY.

SLEEP [IN LAVINIA'S ARMS]. *TA* II.iv.19.

SLIP, -S (n), *17*. *TA* II.iii.86, *Oth* IV.i.9. A sexual escapade or betrayal. Cf. TRICK.

SLIPPERY. *WT* I.ii.273. Sexually unfaithful.

SLUICE (vb), *151*. *WT* I.ii.94. As = to fuck. Cf. POND, RIVER, WASH.

SLUTS. *Tim* IV.iii.135. Drabs, trollops.

SLUTTERY. *Cym* I.vi.43.

SLUTTISH. *TrC* IV.v.62. Licentious and promiscuous.

SMOCK, *5, 57, 149*. *1H6* I.ii.119, *RJ* II.iv.100, *AW* II.i.30, glancingly *AC* I.ii.163. Woman's undergarment (and nightdress), with erotic implication; in *RJ* and *AW*, metonymic for the woman herself. Cf. Jonson, *Alch.* V.iv.126, 'No, my smock-rampant.'

SNATCH (n). *TA* II.i.95. 'A hasty act of kind' (F &H, with illustration from Burton's *Anatomy of Melancholy*, 1621). The connotations include poaching.

SODDEN, *139*. *Per* IV.ii.19, allusively *TrC* III.i.40. Boiled, stewed—whether by being overworked in the brothel (cf. STEWS, STEWED), or treated for venereal disease in the sweating tub, or (most likely) both. Cf. BOILED STUFF, MEAT, POWDERING TUB.

SO-FORTH. *WT* I.ii.218. Used here to suppress some such word as *cuckold*: cf. ETCETERAS, WHAT-YE-CALL'T.

SOIL (n). *MM* V.i.141. Sexual blemish or defilement.

SOILURE. *TrC* IV.i.56.

SOILED HORSE, *130*. *KL* IV.vi.122. A horse stall-fed with fresh-cut green fodder, and hence mettlesome and sexually eager. (There could also be a quibble on SOIL.)

SOLICIT. *Cym* I.vi.146. Sexually.

UNLAWFUL SOLICITATION. *Oth* IV.ii.198. Adulterous wooing.

SON. See SUN and MAKE YOURSELF A SON.

SOUND (adj). *CE* II.ii.91, *MM* I.ii.53. Free from sexually transmitted disease.

SOUTH. *TrC* V.i.17. As reputed source of 'the pox' (syphilis). See also NAPLES, NEAPOLITAN BONE-ACHE.

SOUTHWARD, *54*. *Cor* II.iii.28–32. Probably combining Renaissance notions about venereal infection with the Latin authors' idea that contagion in general was brought northwards in Italy by the south wind. Cf. *Cor* I.iv.30, 'All the contagion of the south'; *Cym* II.iii.131, 'The south fog rot him!'; and ROTTEN.

SPARROWS, *30*. *MM* III.ii.165. As type of lechery. Cf. BOAR, GOAT, MONKEY; and the 'jelly of cock-sparrows' in a list of virility-restorers in Marston, *Malcontent* II.ii.20.

SPEED (vb). *TSh* V.ii.184, *MWW* III.v.60. To succeed or arrive, sexually. Cf. Hulme, p. 98, and *The Passionate Pilgrim*, 17.

SPEND ... MANLY MARROW. *AW* II.iii.279. Quibble, (a) to lose mettle, essence; (b) to expend semen. Cf. Tourneur, *Atheist's Trag.* IV.i.41.

SPIN IT OFF. *TN* I.iii.99. An unclear conceit, perhaps combining (a) Sir Andrew's flax-like hair being spun into yarn by a housewife, (b) his hair being lost through venereal disease caught from a hussy, and (c) the general idea of coital WEAR. See also HAIR, HOUSEWIFE.

SPIRIT. See EXPENSE OF SPIRIT.

SPIT (n). See CUT A MORSEL OFF THE SPIT.

SPITAL, *105*. *H5* II.i.71 and V.i.77. Hospital, here associated particularly with syphilis, MALADY OF FRANCE.

SPITAL-HOUSE. *Tim* IV.iii.40.

SPLEENFUL. *TA* II.iii.191. Passionate, lustful.

SPOILS OF OPPORTUNITY. *TrC* IV.v.62. Easy sexual plunder on any occasion that offers itself.

SPORT (n), *76*, *126*. *TA* II.iii.80 and V.i.96, *VA* 24, *MV* III.ii.216, *Oth* II.i.221 and II.iii.17, *MM* III.ii.113, *KL* I.i.22. As = sexual play or adventure.

SPORTFUL, *57*. *3H6* V.i.18, *TSh* II.i.255. Amorously playful.

SPORTIVE. *R3* I.i.14, *Son* 121. Sexually vital.

SPORT (vb). *VA* 105, probably *WT* II.i.60. Sexually.

SPRAYS (n). *H5* III.v.5. As = bastards.

SPURRING. *Tim* IV.iii.154. Probable quibble, (a) using spurs when on horseback, (b) fornicating. Cf. HACK, RIDE.

SQUASH, *27*. *MND* III.i.181. Mistress Squash is the name Bottom invents for Peaseblossom's mother. A squash is an unripe peascod, but there is probably also a suggestion of the human female's being squashed by the male in coitus. Cf. PEASCOD.

STAB (vb). *2H4* II.i.14-17. Quickly's 'unconscious' quibble—(a) to wound with a dagger, (b) to penetrate coitally. Cf. FOIN, STICK, WEAPON.

STAG, *63*. *TA* II.iii.71. Husband as antlered beast = cuckold. Cf. BUCK, HORN.

STAIN (n). *Luc* 1701, *Tim* V.i.171, glancingly *Cym* II.iv.139. A defilement of chastity.

STAIN (vb). *TA* V.iii.38, *MM* II.iv.55. To mark a woman by sexual assault or betrayal.

STAIR-WORK, *152*. *WT* III.iii.73. Furtive coitus, or its result. Cf. BEHIND-DOOR-WORK, TRUNK-WORK.

STAKE DOWN, *76*. *MV* III.ii.214-15. Quibble, (a) with the bet placed, (b) with limp penis.

STALE (n¹), *41*, *45*. *TSh* I.i.58, *Ado* II.ii.23 and IV.i.63. Originally, a decoy bird: hence = harlot.

STALE (adj), *83*. *RJ* II.iv.130. With pun on the noun.

STALE (n²), *83*. *MWW* II.iii.27, *AC* I.iv.62. Urine. See also BULLY STALE.

STAMP (vb). *Cym* II.v.5. By metaphor of coining = to engender.

STAMPS THAT ARE FORBID, *MM* II.iv.46. Illegitimate children. Cf. *OED* stamp, sb³, 5b, 12b. See also COIN HEAVEN'S IMAGE.

STAND (n). *Cym* II.iii.70. Possible quibble, (a) hunter's hiding-place, (b) phallic erection.

STAND (vb), *68*, *71*. *TGV* II.v.20-1, *TSh* Ind.ii.124, *RJ* I.i.27, II.i.25 and III.iii.89, possibly *TrC* I.ii.123, *Son* 151. Of the penis: to become erect. (With various quibbles.)

—— TO. *Mac* II.iii.32.

—— TO'T, *91*. *2H4* II.i.4, *AW* II.ii.40. Quibble, (a) to stand fast in an affray or battle, (b) to have a penial erection.

STANDARDS, *36*. *LLL* IV.iii.363–5. With suggestion of erect penises. Cf. SUN.

STEAL A SHIVE OF A CUT LOAF, *60*. *TA* II.i.87. To have sexual intercourse with a woman who is already not a virgin. Cf. CUT A MORSEL OFF THE SPIT.

STEW, -S (n), *48*. *R2* V.iii.16, *2H4* I.ii.48, *Cym* I.vi.151. Brothel. (The form *stews* could be either sing. or pl.)

STEWED, *114*. *Ham* III.iv.93, *TrC* III.i.40. Boiled 'in corruption' and in 'the rank sweat of an enseamed bed'. F &H quote the phrases 'beyng a stewed strumpette' and 'strong stewed whore' (1564, 1566). Cf. BOILED STUFF, MEAT, SODDEN, STEW. Associations in Sh.'s mind between stewed food and *stews = brothel(s)* are examined by Armstrong, pp. 113–14.

—— PRUNE, -S, *19, 84, 100*. *1H4* III.iii.112, *2H4* II.iv.138, *MWW* I.i.259, *MM* II.i.87–109. Stewed prunes were (1) included in many diets recommended by physicians for venereal patients; (2) the staple dish served in brothels; consequently (3) associated with dissolute women. *MM* alludes to all these, together with the irrational longings of pregnant women.

STICK (vb, trans), *32*. *TGV* I.i.101. Probable quibble, (a) to slaughter (an unwanted sheep) by stabbing, (b) to fornicate (with a mistress). Cf. MUTTON.

STICK (intrans [IN THE MIRE OF LOVE]. *RJ* I.iv.42. Cf. BOGS.

STING, -S (n), *110, 118*. *TSh* II.i.211–14, *AYL* II.vii.66, glancingly *TrC* V.x.42, *Oth* I.iii.327, *MM* I.iv.59. Sexual urge.

STIR (vb, trans or intrans), *68*. *KJ* I.i.172, *RJ* I.i.8, *MWW* V.v.178, probably *Oth* III.i.27, *MM* II.ii.185. Along with various quibbles, this = to rouse sexually, to move erotically. Cf. Tourneur, *Rev. Trag.* I.ii.181, 'some stirring dish / Was my first father'.

—— UP. *Per* IV.ii.91 and 144. Sexually.

STOCK-FISH, -ES. *1H4* II.iv.241, *MM* III.ii.103. Dried cod—impotent, shrivelled, unappetising. Cf. Marlowe, *Faustus* vi.166, where Lechery declares that she loves an inch of raw mutton better than an ell of fried stockfish.

SAMPSON STOCKFISH. *2H4* III.ii.31. A fruiterer whom Robert Shallow claims to have fought. Cf. other suggestive names, such as GRINDSTONE, HORNER, KEEPDOWN, NIGHTWORK, OVERDONE, TALEPORTER, TEARSHEET, THUMP, VEROLES.

STOLEN HOURS OF LUST. *Oth* III.iii.335.

STONES, *75–6, 83*. *MND* V.i.187, *MV* II.viii.20–4, *2H4* III.ii.316, *MWW* I.iv. 101–2, *Tim* II.ii.144. Testicles (human, as well as animal): with various quibbles. Cf. the Nurse's indelicate reference to a cockerel's stone, *RJ* I.iii.54; and Florio, '*Coglioni*, the stones of testicles of men, or any creature else.'

STRAIN (vb). *H8* IV.i.46. To hug, etc.

STRANGE FOWL. *Cym* I.iv.84. As = would-be adulterous strangers. See also POND.

STRIKE (vb). *TA* II.i.118 and 129. As euphemism (via hunting metaphor) for *to rape*.

STRUMPET, -S, *52, 59, 115, 121, 125, 147*. *1H6* V.iv.84, etc. Harlot.

STRUMPETED. *CE* II.ii.143, *Son* 66. Made a whore of.

STUFF (n), *135, 139*. *Tim* IV.iii.273; *MM* III.ii.4, *Per* IV.ii.18, *Cym* I.vi.24. (1) In *Tim*, = semen. (2) People, especially girls, as the stuff or raw material of the brothel-industry. See also BOILED STUFF.

STUFFED. *Ado* III.iv.58. Quibble, (a) with nose blocked because of a cold in the head, (b) fucked.

STUPRUM. *TA* IV.i.79. Latin for *rape*.

SUBURBS, *65, 156. JC* II.i.285, *MM* I.ii.95–102 and II.i.64, *H8* V.iv.71. Districts outside the city walls, ill-reputed for brothel-keeping and general loose living. Sugden quotes apposite lines from a number of Elizabethan dramatists.

SULLY (vb). *WT* I.ii.326. To soil, physically as well as figuratively. Cf. SHEETS, STAIN. Hamlet's 'sallied flesh' (Q2, at I.ii.129) could also be relevant.

SUN, -S, *36, 57. 3H6* II.i.40–2, *LLL* V.ii.168–71 and probably IV.iii.365. Punning on *son*. Cf. final couplet of Marvell, 'To his Coy Mistress'.

SUPERVISOR, *123. Oth* II.iii.392. Spectator, voyeur.

SUPPLY (vb). *Oth* IV.i.28, *MM* V.i.210. To satisfy, sexually.

SURER SIDE. *TA* IV.ii.126. The mother's side of the family (paternal parentage being hard to verify). Tilley M1205, 'The mother's side is the surer side'.

SURFEIT (vb). *2H6* I.i.246, *MM* V.i.102, *Cor* I.ii.25. Sexually.

SURFEITS (n). *AC* I.iv.27. Sexual excesses.

SURGEON, *53, 139*. Probably *JC* I.i.23, certainly *Per* IV.vi.25. With allusion to treatment for venereal diseases. Similarly ——

SURGERY, *102. 2H4* II.iv.50.

SWEAT (n). *Ham* III.iv.92. Produced by coital exertions.

SWEATING (adj). *VA* 794, *Oth* III.iv.42. Seen as indicating a lecherous disposition. Cf. *Luc* 437–8, and HAND, HOT, LIBERTY, MOIST, REBEL.

SWEAT (vb). *TrC* V.x.54. Undergo treatment for venereal disease. Cf. POWDERED BAWD, POWDERING TUB, TUB-FAST.

SWELL (vb). *TrC* I.ii.261, *WT* II.i.62. In pregnancy. Cf. BIG, BLOW, HIT.

SWORD, -S, *86. Ado* V.ii.18, *TN* III.iv.245, *AC* II.ii.231. With various phallic suggestions. Cf. BUCKLERS, NAKED, PLOUGH.

TAFFETA, *99. 1H4* I.ii.10. Glossy silk, here = typical of the gaudy dress of a 'hot wench'. Cf. Dekker, *1 Hon. Whore* II.i.95.

TAFFETY PUNK, *89. AW* II.ii.21. A flashily-dressed prostitute.

TAIL, *38–9, 110. TGV* II.iii.47, *TSh* II.i.216. (1) In *TGV*, the anus or posterior. Cf. Cotgrave glossing Fr. *cul*: 'An arse, bumme, tayle, nockandroe, fundament.' (2) In *TSh*, the anus may be meant again, but *pudendum* is more likely, if only because Petruchio mentions his tongue, and one would suppose cunnilingus to be what he has in mind. Among other parallels, F&H quote Rochester: 'Then pulling out the rector of the females, / Nine times he bath'd him in their piping tails.' (3) For *penis* as a probable third bawdy sense of *tail* in Sh., see TALE.

DRAGON'S TAIL. *KL* I.ii.189. In astrology, a particular intersection of orbits, one that would encourage some practitioners to expect that Edmund would be 'rough and lecherous'.

TAILOR, *100, 148. MND* II.i.54, *2H4* III.ii.149–59 and 261, possibly *AC* I.ii.158. Hulme, pp. 99–102, argues for three senses of *tailor* equivalent to those of *tail*— (1) posterior, (2) female pudendum, (3) penis (yard). The first would certainly fit *MND*, where the exclamation 'Tailor!' seems to be akin to modern uses of *shit* as a swear-word; and it would add resonance to Falstaff's jokes about pricking the woman's tailor. Senses (2) and (3), however, are to be doubted. The non-Shakespearean parallels are few and remote; and the pejorative jokes,

including all those of *2H4*, can be accounted for by two persistent, though
mutually contradictory, ideas—(a) that women's tailors lacked manliness, and
(b) that they enjoyed exceptional opportunities for sexual intercourse with the
ladies they measured. See further at WOMAN'S TAILOR.

—— MIGHT SCRATCH HER. *Tem* II.ii.52. Because he has the easy access
explained at (b) above.

TAILOR'S YARD. *1H4* II.iv.242. See YARD.

TAINTED OR FREE. *MM* I.ii.43. Infected with, or free from, venereal disease.

TAKE (vb, trans). *VA* 564, probably *RJ* IV.v.10, *KL* V.i.57, *Tim* I.ii.151. Sexually.

—— IT. *R3* III.iii.50.

—— THE BLOW, *119*. *TrC* I.ii.261.

—— UP, *20–1*. *TSh* III.ii.164 and IV.iii.154–8, *MWW* IV.ii.124. By insinuation
this = to lift up a woman's skirts in order to peep beneath. (English women did
not generally wear knickers before the nineteenth century.) Cf. Webster, *Wh.
Devil* I.ii.105.

—— VANTAGES. *3H6* III.ii.25. Coitally.

TALE, *38*, *110*. *RJ* II.iv.92–8, perhaps *AYL* II.vii.28, *Oth* III.i.8–11. Pun on TAIL,
probably as = penis. Cf. HAIR, MAKE IT SHORT, OCCUPY, HOUR, ROTTEN; and
Henry Glapthorne, *The Hollander* (London, 1640; ed. John Pearson, London,
1874) IV.i (Pearson, I, 131), 'speake to her, a woman has ever a hole open to
receive a mans tale'. In *RJ*, however, Mercutio's *double entendres* could be alluding
to his rump or even to a mistress's vagina. As often with bawdy use of *tail*, the
various physiological possibilities are left undefined. Cf. ——

MISTRESS TALEPORTER. *WT* IV.iv.267. Name of a midwife, with quibble
on (a) tale-carrier, gossip, (b) tail-holder—the tail here being (as often elsewhere)
the whole pubic-anal region of any of her patients.

TARQUIN. *Luc passim*, *Mac* II.i.55, *Cym* II.ii.11. As type-figure of lust and ruthlessness. Cf. TEREUS.

TASTE (vb, trans). *VA* 128, *Per* IV.ii.77, *Cym* II.iv.57. To try, or enjoy, someone
sexually.

TASTED HER SWEET BODY. *Oth* III.iii.343.

TAURUS. *TA* IV.iii.69. The Bull (sign of the zodiac): with quibble on HORNS.

TEARSHEET, *104*. *2H4* dram. pers., *H5* II.i.74. Surname of prostitute. See also at
STOCK-FISH, DOLL TEARSHEET.

TEREUS, *137*. *TA* II.iv.26 and IV.i.48, *Luc* 1134, *Cym* II.ii.45. Mythological king of
Thrace, rapist and mutilator of his wife's sister PHILOMEL(A).

THIN ROOFS, *133*. *Tim* IV.iii.146. Heads lacking hair—supposedly as a result of
syphilis (though also, in Renaissance times, a probable outcome of attempts to
cure it). Cf. HAIR, FRENCH CROWN.

THING, -S, *16*, *77*, *85*, *100*, *128*, *165–6*. Probably *RJ* I.iv.24, *MV* V.i.306, *1H4* III.iii.
114–16, *Oth* III.iii.299, *KL* I.v.49, *Per* IV.ii.60. Quibble, (a) an object, entity or
circumstance; (b) the sexual organ, male or female. Cf. AFFAIRS, CASE, ETCETERAS,
WOMEN'S MATTERS; Jonson, *Alch.* V.i.24, 'The boy of six year old, with the great
thing'; Marston, *A &M* IV.i.232, 'I would have sworn I had seen Mellida even
now; for I saw a thing stir under a hedge and I peep'd and I spied a thing; and
I peer'd and I tweer'd underneath, and truly a right wise man might have been
deceived, for it was . . . A dun cow.' Further possible occurrences of the play on
thing—all of them difficult to verify—are in *Son* 20, *TN* III.iv.293, *Per* IV.vi.155,
H8 I.iv.48.

ANOTHER THING, *33. TGV* III.i.341. Female pudendum.

THE —— YOU WOT OF, *19. MM* II.i.107. Venereal disease.

THREE-INCH FOOL. *TSh* IV.i.23. Fool with a three-inch penis.

THREE-PILED. See PILED and FRENCH VELVET.

THROW (vb), *138. Cym* V.v.263. Possible quibble, (a) to cast (a wife) aside, (b) to throw her down for sexual intercourse. Cf. FALL.

—— DOWN. *TrC* II.iii.208. Quibble, (a) to defeat Hector in fight, (b) to throw down Polyxena for coitus.

THRUST (n). *2H4* II.i.18–19. Probably one of Mistress Quickly's unconscious quibbles: (a) sword-thrust, (b) phallus-thrust. Cf. FOIN, STAB, TOOL, WEAPON

THRUST (vb), *68.* Probably *TGV* III.i.371 (cf. SECRETS), *VA* 41, *RJ* I.i.16, probably *AW* I.i.207. To push oneself forward, or another person backwards, for sexual intercourse: used with various *double entendres.* Cf. SECRETS, UNDERSTAND.

THUMP (vb), *153. WT* IV.iv.196. Possibly = to assail, sexually. Partridge cfs modern *bang.* See also JUMP and F&H *tump.*

PETER THUMP. *2H6* dram. pers. and II.iii.79–84. The armourer's man. Cf. HORNER.

TICK-TACK. *MM* I.ii.189. Strictly a form of backgammon in which pegs were put into holes to keep score; but here = fornication.

TILLAGE. *Son* 3. Sexual digging, with a view to planting seed. Cf. EAR, HUSBANDRY, PLOUGH, UNEARED WOMB.

TILTH. *MM* I.iv.44.

TIRE ON. *Cym* III.iv.93. To prey on, or feed ravenously on, sexually. Cf. PREY.

TISICK, *118. TrC* V.iii.101. A phthisic, a chronic cough—here the first of several symptoms consistent with the secondary phase of syphilis. See BONES, RHEUM IN MINE EYES.

TOMBOYS, *135. Cym* I.vi.121. Harlots.

TONGUE, *38, 137. TGV* II.iii.45–7, *TSh* II.i.216, glancingly *Cym* II.iii.14. With allusion to cunnilingus or (in *TGV*) the nearest homosexual equivalent. Cf. TAIL, TALE.

TOOL, *68. RJ* I.i.30, *H8* V.iv.34. As = *penis,* with quibble on *sword* in *RJ.*

COINER WITH HIS TOOLS. *Cym* II.v.5. Quibble, (a) tools for stamping illicit coins, (b) his sexual organs, for engendering a bastard.

TOP (vb), *123, 125. Oth* III.iii.393 and V.ii.137. To copulate with (a woman). Cf. LEAP, MOUNT, TUP, VAULTING VARIABLE RAMPS.

TO'T. *MM* II.i.222. As = GO TO'T.

TOUCH, -ES (n), *146. Oth* IV.ii.83, *MM* III.ii.22. Erotic caress.

TOUCH . . . FORBIDDENLY. *WT* I.ii.416–17.

TRADE (n). *MM* IV.iii.18, *Per* IV.vi.66–9. Prostitution.

HOLD-DOOR ——. *TrC* V.x.50. Brothel-keeping.

TRADERS IN THE FLESH. *TrC* V.x.45. Brothel-keepers (perhaps with quibble on brothel-users). Cf. PAINTED CLOTHS.

TRADE (vb), *78. MWW* I.iii.69, *AC* II.v.2. To engage in sexual business.

TRADING. *1H4* II.iv.358.

TREASURE, -S (n), *165. Son* 136, *MM* II.iv.96, *Cym* II.ii.42. Of a woman's love, body or HONOUR. Cf. JEWEL.

LAVINIA'S TREASURY. *TA* II.i.131. As = vagina.

TRICK, -S (n), *155. R3* I.i.14, glancingly *TrC* V.ii.24, *MM* III.i.117, *H8* I.iii.40. A sexual device or ploy. Cf. Heywood, *WKK* vi.169; and JUGGLING.

TRIM (vb), *39*. *TA* V.i.93–6. Quibble, (a) to barber, cut or prune, (b) 'to deflower, to possess a woman' (F &H, citing parallels from Chapman, Fletcher and others). Cf. UNTRIMMED BRIDE.

TRIP (vb). *Per* II.iii.103. Quibble, (a) to dance gaily, (b) to stumble, falling from chastity.

TROILUS. *TN* III.i.51. As one of a fornicating pair. Cf. CRESSIDA, PANDARUS.

—— THE FIRST EMPLOYER OF PANDERS. *Ado* V.ii.31.

TROT (n). *TSh* I.ii.78, *MM* III.ii.47. Bawd.

TROUTS. See GROPING FOR TROUTS.

TRUANT WITH YOUR BED. *CE* III.ii.17. To sleep away from home, adulterously.

TRULL, -S, *55*, *61*. *1H6* II.ii.28, *3H6* I.iv.114, *TA* II.iii.191, *AC* III.vi.95, *Cym* V.v.177. Harlot, slut.

TRUNK-WORK, *152*. *WT* III.iii.72. Furtive coitus, or its result. Cf. Iachimo's trick in *Cym* II.ii; and BEHIND-DOOR-WORK, STAIR-WORK.

TRY EXPERIMENTS. *TA* II.iii.69. Sexual experiments, related to the horning (l. 67) of Saturninus, Tamora's husband.

TRY WITH TONGUE, *137*. *Cym* II.iii.14. Probable quibble, (a) to serenade with singing, as opposed to the fingering of musical instruments; (b) to probe cunnilingually.

TUB, -S, *104*. *H5* II.i.72, *MM* III.ii.54, *Tim* IV.iii.87. Barrel in which venereal patients would sit to be sweated, and/or fumigated over roasted mercuric sulphide. Cf. BATHS, HOT-HOUSE, POWDERING TUB, SWEAT.

TUB-FAST. *Tim* IV.iii.88. Low diet prescribed for venereal patients. Cf. STEWED PRUNES.

TUMBLE (vb), *116*, *152*. *Ham* IV.v.60, *AC* I.iv.17, *WT* IV.iii.12. Coitally. Cf. Middleton, *WBW* IV.ii.104, 'can sing and dance—and tumble too, methinks.'

TUN-DISH. *MM* III.ii.162. Literally, a type of funnel: here made = phallus.

TUP (vb), *122*. *Oth* I.i.90. Of a ram with a ewe: to mount, to copulate.

TURD, *83*. *MWW* III.iii.210. Dr Caius's Fr. pronunciation of *third* yields pun on *turd*, literally = a lump of dung, but also common as a term of personal abuse.

TURK, *129*. *AW* II.iii.87, *KL* III.iv.88. The Grand Turk, Sultan of Turkey, as type-figure of ambisexual lubricity. Cf. Jonson, *Volpone* I.v.88, 'The Turk is not more sensual in his pleasures . . .'.

TURN, -S (n). *TA* II.i.129, *AC* II.v.59, *Cym* II.vi.142. Sexual bout, performance, or betrayal.

SERVE . . . TURN, -S, *61*. *TA* II.i.95, *LLL* I.i.278. Quibble, (a) to fulfil someone's needs, (b) to satisfy them sexually.

TURN (vb), *132*, *150*. *TGV* II.ii.4, *MND* III.ii.91, glancingly *TrC* V.iii.110, *Oth* IV.i.255–6, *Tim* IV.i.3, *AC* IV.xii.13. To be sexually unfaithful or treacherous. (Sometimes with quibbles on other senses.)

—— TO. *MV* I.iii.78 and (by Portia's quibble) III.iv.79–80. To become coitally available to or ready for.

TURNBULL STREET, *103*. *2H4* III.ii.297. Sugden: 'In our dramatists the commonest spelling is Turnbull, but we also find Turnball, Townbull, and Tunbold as variants. It was the most disreputable street in London, a haunt of thieves and loose women.'

TURRETS. *Luc* 441. As = breasts. Cf. SCALE.

UNCUCKOLDED. *AC* I.ii.68. Not betrayed by an adulterous wife.

UNDER YOU. *LLL* IV.ii.72. Quibble, (a) under your tuition, (b) beneath you during coitus.

 UNDERMINE, *89. AW* I.i.118. To defeat chastity or HONOUR by penetration from below. Cf. BLOW UP.

 UNDERMINERS AND BLOWERS UP, *89. AW* I.i.119.

 UNDERSTAND THE CASE. *Cym* II.iii.75. Probable quibble, (a) to comprehend the state of affairs, (b) to grasp the legal position, (c) to have an erection below a woman's vagina. Cf. CASE, and *TGV* II.v.29, 'Why, stand-under and understand is all one.'

 UNDERTAKE, *85. TN* I.iii.55. To take a woman beneath one, for sexual intercourse.

UNDO, *62. TA* IV.ii.72-3, probably *Cym* II.iii.73. To ruin, through seduction.

UNEARED WOMB. *Son* 3. A womb without seed. Cf. EAR, HUSBANDRY, PLOUGH, TILLAGE.

UNGENITURED. *MM* III.ii.163. A nonce-word, either = *impotent* or = *without testicles*.

UNMANNED. *RJ* III.ii.14. Quibble, (a) untrained, like a young falcon; (b) virgin.

UNPAVED, *137. Cym* II.iii.30. Without testicles, without STONES.

UNPROPER BEDS. *Oth* IV.i.68. Marital beds shared with wives' illicit lovers. Cf. COMMON.

UNPROVOKE. See PROVOKE . . . UNPROVOKE.

UNSEDUCED. *Cym* I.iv.55.

UNSEMINARED. *AC* I.v.11. Castrated, deprived of semen.

UNSTANCHED WENCH. *Tem* I.i.47. A girl menstruating without absorbent padding. (For what is probably Sh.'s only other allusion to menstruation, see PAINS.)

UNTRIMMED BRIDE. *KJ* III.i.209. Probable quibble, (a) not yet decked-out for her wedding, (b) still-virgin. Cf. TRIM.

UNTRUSSING. *MM* III.i..169. Untying one's hose, for sexual intercourse.

UNWHOLESOME. *Per* IV.ii.20. Sexually unwholesome, because of venereal disease.

UPSHOOT, *36. LLL* IV.i.129. Quibble, (a) in archery, the best shot so far; (b)penial ejaculation: cf. CLEAVING THE PIN.

URINAL, -S. Urine-flask. See KNOG [HIS] URINALS and CASTALION-KING-URINAL.

 URINE. *MM* III.ii.104, *Mac* II.iii.26. Cf. LIE, LYE, STALE, WATER.

USE, -S (n), *163. TSh* IV.iii.158, *RJ* III.v.226, *2H4* II.i.111, *TN* III.i.49, *AW* IV.iv.22, *Son* 20 and 134. Sexual use, employment or enjoyment: with various quibbles, mainly from usury. See *OED*, sb, 3b; and Tourneur, *Rev. Trag.* II.ii.99, 'Her tongue has turn'd my sister into use.'

USE (vb), *130. TA* IV.ii.40, etc. Sexually.

USURIES. *MM* III.ii.5-6. One of two—'the merriest'—is prostitution. Cf. USE, and Tourneur, *Rev. Trag.* IV.iv.103, 'put myself to common usury'.

VARLET. See MALE VARLET.

VAULTING VARIABLE RAMPS. *Cym* I.vi.133. Copulating with promiscuous hussies. Cf. LEAP, MOUNT, TOP.

VELVET. See FRENCH VELVET and PILED.

VENICE. *Ado* I.i.251. Among the Elizabethans, a byword for its sexual immorality. Cf. Jonson, *EMI* II.v.46, etc.

VENT (vb). *Cym* I.ii.3, *Tem* II.ii.104. To emit from the body.

VENTURES (n), *135*. *Cym* I.vi.122. Prostitutes.

VENUS, *154*. *TA* II.iii.30, *VA passim*, *AC* I.v.18, *Tem* IV.i.87–98. Goddess of love, with particular emphasis on her carnality or her adultery with MARS. See also VULCAN'S BADGE.

VEROLES, *139*. *Per* IV.ii.104–13. Name of a venereally-diseased Frenchman, customer of the brothel. From Fr. *vérole* = pox. Cf. MOUNSIEUR BASIMECU, GRINDSTONE, HORNER, NIGHTWORK, TEARSHEET.

VICE. *Ado* V.ii.21. Multiple quibble, (a) a screw, (b) a penis, (c) a sinful act.

VIOLATE . . . HONOUR. *Cym*, V.v.284–5, *Tem* I.ii.346–7. To rape. HOT AND FORCING VIOLATION. *H5* III.iii.21.

VIRGIN (n and adj), *51*, *1H6* V.iv.50, etc.

   VIRGINITY, -IES, *51*, *89*, *132*, *139*, *140*. *LLL* I.i.276, etc.

   VIRGIN-VIOLATOR. *MM* V.i.41.

VIRGINALLING UPON HIS PALM. *WT* I.ii.125–6. Quibble, (a) fingering his hand as though it were a keyboard instrument, (b) playing with it girlishly.

VIRGO'S LAP, *64*. *TA* IV.iii.64. Middle of the constellation Virgo (the virgin). The arrival of an arrow there gains much of its sexual significance from LAP.

VIRTUE. *KJ* II.i.98, *2H4* II.iv.46, *Oth* IV.i.8. Used with varying degrees of sarcasm.

VOCATIVO, *82*. *MWW* IV.i.46. See FOCATIVE and O.

VULCAN'S BADGE, *60*. *TA* II.i.89. The reputation of being a cuckold: in myth, VENUS, adulterous wife of the fire-god Vulcan, was caught *in flagrante delicto* with MARS.

WAGTAIL. *KL* II.ii.65. Here, an unspecific term of abuse. But cf. TAIL, TALE.

WANTON (n and adj). *1H6* V.i.23, etc. Loose, lascivious person.

   WANTON (vb). *TA* II.i.21. To frolic sexually.

   WANTONLY. *Son* 54.

   WANTONNESS. *KJ* IV.i.16, etc.

WAPPENED WIDOW. *Tim* IV.iii.37. *Wappened* is of uncertain meaning: probably = 'stale, sexually exhausted'. Widows, in Elizabethan drama, are often assumed to be promiscuous.

WARM, -ER, *152*. *VA* 605, *1H4* IV.ii.17, *WT* III.iii.73. Sexually ardent. Cf. HOT.

WASH (vb), *63*. *TA* V.i.95. Quibble, (a) to wash, as a hairdresser might wash hair; (b) to fuck: cf. SLUICE.

WASTE (n). *MWW* IV.ii.189. In law, spoliation by a tenant; hence a metaphor for seduction.

WATER. *2H4* I.ii.1–2, *TN* III.iv.102. Urine.

   MAKE ——, *31*. *TGV* IV.iv.36, *TN* I.iii.123, *MM* III.ii.104. To urinate.

   BREATHE IN YOUR WATERING. *1H4* II.iv.15. To fart during urination.

   WATER AND BRAN. *MM* IV.iii.152. Diet to restrict lechery. Cf. *LLL* I.i.280, 'bran and water'; and *MM* III.ii.97, 'impossible to extirp [lechery] quite, friar, till eating and drinking be put down'.

   WATER . . . BY THE MILL, *60*. *TA* II.i.85. Cf. Tilley W99, 'Much water goes by the mill that the miller knows not of'; STEAL A SHIVE; CUT A MORSEL OFF THE SPIT. Demetrius is arguing that adultery is safe and easy.

WAY OF WOMENKIND. See at GO.

WEAPON, -S, *3*, *18*, *68*. *RJ* I.i.32 and probably II.iv.55, *2H4* II.i.16 and II.iv.196. Quibble, (a) sword or dagger, (b) penis. Cf. Tourneur, *Atheist's Trag.* II.v.100, 'Nay, husband, . . . he was ready even to have drawn his naked weapon upon me'.

WEAR (vb), *107*. *TSh* III.ii.117, *AYL* II.iv.49. Implying coital wear-and-tear. Cf. GRINDSTONE.

WEIGHT. *Ado* III.iv.24, *AC* I.v.21. Man's weight, borne by woman during coitus: with quibbles. Cf. BEAR, BURDEN, HEAVIER, UNDERTAKE.

WENCHLESS. *Per* IV.ii.4. Without girls, in the brothel.

WHALE TO VIRGINITY. *AW* IV.iii.215. A ravenous devourer of virgins.

WHAT UPWARD LIES. *LLL* IV.iii.276. Rosaline's private parts, visible if she walked on streets paved with eyes. (Elizabethan women wore no knickers.)

WHAT-YE-CALL'T, *19*. *AYL* III.iii.67. Touchstone's euphemism for the name Jaques, avoiding the sound *jakes* (Kökeritz, p. 118). Cf. ANOTHER THING, LOWER PART, THE THING YOU WOT OF.

WHETSTONE. *TrC* V.ii.74. Cressida, as habitual sharpener of men's sexual appetites. Cf. EDGE, GRINDSTONE, SHARPEN; and Tilley W299, 'A whetstone cannot itself cut but yet it makes tools cut.'

WHIPPING-CHEER. *2H4* V.iv.5. 'Entertainment' with the whip—the recognised punishment for Elizabethan prostitutes when convicted.

WHITE STOLE OF CHASTITY . . . DAFFED. *LC* 297. Virginity given up.

WHORE (n), -S (n), *20*, *48*, *82*, *103*, *120*, *125*, *129*, *133*, *150*. *1H6* I.iii.35, etc. A prostitute or quasi-prostitute. See also HOAR (adj).

WHORE (vb, trans and intrans), *133*. *Ham* V.ii.64; *Oth* V.i.116, *Tim* IV.iii.148. (1) To make a whore of someone; (2) to work or behave as a whore. See also HOAR (vb).

WHOREMASTER, *128*. *1H4* II.iv.456, *MM* III.ii.33, *KL* I.ii.119, *Tim* II.ii.108–17. A user of whores, a 'client' of prostitutes.

WHOREMASTERLY (adj). *TrC* V.iv.6.

WHOREMONGER. *MM* III.ii.34. A pimp.

WHORESON (n and adj), *9*, *118*, *127*. *TGV* II.v.41, etc. Literally, 'son of a whore', but usually with negligible metaphoric life. Sometimes quite affectionate, as in *Ham* V.i.171.

WHORISH LOINS. *TrC* IV.i.65. Helen's.

WILL (n), *118*, *164–5*. *Luc* 247, etc. See especially *MWW* I.iii.46, *AC* II.v.8, *Son* 134, 135, 136 and 143. Four sexual senses of the word can be distinguished: (1) sexual energy, libido, (2) lust, (3) penis, (4) vagina. Sh. quibbles amongst these, as well as on non-sexual meanings.

WINCHESTER GOOSE, *48–9*. *1H6* I.iii.53; and cf. l. 35 (to Winchester), 'Thou that giv'st whores indulgences to sin.' In the suburbs of London, the liberty of the Bankside, sheltering a number of brothels, was under the jurisdiction of the Bishop of Winchester. Hence, apparently, *Winchester goose* as a cant term for (1) a syphilitic chancre; then (2) a sufferer from it; and (3) any prostitute, who would spread the infection. Cotgrave glosses Fr. *clapoir* (n), 'A botch in the Groyne, or yard; a Winchester Goose.' Armstrong, pp. 59 and 63, notes that the erotic associations of the goose are very ancient, and that Sh. several times juxtaposes the ideas of goose and blindness: 'at the back of Shakespeare's mind was the realisation that syphilis causes blindness'.

GALLED GOOSE OF WINCHESTER. *TrC* V.x.53. Quibble, (a) an angry goose, (b) an angry and suffering prostitute.

WIND INSTRUMENT. *Oth* III.i.10. As = anus.

WINDOW. See IN AT THE WINDOW.

WITCH. *MWW* IV.ii.151-7, *WT* II.iii.67-8. With emphasis on procuring as an expected sideline for witches. Cf. AUNT OF BRAINFORD.

WITHERED PEAR. *AW* I.i.160. As = virginity.

WITHOUT HIS ROE. *RJ* II.iv.37. Probably a multiple quibble: Romeo (a) without *Ro*, = only half himself; (b) post-coitally exhausted (Mercutio would suppose); (c) thin and languid, like a herring that has shed its roe. Cf. FISH.

WIT-OLD. *LLL* V.i.54. Quibble, (a) senile, (b) a wittol, a cuckold.

WITTOL. *MWW* II.ii.267. Complacent cuckold.

WITTOLLY KNAVE. *MWW* II.ii.241.

WOLVES IN PRIDE, *123*. *Oth* III.iii.401. Sexually excited wolves.

WOMAN'S TAILOR, *100*. *2H4* III.ii.149-59. Feeble's name derives from a long-lived cliché about women's tailors, the idea being that they were effeminate or at least weak. This nourishes Falstaff's quibbles on PRICK (cf., especially, PRICK OUT (vb)). But a tailor, measuring women and holding out his YARD, was also considered to have unique opportunities for venery; hence, perhaps ——

——, RUN OFF. *2H4* III.ii.261. Possible quibble, (a) to run away in a military retreat, (b) to ejaculate in coitus or *coitus interruptus*. Cf. RUN AWAY.

WOMEN. *3H6* III.ii.124, etc. As sexual material or quarry.

WOMEN'S MATTERS, *53*. *JC* I.i.22. Quibble, (a) their concerns, (b) their THINGS, pudenda. Cf. AFFAIRS, MEDDLE; and Marlowe, *Faustus* vii.21.

WOODMAN. Probably *MWW* V.v.24, certainly *MM* IV.iii.160. A hunter—here, of women.

WORK, -S (n). *MV* I.iii.81, *Oth* V.ii.212. Sexual activity or effort.

WORK (vb), *122*. *Oth* II.i.114. Sexually. Cf. PLAY.

WORKMAN. *Cym* IV.i.5. Skilled sexual workman.

WRACK (n). *Luc* 841, *AW* III.v.22. Ruin of honour or maidenhead.

WRECK (vb). *Ham* II.i.113. To ruin, by seduction.

YARD, *3*. *LLL* V.ii.659, *RJ* I.ii.40, probably *1H4* II.iv.242. Quibble, (a) clothier's measuring-yard, (b) penis. *OED* gives 1693 as its earliest date for *penis* = the male sexual organ; previously, *yard* was the normal English word for this. Cf., also, FOOT, MEDDLE, TAILOR; the draper's-shop scenes of Dekker, *1 & 2 Hon. Whore*, and Middleton, *Mich. Term*; and Middleton, *ibid.* V.iii.166, where Shortyard is banished—'Henceforth no woman shall complain for measure.'

YIELD (vb, trans and intrans). *MM* II.iv.103 and 164, V.i.101, *Cym* I.iv.101. Sexually.

YOKES. *MWW* V.v.105. As = HORNS.

BEARING YOKE [ON BREASTS]. *Luc* 409. As = man, coitally superimposed on the two upturned breasts. Cf. BEAR, BURDEN, HEAVIER, WEIGHT.

Index

Colman
(s) Shakespeare, William.
Criticism.